THE COHOUSING HANDBOOK

The Cohousing
HANDBOOK

Building a Place for Community

Chris Hanson

Hartley & Marks
PUBLISHERS

Published by

HARTLEY & MARKS PUBLISHERS INC.

P. O. Box 147   3661 West Broadway
Point Roberts, WA   Vancouver, BC
98281   V6R 2B8

Library of Congress Cataloging-in-Publication Data
    Hanson, Chris, 1949–
    The cohousing handbook: building a place for community / Chris
Hanson.
        p.   cm.
    Includes bibliographical references and index.
    ISBN 0-88179-126-1
    1. Housing, Cooperative.   I. Title.
HD7287.7.H36   1996
334'.1—dc20   96-16559
                                                        CIP

Design and composition by The Typeworks
Set in MINION

Printed in the U.S.A.

Contents

development. Construction documents. Construction supervision.
Post-occupancy evaluation.

Acknowledgments

For helping me understand, I would like to thank the members of the Winslow, Cardiff Place and WindSong communities. They have shown me what is possible. I would especially like to thank Lynn Perkins, whose drive and undying enthusiasm kept us going at Winslow in those early days. I also want to thank all those who are now living in cohousing who make their homes, their hearts and their lives available to those who still dream of creating cohousing for themselves.

Thanks to my editor, Brian Scrivener who helped me get it all organized. A special thanks to Vic Marks and the staff at Hartley & Marks Publishers for their patience, humor and continued encouragement. They were a pleasure to work with, even though they didn't tell me how much work this was going to be.

Thanks also to the people whose contributions appear in this book: Tom Moench at Winslow Cohousing; Katie McCamant at Doyle Street Cohousing; Zev Paiss at Nyland CoHousing; Patsy Casey at Winslow Cohousing; Fritz Radandt at Cardiff Place Cohousing; Terry Lyster, Urban Development Consultant; and David Simpson, Architect.

And finally, a special thanks to my wife, Noj, and my family and my friends, for understanding and accepting that cohousing has not been my work in recent years, it has truly been my life. And to Katie and Chuck, for their work, and just for being friends.

Chris Hanson,
Spring 1996

Foreword

The desire to live in community is as old as civilization. For most of human history we have lived in extended families, villages and tribes. The desire to connect with the people who live near us runs very deep. As our modern lifestyles stretch our ability to stay connected with friends and family, a growing desire to find connection and belonging can be seen in our culture.

Enter cohousing. While not a solution for all the ills of society, it begins to address some of the stresses of our daily lives. Both the process of putting together and living in a cohousing community add a dimension to daily life which, for many, satisfies a deep longing. Perhaps it is the memory of knowing and caring for the members of our community. Perhaps it is the feeling of safety created by knowing the people who live nearby and who take a role in the lives of our children. However, creating cohousing is not a simple task. In actuality, it may end up being one of the most challenging (and rewarding) adventures many people will encounter.

When beginning any adventure the use of a road map is essential. With *The Cohousing Handbook* Chris Hanson has provided just such a map. Using his extensive experience in the world of cohousing development, Chris has clearly explained what for some may feel like an almost impossible task. This handbook can guide a group of cohousing enthusiasts through the long and sometimes confusing maze of real estate, design, political, social and construction issues that are sure to come up. Cohousing groups can build on the experience of past groups and professionals with this step-by-step guide to building our dreams. Chris has created a straightforward tool for guiding even totally inexperienced groups through the myriad steps toward successfully planning, building and moving into a cohousing community.

I encourage groups to really USE this book. By the time the first residents move into their homes this handbook should be highlighted in several colors, page corners folded, and have notes in the margins. Don't sit down and read *The Cohousing Handbook* through from cover to cover. Bring it to every community meeting and refer to it whenever questions come up. Working cooperatively with people is often a challenge. It is an experience which brings out many deeply held feelings concerning power, self-esteem, tolerance and the ability to both listen and be heard. *The Cohousing Handbook* is like having an outline along for what I sometimes refer to as "the longest and most expensive personal growth workshop you will ever take."

Zev Paiss
Managing Editor
The CoHousing Journal

1

Introduction

Why community? • What is cohousing? • What is this book? •
Don't read this book! • Theory and practice • The creative
process • Setting goals and achieving them • Short answers to
a few common questions

Why community?

The movement back to community

Everywhere, people talk about feeling isolated, or about not feeling safe in
their own home. In today's fast-paced world of competition and lonely individualism we need a place to belong, where we feel safe and supported.
And yet, when we need to get away, we need a place to be by ourselves –
quiet, separate and secure.

The romantic image of the log cabin in the woods has led to the urban
isolation of our single-family neighborhoods, making our homes too separate and autonomous. We don't know our neighbors, and have solved our
need for privacy and security through independence and isolation. Our
rugged individualism has led us to the point of feeling detached from the
world around us, as if somehow we don't belong anymore.

As a result, many of us are looking for community in our lives, for a
place where we can belong. We are looking for a way to end our isolation,
to live a more meaningful life, and to feel connected again.

There are many wonderful opportunities to experience community – in the workplace, after church or with your book group. But this book is about making a place to *live* in community. It is about making it possible to experience community every day, right where you make your home.

What is cohousing?

A brief history of cohousing

Cohousing started in Denmark in the late 1960s when a group of dual income professional families were searching for better child care and a way to share evening meal preparation. Nearly 200 projects have been completed in Denmark since the first community was completed in 1972. In 25 years it has matured into an intergenerational mix of family types, attractive to young families and single parents, as well as retired couples and singles. In North America more than 25 cohousing communities have been completed, and hundreds of groups are meeting regularly trying to make their projects happen.

In 1988 the book *Cohousing, A Contemporary Approach to Housing Ourselves*, was published in North America. In it, Kathryn McCamant and Charles Durrett coined the term 'cohousing' to describe the Danish 'Bofællesskaber,' directly translated as living communities. The idea resonated with many of us on this side of the Atlantic. Within months, many groups got started on their path to creating and living in a cohousing community.

McCamant and Durrett identify four common characteristics of cohousing in Denmark:

- Participatory Process: Residents organize and participate in the planning and design process for the housing development, and are responsible as a group for the final decisions.
- Intentional Neighborhood Design: The physical design encourages a strong sense of community.
- Extensive Common Facilities: An integral part of the community, common areas are designed for daily use, to supplement private living areas.
- Complete Resident Management: Residents manage the development, making decisions of common concern at community meetings.

From my experience with cohousing in North America, I would add the following:

- Optimum Community Size: Communities seem to work best when they contain between 12 and 36 dwelling units. Smaller or larger groups can work, but they have special challenges. Some are too intimate, or have limited funds for common facilities. Others are too big to get to know everybody, or too administratively complex.
- Purposeful Separation of the Car: In addition to intentional neighborhood design, separation of the car from the dwellings is a key feature of successful cohousing community design. Encouraging people to interact with other people requires that cars be parked away from the private residences. (See Chapter 7, Design Considerations.)
- Shared Evening Meals: Cohousing groups usually choose to share several evening meals together each week in their common house. A tradition started with the early communities in Denmark, it effectively brings residents together for a convenient and pleasurable time of fellowship and sharing. Menus, who cooks and how often, paying for meals and so on, are managed in a variety of ways. The level of participation also varies from group to group.
- Varied Level of Responsibility for Development Process: The control of design decisions and the responsibility for the development process vary from one group to the next. Some groups have maintained complete control, acting as their own developer. Other groups have had more limited input during the development process, simply purchasing the final housing product.

How does cohousing fit into the community movement?

Living in cohousing is experiencing life in community. But is it another form of "intentional community"? In my opinion it is not – at least not directly. Intentional communities are usually based on an ideology, and sometimes on charismatic leadership, often sharing a common purpose, or a common religion, for instance. They emphasize community at the expense of privacy. It seems to me that cohousing is a means for people to make a major step toward community without giving up their privacy, or control over their personal lives.

Cohousing is also a housing type. It is a way of creating a built environment that supports ongoing community interaction through four main design features. These include: separation of the car from the private residence, pedestrian pathways linking the access to each residence, locating the active area of each home (the kitchen) on the pedestrian pathway side of the house, and a centrally located common house. (See Chapter 7, Design Considerations.) None of these features is new, but they are combined in cohousing with the intent to facilitate ongoing community interaction. Some would say that cohousing is a balance of community and privacy reminiscent of an old-fashioned pre-automotive village.

How does cohousing relate to eco-villages?

The concept of the eco-village is based on the desire to create ecologically and socially sustainable communities. Cohousing is often seen as an ingredient of the eco-village, because it addresses many of the social issues of community, but the eco-village movement conceives of a more radical change in our relationship to the planet.

Cohousing is not itself an eco-village since it is a small part of the larger community in which it is located. It is normally attached to the existing infrastructure where it is located, whereas the goal of the eco-village is to establish a sustainable, non-consuming infrastructure, including agriculture, commercial activity, and the appropriate use of power and water. The eco-village is a total and comprehensive move toward environmentalism. Interest in the concept of eco-village is just beginning and the definition of eco-village is still not clear. Most cohousing people are concerned about environmental issues and many would call themselves environmentalists. Many who are already a part of cohousing are supportive of the idea of building eco-villages, whether they are living in cohousing now, part of a group in the development phase or still just thinking about it. Of the many cohousing groups I have worked with in the past six years, most have identified the environment as one of their top priorities in the development of their community.

What is this book?

A practical guide to getting it built

Much of this book is about the patterns and methods that have led to success for those who now live in cohousing in North America. Understanding

Existing cohousing communities

Winslow Cohousing
353 Wallace Way NE
Bainbridge Island, WA 98110
(206) 780-1323

The Winslow Cohousing community is located in a small town of about 2,500 people on an island in Puget Sound. The community is centrally located, a few short blocks from the ferry terminal, main street and the public schools complex allowing for a completely car free lifestyle. The commute to jobs in Seattle requires a 30 minute ferry ride. A 2nd generation cohousing community, Winslow Cohousing has an open pedestrian street and tightly clustered townhouses and apartments. Parking is clustered in one landscaped lot at the edge of the property.

Number of Units:	30 units
Property Size:	4.8 acres
Housing Form:	24 townhouses and 6 apartments
First Meeting:	February 1989
Land Secured:	April 1989
Move In:	February & March 1991
Project Budget:	$4,100,000
Housing:	33,000 sf
Common House:	5,000 sf
Circulation:	outdoor pedestrian pathways

these patterns will help you and your group be successful in creating your vision of community, whether it is the renovation of an old building in the inner city, or the creation of an entirely new eco-village for 5,000 people.

From a broader perspective, this book is about the process of building and creating as a community. The examples I use are from cohousing, but the material applies equally to other collaborative efforts, such as the growing eco-village movement.

DON'T READ THIS BOOK!

Please *use* this book, don't just read it. This book is meant to be useful in many different ways, but you will benefit most if you do more than just sit

Cardiff Place Cohousing
1246 Fairfield Road
Victoria, B.C. V8V 3B5
(604) 920-7984

The Cardiff Place community is in Victoria, the provincial capital of British Colum-
bia, located on Vancouver Island. Known as the city of gardens, Victoria has a popu-
lation of about 250,000 people. Cardiff Place is located about 15 blocks from the
inner harbor, and walking distance to shopping, public schools and the city center.
As a 3rd generation cohousing community, members of Cardiff Place share a reno-
vated turn-of-the-century mansion and a new four story apartment building. The
single parking lot is partially under the new building and on the surface, below the
original grade in back of both buildings.

Number of Units:	17 units
Property Size:	.5 acres
Housing Form:	17 apartments
First Meeting:	September 1991
Land Secured:	December 1992
Move In:	September 1993
Project Budget:	$2,300,000 (C$3,100,000)
Housing:	16,000 sf
Common House:	2,600 sf
Circulation:	2,500 sf of hallways and lobby

down and read it. The creative process is not linear, and this book is not intended to be used in a linear way. Try opening it at random and reading
any one section. See where your interest takes you. Consider reading a
chapter or a section before a group meeting when you will be discussing
that topic. Or read a few paragraphs out loud and discuss them at your
meeting. If nothing else, it will help you learn the language of development
as a group, a language you can then share.

You will find throughout this book that my recommendations tend to
be action-oriented. The focus on getting the project built was uncomfort-

**WindSong Cohousing
20543 96th Avenue
Langley, B.C. V1M 3N6
(604) 888-8683**

The WindSong Cohousing community is located in the Walnut Grove neighborhood of Langley, a suburban area about 25 miles east of Vancouver and 8 miles north of the U.S. border. On a bus route 1 mile north of the local shopping area, members who commute to jobs in Vancouver experience a 60 minute drive, or a combination of bus and light rail travel. The buildings cover less than 2 acres of the property. A 3rd generation cohousing community, WindSong has a glass covered pedestrian street connecting townhouses and apartments, and an underground parking facility.

Number of Units:	34 units
Property Size:	5.9 acres
Housing Form:	26 townhouses and 8 apartments
First Meeting:	February 1991
Land Secured:	April 1993
Move In:	July 1996
Project Budget:	$5,000,000 (C$6,900,000)
Housing:	37,000 sf
Common House:	6,000 sf
Circulation:	12,000 sf of glass covered street

able to many early members at Winslow. Many would-be participants left because their need for process wasn't satisfied. For some, getting to know their neighbors or feeling good about one another was more important than getting the project built.

By all means, criticize what you read here. Comment in the cohousing-L discussion on the Internet. (See list of resources.) Or write to me directly. I look forward to hearing from you, whether you agree with my opinions or not. Tell me about your experiences getting a project built so we can include them in the next edition of this book.

I recommend that you use this book as a measure of what has been done before you, so that you are better able to measure what course of action you will choose. In this book I refer to examples from the United States and Canada, primarily the Winslow, Cardiff Place, and WindSong communities. I will show you how people have successfully created cohousing. I will also identify some of the beliefs, attitudes and fears that resulted in patterns of behavior which were not successful. By being aware of these patterns, you can help your group avoid getting stuck in them.

I hope that people who are trying to create community for themselves will be able to listen to and learn from the examples of others. As strong-willed as you must be to succeed, I hope you can open yourself to benefit from the extensive experience of those who have created cohousing before you.

Theory and practice

"But our group is different!"

Most of what you will be doing to create your community is very similar to what others have done. Some might say, "But our group is different. We can do it ourselves, and we will do it our way." I am not suggesting that you should give up on that dream. Your dreams are very personal, and in many ways they are unique; eco-village, cohousing or collaborative community, your community will be different from any other in many ways.

However, the creative process has remarkable similarities. There are clear patterns of attitudes, activities and behaviors, as well as fears, that come into play. The problem-solving process and the design process will be essentially the same as with other groups. The patterns of finance, permits and construction are common to the development industry as a whole. Other issues are common to group process and decision making.

While the process of creating your project will be very similar, what will be different are your dreams and your experiences. Your investment in your cohousing dream will be both financial and emotional. You will care about what you are doing, possibly unlike anything you have cared about before. In addition, you and your group will create a final product, the physical manifestation of your creative efforts, that will be uniquely yours. It will belong to you as a community and you will live with the results. Your architects can't take credit for it; they just drew what you asked them to draw. Neither can McCamant and Durrett, who brought this idea to North America. Neither can I, for even if you use this book carefully and completely, it will only serve as a guide to the process, not the product.

The creative process

Building a place to live in community requires that you be proactive. You will be building something real from what started as a dream. The successful creative process rests on three foundation stones. They are:

1. Defining a vision: Nothing can replace a clear image of your hopes and dreams. What will your community look like?

2. Understanding the existing conditions: Knowing and accepting the current reality in which your creative process will occur. What do the banks and the building officials expect? What does the zoning allow?

3. Identifying the pathways: Seeing the necessary course of action from the current reality to the vision you have defined. How do you get from here to there? How will you supply the water? Can the zoning really be changed?

In the past most creative process has been accomplished by the individual or the hierarchical organization led by an individual. In the future, as more and more people seek to build community, and as they attempt to cooperate in sustaining this spaceship we call earth, the creative process will need to be accomplished by groups of people working together cooperatively. It seems that the cohousing experience has opened the door to this change. Cohousing demonstrates the capacity for a group of individuals to set aside their personal issues, and their fears, to work together for a greater good.

Setting goals and achieving them

While this book is about the process of creating community, it is intended for those who want to create the product. It is for people who want to build a place for community. It may be of interest to the academic, or to a cohousing discussion group (sometimes ungenerously dubbed the "cohousing encounter group"), but I wrote it for those who want to get something *built*.

To be successful you will want to set goals for yourself and your group. You will define what it is you want and how you are going to make it happen. For cohousing groups that are not successful the missing factor tends to be the ability to identify and accept achievable goals.

Short answers to a few common questions

How does a group get started?

Imagine a couple of friends are sitting around after dinner talking. Anne speaks of her recent look at a cohousing book and says, to no one in particular, wouldn't that be wonderful? Do you think we could do something like that? Mike asks a few questions, open to the idea, but a bit skeptical. The discussion leads to a vision of what their cohousing community might look like, envisioned as an ideal place to live. It would be a place to come home to after work and share a few evening meals together, raising kids, pursuing personal interests or retiring. A permanent place where they would want to stay for the rest of their lives. Gradually, Anne and Mike define a vision of how they want their ideal community to be, purely imaginary at this point, but alive in the hearts and minds of these two friends.

Anne suggests having a meeting, inviting anyone they know who might be interested. Let's see who comes, and how many people share our dream. Let's make a poster and put it up in the grocery store, maybe the video rental store and the laundromat. We'll post it on all the bulletin boards we can find. Isn't there a free public information service on the cable channel? We'll let them know, too. Does the newspaper have a free service?

Mike agrees to arrange for a place to meet. Hire the fire hall, or the basement of the local church might do. He asks Anne, how many people do you suppose will come? At least a few, I should think, maybe 10 or 12. But what if 30 or 40 people show up, how will we handle it? Maybe we should rent a place that's cheap, but big enough to handle a crowd if we happen to get a lot of interest.

Three weeks later twelve people show up at the first meeting, eight women and four men. It begins as a presentation about cohousing taken mostly from McCamant and Durrett's book. Then Anne shares her ideas of what she would like her community to look like. Someone suggests that they meet on Thursday evenings for awhile to continue the discussions. Anne is thrilled. Mike isn't so sure this is the right thing for him. It looks like it might eat into his free time, and besides, it's not practical.

This is just one of many scenarios, but cohousing groups generally start from the ground up. Someone has the idea and says, "Hey, let's do this!"

How are members selected?

Is there a member selection process, or do we need to establish one? Many groups ask this question, and some have even implemented such a process. Conveniently, cohousing is a very effective self-selection process.

The opportunity exists to choose your neighbors, but the fact is that most people who choose to be in cohousing are people you will be happy to have as neighbors. It seems that those groups who have implemented complex methods of determining who will be able to join their group have either failed to create cohousing, or they have had to change or eliminate their process of member selection.

How is cohousing different from a co-op or a condo?

The completed cohousing project can be owned and operated as a cooperative or as a condominium (strata title in Canada). Some would think that the best ownership structure for cohousing is the cooperative model because of the cooperative nature of the community that intends to live there. However, a condominium ownership structure can be operated just as cooperatively, and in many places it is much more easily financed than the true cooperative. (See Chapter 9, Legal Issues, for a discussion of ownership options; see Chapter 10, Finance and Budget, for a discussion of financing implications.)

What is it going to cost?

To date cohousing is rarely subsidized. Participants are generally those who can afford to buy their own home.

Some people want to know firm prices before they will get involved, not wanting to "waste their time" on something they can't afford. The answer to this question may seem amazing, but within certain practical limits, your unit in cohousing can cost almost anything you are willing or capable of paying. The key is that you must be willing to trade off size, quality or location to achieve the price you want to pay.

A normal part of the process of creating cohousing is that the group participates in design and development. This means that a group must come together long before anyone knows what final construction costs are going to be, so they can direct the design process. With the help of their design professionals, members of the group establish size, quality and cost guidelines for the project. Essentially, members determine what they want to pay, and the project is designed to match those identified needs, including unit prices. (See Chapter 7, Design Considerations, for discussion of affordability and what you can afford.)

How do I sell my unit when I have to move?

Most groups choose to set up their ownership structure to allow members to sell their units themselves to anyone they wish. This facilitates the acquisition of financing and allows those with assets to feel they have a secure investment. It doesn't control the increasing cost of owning real estate, which will have a long term effect on affordability. (See Chapter 10, Finance and Budget, for a discussion of affordability issues.)

The legal structure can be a condominium, strata title, equity co-op or fee simple land ownership. Local laws and customs will have a significant effect on which ownership structure you will choose. (See Chapter 9, Legal Issues, for a more complete discussion of ownership structures.) Local laws and customs will have a big effect on what ownership structures you can get financed, for both the construction phase and for your private mortgages. (See Chapter 10, Finance and Budget, for a more complete discussion of mortgages and financing.)

How long does it take?

It could take several years, or it could take only a few months. Cohousing is created in a variety of different ways that will influence the length of time it takes to get your project built. (See Chapter 3, Development Process, for a discussion of the various development options.)

If you choose to build your cohousing project from scratch, finding raw land and designing a project to fit your specific needs, then your project will take several years to complete. Many groups have followed this path, and the process seems to take a minimum of two years, and more often three to five years.

If you choose to purchase and adapt a project ready to start construction, or a building which can be remodeled to fit your needs, the time frame can be much shorter. The members at Cardiff Place moved in nine months after locating a project which was ready to start construction. (See also Chapter 12, Scheduling and Planning, for comparative charts.)

Keep in mind that if your group gets bogged down in the process of creating the product, your project will never actually get built at all.

Can I have a single-family home?

Yes you can. However, cohousing is usually designed as clustered multi-family housing. Like a single-family home, each home is self-sufficient with private living, dining and kitchen areas. As people get to know one another and trust that their personal needs will be met and respected, they move as a group toward clustering their homes to achieve larger community goals.

The benefits of clustering (and/or stacking) the private dwellings include: environmental protection, energy conservation, reduced infrastructure costs, increased open space and the promotion of human interaction. (For a more complete discussion of the environmental benefits of clustering and stacking, see Chapter 8, Environment.)

Cohousing groups often design smaller, more efficient private units so that they can accommodate a larger "common house." Residents often choose to include amenities such as a kitchen and dining area, children's play areas, laundry, a library or lounge, guest rooms and workshop facilities in their common house. Unlike housing built by a developer, a single cohousing project generally will have many unit types, ranging from studios to four or five bedrooms. This range of choices better serves the diverse needs and family types of a cohousing community.

Will I own my own home?

As a matter of financing convenience, most cohousing communities in the U.S. and Canada have chosen the condominium or strata title legal ownership structuring (the word "condominium" here refers to the legal structure and not the housing form). In this ownership model each household owns its own home together with a share of the common facilities.

After working together as a group for awhile, many would prefer philosophically to be organized as a cooperative housing association, more consistent with the goals of shared resources and the anticipated experience of community. A number of groups have successfully adopted the cooperative ownership structure, but only because they were able to locate the required financing. (See also Chapter 9, Legal Issues, for a discussion of ownership options.)

Can I build my house myself?

Normally a licensed contractor does the construction. This is what the banks expect, and what they will generally require. But, if you have all the necessary cash on hand you could build it yourself. Commonly referred to as sweat equity construction, the limitation on how much you can build yourself, either as a group or as an individual, is based on how much financing you need from a lender and what that lender will allow.

Generally, if you are paying cash, you can do as much of the construction as you want, subject to the needs of other members. But if you have to borrow money you will have to live with the rules and requirements of mortgage financing. Normally, a bank won't let you build by yourself because they won't have adequate security for the money they lend to you during the construction process. It is possible to work out a deal to allow some sweat equity construction. But remember, keep the focus on creating a place for community to happen balanced with your own building agenda. (See also Chapter 3, The Development Process, and Chapter 10, Finance and Budget.)

For those who really want to save money by building it themselves, I recommend designing and building a small basic core, using normal bank financing. Plan to add on or remodel on your own after the project is complete to create the home you really want.

Can I rent my unit if I am going to be away?

Say you want to be able to travel for awhile and you would like to rent your unit while you are gone. Will this be possible? Does it make sense for a cohousing community of owners to allow for rental units?

Some groups choose to have control over rentals, fearing that renters will not be as committed to sustaining community as owners. However, most of the time I find that the control of rental units is not necessary. Most often, when cohousing groups deal with this issue they decide that all initial owners will have the right to rent their unit out any time they want. Often, when thinking about controlling rentals, members themselves don't want to be controlled.

In the end, you will decide as a group how you want to deal with rentals. This means that if you join a cohousing group that has not yet made a decision about rentals, you can make a proposal that meets your needs, and seek the support of the rest of the community. It also means that if you really need to rent out your unit, for instance when you are out of the country traveling, you can be sure, because of the consensus process, that the group won't deny you that right. (See the section on consensus in Chapter 2, Forming a Group.)

All those meetings – do I need to be there?

Someone does. The whole reason for the meetings is for the group to work together to define what it wants, and then to find a way to make those dreams come true. If you don't participate, or if you let others do most of the work, you will be giving up your control to others, and you won't be participating in "building community" together.

Some say you will miss out if you don't participate in making your community what you want it to be. Some say you won't be a part of the community that is being created. However, it is important to recognize that some people are simply too busy to be actively involved during the development process. Very busy people who want to live in cohousing often join the group and give someone else their proxy when they can't get to meetings. And of course many people come in as members late in the process and are not involved until the project is almost complete. (See Chapter 2, Forming a Group.)

What kinds of people live in cohousing?

It may seem like a strange question, but I am often asked that by developers or bankers, or other professionals in the housing industry who find it difficult to understand who these strange people are who would give up their single-family homes in suburbia to live together in something called cohousing.

Any answer to the question would be only a generalization, but let me generalize a bit. (For an expanded discussion, and additional generalizations, see Chapter 11, Marketing and Membership.) Who is attracted to cohousing? First of all, they tend to be people who have thought about this idea of creating community long before they heard the term cohousing. (Note that I use the word "tend" very intentionally.) In my case I was developing ideas about what I called "shared housing by design" and meeting with friends regularly in an effort to create something like cohousing back in the early 1980s. Many cohousers relate similar stories, previous thoughts or attempts to create something like what we now call cohousing.

Additionally, cohousing people tend to be what I call "experienced and successful controllers." They are accustomed to controlling the world around them, at least more so than the average person. They tend to be well educated by choice, often with a very broad range of personal and academic interests. Often they are educated later in life, as "mature students." They tend to be people seeking to improve their quality of life, and have been on this quest for many years. They also tend to be people who are interested in the larger community around them, and are often very active in local or regional issues and events. An amazing number of cohousing people are on citizen advisory panels, school boards or planning agencies, or even are elected officials in their local government. They tend to be people who think globally and act locally. To the best of their ability they take responsibility for themselves, and for the world they experience, and for the world their children will inherit.

None of this may make any difference to you, but it's interesting to think about who your fellow cohousers are, who you are attracting to your group, and what kinds of people you might be living with in your community.

2

Forming a Group

Identity and becoming • Another being in the room •
We are each different – finding out who you are • Personal
strengths • Checklist of beliefs, purpose, and vision • Group
process and group dynamics • Managing meetings • Colors
of Empowerment • Maintaining records • Effective meetings •
Facilitating the meetings • Decision making • Organization
development • Structures and processes • Special issues •
Key structures • Key processes • Conflict and change •
The sentence • The greater good round robin,
building consensus

Identity and becoming

I arrived early, eager to get started, and not wanting to miss anything. As
people began to arrive I offered to transfer the agenda to a large piece of
newsprint, then tape it up on the wall. Nothing special for the group to deal
with today, just routine committee reports and a few items for discussion.

As people got settled the meeting was called to order. We did a check-
in, a round robin wherein each person said a few words about him or her-

self and how he or she felt as we started the meeting. During the check-in Anne expressed an uneasiness about the stability of the group. It seemed fragile to her and she was concerned about putting any more money in.

During the review of the proposed agenda, someone suggested adding the "fragile group" topic for discussion, suggesting that they, too, were feeling uneasy. I didn't know what this meant, or why people would want to talk about it.

I don't really know what happened during the next few minutes because I was thinking about the idea of a "fragile group." I couldn't figure it out. We had some money collected, we had a deal on a piece of land. We were reviewing the various design options for how we could develop that land. Everything seemed to be going smoothly. Why then did these people want to talk about the group being fragile?

My mind continued to wander during the committee reports. I think Bob told us how much money was in the bank, and what bills were expected in the next few weeks. I wasn't listening because I trusted Bob and knew he would take care of things. Soon enough it was time to talk about this curious subject of our "fragile group," and they had my full attention. Anne restated her concern and several people raised their yellow cards to ask questions. I was the third person to get my card up so I had to wait my turn. Joan asked Anne about her feelings (see Using Colored Cards in a Large Group, later in this chapter): Was there an event that triggered these feelings? Anne couldn't think of anything. Bob asked Anne if there was something she thought the group should do. Again, Anne couldn't think of anything.

Ah! My turn. The four or five more people who also put their cards up would have to wait. I got to ask my question. "Anne, don't you feel good about the fact that we have land, we have some money in the bank, and we're in the middle of the design process? I think we're doing great." Her answer surprised me, because I thought she would say, "Yeah, you're right, I guess I feel O.K." Instead, she said, "The land and the money don't mean anything to me. It doesn't feel like this group has come together yet. We haven't really become anything, except a bunch of dreamers. We don't know who we are, or what we want as a community." Stunned, I sat back.

I tried to listen to the other questions. I tried to understand what she had said, but it made no sense to me. Everything was in order, why didn't she feel fine?

When all the questions had been answered, the first blue card was called. Terry had a comment to make, and when she suggested a ritual at the start of every meeting, I couldn't believe it. Amazingly, Anne thought this might help. What were they talking about – a church service? Saying the pledge of allegiance?

Well, that's how it started. At the next meeting we started with a ritual. Terry and Anne had worked on it during the week, and when I arrived on Saturday morning there was a chair in the middle of the room with a candle on it. The rest of us sat around the edge of the room, as usual. When the meeting was called to order we began with a check-in, as usual. As it got closer and closer to my turn to speak, I felt stranger and stranger about what I should say. When it was my turn, instead of the usual "I feel fine, I'm happy to be here, and last night we won our soccer game," I blurted out that I was confused and that I didn't understand why we had to do this ritual thing, and that it made me very uneasy. I didn't really know I felt this way until after I had said it.

Something happened that day that made our community possible. Money, meeting, records, and legal documents – these didn't add up to our group's identity. It required something more. I had to come to an appreciation of other members' needs for process, just as they came to respect my need for getting things done. I realized, for the first time in my life, the value of a simple ritual. Together we were looking for a balance between task and process. We were trying to find an identity, a way of becoming something different from all the individuals in the room. I began to realize that we were indeed creating a new being.

Another being in the room

A room full of individuals will not create a community. Learning to work together, to define yourselves as a group is the key to finding your identity as community. To be successful as a community, you will need to be able to make decisions, to work together effectively, and to speak with one voice. You will have to create an image of steady confidence.

To reinforce the image you are trying to create, consider the following exercise for a single meeting, or establish it as a ritual for every meeting.

Place a chair or a small table in the middle of the room in which you are conducting your meeting. Create a sign, a large label that you can tape to the chair, indicating the name of your group. (If you haven't agreed on a name, call it anything for the moment. Consider using FRED, or Green Acres, or call yourselves "The New Cohousing Group" or "The Sunday Evening Group." Agree to choose a name later.)

Collect all the records of the group, meeting minutes, decision logs, etc. and place them under the chair.

Pull together any evidence of the group's financial capacity, such as a checkbook that belongs to the group, cash donated or collected at the current meeting, anything to give evidence of your commitment. Place these under the chair. (The money part is especially important in our society.)

Place a candle on the chair.

To start your meeting light the candle and have everyone close their eyes for a few moments and visualize the chair in the middle of the room, imagining it coming to life with these things you have given it. Imagine that this is the infant you are supporting and nourishing, trying to help it grow into an adult community. Think of yourselves as responsible for empowering this new entity, making it possible for it to take on a life of its own.

Having done this at least once, especially if there is a member of your group who is skilled at leading visualization exercises, you should begin to experience a change in the way individual members relate to the group as a whole. People will tend to think more about how a particular decision will affect the community, and not just themselves as individuals, or their family.

We are each different – finding out who you are

A collection of individuals

The members of your group started as a collection of individuals. Most of them will have worked on personal growth and awareness. They generally respect the rights of others and they take responsibility for their own lives. Because of all they have learned about themselves, they now sense that it is time for a measure of community in their lives. They are ready to come together and find a balance between community and privacy.

After months of meeting every Saturday for four or five hours, a member of the Winslow Group said, "I'm finding that I like this group best when no one is talking." At another point a different member said, "I don't know if we will ever get this built, but I sure enjoy these meetings."

We all have different needs, different expectations, and different perceptions about the world we experience. Many groups find that they need to explore their differences together to better appreciate one another, and to build the trust that's necessary to be successful in creating community. A number of resources are available to help you develop a common language and understanding of personality types, personal strengths, learning styles, and group dynamics.

Controllers

I like working with controllers. Cohousing groups are full of controllers – proactive people who take responsibility for the world they experience and are trying to make the world a better place. Often well-educated and articulate, controllers are used to getting their own way.

The early participants in the development of cohousing in North America were pioneers – risk-takers with the self-confidence that comes from successfully controlling the world around them. When controllers butt heads, each wanting to do things their own way, they create drama and apparent conflict and discord. Lots of energy, lots of feeling, and lots of caring are the hallmarks of controllers. Although this strife and conflict is unsettling to non-controllers, those who find a way to become a part of the process are rewarded. Because a group is full of controllers, no one person can step forward and lead. This lack of leadership leads to the development of consensus as the model for decision-making, since consensual decision-making is non-hierarchical and empowers everyone to direct the course of events.

Controllers are intimidating to many, but more often than not, it is their guts and determination that will actually get the project built. The key for cohousing controllers seems to be finding the balance between standing up for what they "know is right" and letting go of those issues that don't really matter.

Personality types

In November of 1989 I participated in the Myers-Briggs Type Indicator (MBTI) testing, as did most members of the Winslow Group. What we found was helpful to understanding who we were as individuals and how that might affect our relationship to the larger group. (See the book *Gifts Differing* by Consulting Psychologists Press, 1980. The Myers-Briggs Type Indicator is a registered trademark of Consulting Psychologists Press, 577 College Avenue, Palo Alto, CA 94306.)

The MBTI uses four scales to measure your personality type based on your personal preferences, determined by answering a series of questions. They are:

- Extroversion(E) ———— Introversion(I)
- Sensing(S) ———— Intuition(N)
- Thinking(T) ———— Feeling(F)
- Judging(J) ———— Perceiving(P)

After we each answered all the questions and turned in our forms for scoring we found some interesting patterns and learned some valuable lessons about ourselves, as individuals, and as a group. My personality type was characterized as an Intuitive Extrovert (ENTP: E5, N33, T17, P29). I learned that many people in our group had significantly different personality types from mine, and it became obvious that I needed to take this into account when dealing with other members. For the first time I could appreciate why each of us solves problems so differently, and why some have such a voracious appetite for more and more information.

The materials that came with the tests were very helpful in understanding and appreciating these differences. They state, "The questions in the Myers-Briggs Type Indicator are not important in themselves, but they do indicate basic preferences that have far reaching effects. There is no right or wrong to these preferences. They simply produce different kinds of people who are interested in different things, are good in different fields and often find it hard to understand each other. People with preferences opposite to yours tend to be opposite to you in many ways. They are likely to be weak where you are strong, and strong where you are weak. Each type has its own set of strengths and abilities."

If you feel this might be helpful for your group there is a paperback which is based on the Myers-Briggs Type Indicator called *Who Am I?: Personality Types for Self Discovery*, by Robert Frager.

Many other books and tools are available which can assist you in finding yourselves as individuals in a group, helping each of you appreciate the strengths and compensate for the weaknesses of each. A transactional analysis approach is offered in two books: *Egograms*, by John M. Dusay, M.D. and *Games People Play*, by Eric Berne.

BY TOM MOENCH

Personal strengths

People bring a range of personal strengths to the world. Personal strengths come naturally and give each individual a special way of establishing goals and relating to others. There are three pairs of strengths, a primary pair: Acting/Thinking – and two secondary pairs: Independent Acting/Relational Acting – and Conceptual Thinking/Practical Thinking. The characteristics for each are listed below:

ACTING
Doing, feeling, boldness
- Independent Acting: self-confident, trusts own ideas first
- Relational Acting: shows confidence in others, trusts others' ideas first

THINKING
Thoughtful, reasoned, planful
- Conceptual Thinking: looks to the future, motivated by possibilities, likes ideas
- Practical Thinking: solves current problems, motivated by necessity, likes reality

The secret to appreciating others and developing better working relationships is to develop balanced strengths between your strength pairs. As in "handedness" – right or left – each of us has a dominant strength in each pair and a supportive strength, making eight different styles. Most people are not aware of their own style, how to use it, how it aids cooperation or causes conflict in relating to others.

Membership surveys: figuring out who you are

Many groups find it helpful to do surveys of the membership to find out what people want, who they are, what they expect, how much money they have, what skills they bring, and so on. While surveys can be very useful, I would recommend caution in evaluating and using the results.

If you're so inclined, use a survey to determine what issues are important in your group, but be careful not to assume you have learned what people really want. I have found that in answering a membership survey people relate their feelings and attitudes out of context of the spirit of community. Respondents tend to present personal issues, attitudes and concerns without looking at their desire for a relationship with community. In my opinion, a membership survey only serves as a tool to find out what people think they want before they have talked to other members of their intended community. Imagine how different the results of a survey might be if, for instance, the group were to sit down and discuss each survey question together, considering the pros and cons and the long range community impacts. When we listen to others we care about, we tend to temper our opinions and adjust our expectations.

For example, a member of one cohousing group indicated on an early survey that she did not want the community to own or be responsible for a hot tub. The reason she offered for this requirement was that it would be too expensive and would only be of benefit to a few members. At a meeting of the membership to discuss this and other issues that had come up on the survey it was discovered that her real concern was one of modesty. She didn't feel it was right for people to be using a hot tub without the benefit of clothing, and since she assumed that everyone else would want to do so without clothing, she did not want the community to own a hot tub. Needless to say the discussion around this issue was interesting, but in the end the group agreed to protect her sensitivity to nakedness by scheduling the use of the hot tub with "clothing only" and "clothing optional" periods.

It should be noted that this occurred very early in the group's process of getting to know each other, long before the project had ever been designed or built. The member with the concern about nudity left the group long before the project was completed. When we moved in no hot tub was included for financial reasons, but many years later a hot tub was finally installed.

BY TOM MOENCH

Checklist of beliefs, purpose and vision

Core beliefs

- Have we defined our core values, beliefs and shared commitments?

Purpose

- Have we defined our purpose?
- Have we documented why we want to dedicate a portion of our lives to producing these dwellings and relationships?
- Have we considered what the world would lose if our group ceased to exist?
- Have we answered the question "Why don't we just shut the doors and sell off our land?"
- Is the underlying purpose sufficiently enduring to guide the establishment of new visions and goals once the current ones are achieved?

Vision statement

- Is our vision statement a clear, concise and compelling statement of the overall goal that individuals can identify with and which serves to unify the group effort?
- Does it reach out and grab people?
- Do people "get it" right away with little or no explanation?
- Is it measurable so we will know when we have achieved it?
- Does it have a specific time frame for its achievement?
- Does it seem unreasonable, or too much?
- Is our vision possible in the current building and lending environment?

Description

- Do we have a specific description of what our community will be like when the vision is achieved?
- Is there a specific description of what life will be like when our vision is achieved?
- Does the description generate excitement?
- Does it describe an end goal?
- Does it express passion, emotion, conviction and commitment and capture our guiding philosophy?

Group process and group dynamics
Managing meetings

Regular meeting times

Establishing regular meeting times, and preferably a regular meeting place, really helps. If you don't need to spend time at the end of every meeting figuring out where you are going to meet next week, you will have more time and energy to focus on getting your project built. Regular meeting times and locations also help with membership and marketing because you can get a consistent message out, and your posters don't go out of date.

Child care

The whole group benefits if you can arrange child care for meetings. Groups that include parents or that want to encourage families with children should pay particular attention to how well they handle this issue.

Your choice of a meeting location will have a major impact on child care. How separate is the area for the kids? Will they distract the adults at the meeting? Will they interrupt the meeting looking for mom or dad? These problems are not difficult to solve, but they should be considered.

Paying someone, not a member of the group, to look after the kids can be a big help for everyone. Try to find a good place for the kids to play and do activities. Many groups find that child care during meetings is so beneficial to the group as a whole that the group picks up half the cost of hiring the child-care person, with the parents paying the rest.

Maintaining records

Recording agreements

Organizing the affairs of your group generally begins with keeping records of decisions you have made together. Taking minutes in the traditional way is a good start, however, most cohousing groups find that over time the mountain of paper that is generated is not very practical. As soon as possible, begin keeping track of your decisions.

Decision log

In hindsight you will find that nothing that happens at your meeting makes much difference except for a clear statement of what you agreed

BY TOM MOENCH

Colors of empowerment

Using colored cards in a large group

Large groups of people (greater than 12) discussing a subject usually call on hands as a fair way to allow participation and do so in the order the hands were raised. At any given time people have questions, opinions, and information they wish to share. Going through hands in the order raised leads to a disconnected and relatively unfocused discussion. The result is that the non-linear communication dynamics of the group are constrained by the linear nature of the facilitation process.

People with questions cannot hear and understand more information until the current gaps in their knowledge are addressed. People who have comments to make before those with questions will not be heard by those with questions. The discussion will have to return to that point in the future and the contributor will feel discounted or unacknowledged. The consequence to the group is that many people feel unheard and frustrated.

The "Colors of Empowerment" process is a method which addresses these dynamics and allows people to engage in the discussion both at a time most appropriate for them and for the group as a whole. It is a non-linear facilitation process which addresses a large group's non-linear dynamics. Using color cards, the presenter or facilitator knows where people are in the discussion and calls on them accordingly. Red and orange are process cards which help manage the flow of the discussion process and acknowledge emotional issues. Green, yellow, and blue are discussion cards which help focus on discussion content.

Red, the process card

The process card empowers participants to help facilitate the meeting by refocusing on outcomes or making suggestions regarding the process.

Orange, the acknowledgement card

The acknowledgement card empowers individuals to acknowledge others in one of two ways:

1) State appreciation of someone for contributions made to the group (i.e., thank yous).

2) Stop the process and acknowledge someone's underlying concern by asking them what is bothering them until it is understood.

"You let the feeling live, it dies in the birthing. You deny the feeling life, it struggles for life." – Stephen R. Covey

Writing the process down so the person feels understood and affirmed will also help the group get unstuck, the sign that an underlying concern is not being heard is when someone keeps repeating the same statement.

Green, the "I can answer that" card

This card enables everyone to respond to yellow cards and bring missing information to the table or suggestions for facilitating understanding in another.

Yellow, the clarification card

The clarification card empowers individuals to ask for the information they need to participate in the discussion to make informed decisions. The key premise is that a group cannot proceed toward a consensus if anyone is missing information and understanding.

Blue, the comment or opinion card

The comment card allows people to be recognized and heard and contribute to the discussion.

There is an important distinction between blue and green cards. The blue card is a personal opinion which may or may not be substantiated beyond your own feelings, thoughts or values. It is an "I" statement. The green card is for sharing information you feel is pertinent to a question raised to which you may or may not agree. Such information might include conveying a response from an attorney, the IRS, the city government, another person or a historical perspective. A green card is not used to share your ideas and biases, but to try to help others clarify their confusions. It is information that addresses the learning need of one or more individuals in the group.

to. It can be helpful to provide a brief description of the discussion that led to the decision, or a summary of the rationale for the decision, but what is important is the decision itself, clearly stated and agreed to by consensus.

Some groups find it useful to publish a summary of their decisions regularly, making it easier to share the growing identity of the group with new or prospective members. Some groups even index and cross reference their decision records by subject, date and sometimes even by person. These techniques may seem like overkill, but they do make it easier to find decisions later.

BY TOM MOENCH

Effective meetings

The amount of time spent in meetings to successfully complete a project is staggering. Creating effective meetings through good planning and facilitation makes the experience far more enjoyable and successful. The key steps to having good meetings include:

Compile agenda items

Compile agenda items from the previous meeting, task groups, board or individuals at least 48 hours before the meeting. Establish for each item a desired outcome (e.g., decision, status, understanding), the presenter of each item, and the estimated time to complete. Remind presenters they are responsible for providing handouts or audiovisual aids as needed (including spare copies of the minutes of the group secretary and answering questions and providing information about the content of the agenda items).

Determine agenda order

Determine the order for achieving the outcomes. Start with a community building activity or sharing. Usually it is best to deal with critical issues early in the meeting. Factor in breaks and meals. If possible mix the more demanding development issues with community-related items to give some changes in thinking and feeling for the members.

Collect meeting supplies

Collect the supplies you will need to facilitate the meeting, including chart paper, pens, tape, bells for breaks, and Colors of Empowerment cards.

Write out agenda

Write out the agenda. Type it up as a handout and/or post it on chart paper in bold letters in front of group the day of the meeting. Providing an agenda before the meeting allows people a chance to read it and begin to get prepared for the meeting. For each item include:

a) Topic and objective

b) Presenter

c) Estimated time to complete

Facilitating the meetings

Some key points to keep in mind when facilitating a meeting are:

- Recruit minute takers before the meeting (set up a computer if necessary).
- If possible have everyone sit in a circle.
- Open the meeting with a coming together activity.
- Have guests or visitors introduce themselves or be introduced.
- Review the agenda, desired outcomes, presenters and allotted times.
- Make sure you have a quorum.

Confirm the minutes and decisions of the last meeting. Read the minutes and make sure that your recollection of the meeting jives with the minute takers'. Address any gaps or misperceptions. Remember the minutes become the official history of the group.

Begin the discussion and pace it using the Colors of Empowerment, periodically summarize, restating or paraphrasing ideas to clarify understanding in the group. Have a second person write on newsprint on the wall the main points being shared in the discussion because many people are visual learners, not auditory.

Use small group breakout sessions, splitting into groups of three to five, when people need to explore an issue to gain understanding and make a decision. Organize a round robin if discussion is getting emotionally charged and people need to feel heard by others.

Test consensus by asking those expressing opposition to an action, "How do you feel the action being considered is detrimental to the welfare of the group?"

Adhere to scheduled breaks.

Get group agreement for any extension of agenda item times.

Close the meeting. Have the minute taker state all decisions made during the meeting for affirmation. End with the group coming together and affirming their work.

Organization development

Basic organization development

At some point in the evolution of your group it will be important that you, as a group, establish a relationship with the outside world. It is at this point that you will want to sign a contract, or borrow money, or purchase that perfect piece of land. In preparation for this time you will want to clearly establish an identity for your group, both legally and socially.

Legal requirements

Eventually, your group will need to form a legal entity so that you can buy land and enter into contracts. Most groups struggle with the decision about legal form and spend significant sums of money trying to figure out which is best. I suggest that you delay forming a legal entity until you have to, and then do so quickly and simply without a lot of fuss and bother. If you are comfortable doing so, use a self-help book that includes standard forms and bylaws.

At some point you will want professional legal advice on behalf of the group. It is important to recognize that this is different than providing legal advice for the individual members of the group, since the best interests of individual members will often differ from the best interests of the group. For a detailed discussion about the legal aspects of developing a project see chapter 9, Legal Issues.

Financial requirements

Creating cohousing costs money, and getting money "on the table" is a major challenge for all cohousing groups. The money issues are quite simple. How can any one person or family trust that the group is going to create the community they want? How do they know they are going to have their

BY TOM MOENCH

Decision making

How can you make decisions effectively? There are numerous kinds of decision making, each used under different circumstances. When and how they are used is important.

Good decision making goes back to clarity of role definitions and where the authority to make a decision resides. In every association final authority lies in the membership. How the membership wishes to distribute that authority is a matter of choice and a critical choice.

Ironically, many cohousing groups wishing to promote community and the common good choose unanimous voting (wrongfully called "consensus") for most of their membership decisions and inflict upon themselves many of the worst aspects of individualism. Unanimity has the advantage that everyone gets to be heard if they want to and to have a final say in the decision (i.e., the right to veto or block). Unanimity is the most difficult form of decision making. Deep polarizations can occur, deeper than by majority voting because one person can paralyze an entire group and the larger a group is the greater the potential for polarization. Polarization leads to mistrust and resentment.

True consensus is the most inclusive form of decision making. Unlike unanimity, it is the group that decides whether to honor an individual dissenter. The dissenting voice has the right to be heard but not to veto and the responsibility to accept the will of the group when a dissent is not accepted. In every consensus decision making opportunity each member has three choices:

1) Affirm the decision

2) Step aside and agree not to impede implementation, or

3) Request that the group delay implementation of an action until you can make a case for why it is detrimental to the welfare of the whole group.

The advantage of true consensus is that every person has the opportunity to be heard and understood. A reason for everyone sharing is to let go of our individualism in favor of the common good. Letting go of self-centered perspectives is an emotional process. When we are allowed to express feelings we are better able to let go of our fears and be open.

"The deepest need of the human soul is to be understood — acknowledged — affirmed."
— Stephen R. Covey

It is helpful to keep in mind that groups make mistakes just as individuals do. And as individuals learn from their mistakes so can groups, especially if they have an honoring consensus process. If you find yourself in disagreement with a group consensus assume two things: 1) the group will learn from this mistake and 2) maybe, just maybe, the group knows something you do not.

Before choosing consensus as a decision-making option, because of the skill level and emotional flexibility required, it might be useful to make decisions by a super majority vote of three-quarters. If a consensus building process is used and everyone is heard and understood then the votes will usually happen without the divisiveness of blocking behavior. During the development phase the ability to move forward as a group is important.

needs met? Will they end up with a home that they can afford? And the big question for most people is: How much will it all cost?

In my experience the only way to get past these hurdles is to start by getting to know one another, and building trust. Work up to putting small amounts of money in a common pool and decide together how you are going to spend it – on photocopies, a special workshop, or an ad in the local paper. You can build trust by spending money together, and by demonstrating during the process that you care about one another.

Generally speaking, successful groups start off with a few hundred dollars per family in the common pot. As the financial needs go up, more money is contributed per household. This incremental commitment allows people to get their feet wet, gradually testing their relationship to the group. As they experience success, they will feel more comfortable putting in more money.

As a group you will need a few thousand dollars to establish your identity and pay for the basic day-to-day costs of administering your affairs – copies, supplies, meeting rooms, ads, etc. When you are ready to look for a site (land or an existing building) you will need tens of thousands of dollars to pay for professional assistance in evaluating property and planning for your use of it, as well as any down payment money or deposits which might be required on the purchase. (See Chapter 3, The Development Process, and Chapter 10, Finance and Budget, for a more complete picture of financial requirements.)

BY TOM MOENCH

Structures and processes

People underestimate the role of structure and process in shaping relationships in community. We believe that architecture and site location will help create interdependence, interaction and support the emergence of community.

Organizations also have structures which are less tangible, but influential in shaping our behavior and feelings. By structure we mean the particular patterns of relationships, such as, neighbor-neighbor, neighbor-member, father-child, developermember. We might think of each role in this complex web of social relationships as wearing a different hat. Different hats have different expectations, authority to act and boundaries. The way two neighbors expect to treat one another as equals may be startlingly different than the expectation of a board member representing the group in dealing with a member who is delinquent in paying a community bill.

Key structures

The membership

The membership is the source of all organizational authority. At times it makes sense to delegate that authority. Some authority will always remain in the membership, some will be assigned to a management team and some may go to individuals or task groups.

Board of directors or management team

The purpose of the Board or management team is to manage the project, keeping the interests of the membership in mind, while implementing policies set down by the group as a whole.

Membership meetings

General meetings of the membership are a time for the membership to work on vision, values, general policies, site programming and design approval – to make essential decisions that will affect all members. General meetings should focus on issues and decisions that cannot be delegated to a board or task groups.

Task groups

The best structure for coordinating necessary activities is the task group. They allow people to pool their collective wisdom, knowledge, and skills in creative tasks. They are different from committees in that their focus is on getting a job done, as opposed to just talking about the problem.

Gatherings

The primary purpose of the common house in your completed community is as a place to gather. A place for shared meals, parties, celebrations, sharing circles and so on. Since community emerges when our bodies, minds, hearts and souls come together, you will want to create places and events for these gatherings.

Key processes

The following processes shape the behavior of people using them and determine the quality of whatever outcomes those processes are intended to create. Take care in defining and improving your processes.

Leadership

Leadership is often a process by which one person initiates a direction for one or more persons and engages them to move along together with competence and commitment. Leadership begins with wanting or loving something so much you want to see it exist and then using your skill and knowledge to engage others in creating it. Leadership requires follower-ship.

Enrollment

If your group has a clear vision – values, beliefs, purpose and tangible image – it has a greater potential to attract and enroll people. What steps will you take to let others know about your vision (e.g., the Internet, local newspapers, community/cohousing journals)? Do new members select you by informed choice or will you screen them by a set of criteria?

Initiation, continuity and leaving

Joining and leaving a group can be difficult, both emotionally and mentally. How will you initiate people into your vision and history to give them a sense of belonging? How will you find a role for them to contribute? What and how will you learn from them?

When people choose to leave a group, especially a community, there is an opportunity for learning about the community and a need to deal with their departure. How can you learn from people who are leaving – the good and affirming aspects of their experience in community and the areas that need healing? What ritual can you use to acknowledge the transition of those departing? How will you take this information and affirm or heal the community?

Rituals

What, if any, rituals might be used for ground breaking, births and deaths in the community, the coming of age for young men and women, and birthdays or events of religious or spiritual significance (e.g., various New Years, Christmas, Hanukkah, the solstices)? Rituals are at the heart of building community.

Effective meetings

The amount of time spent in meetings is staggering. Creating effective meetings through good planning and facilitation can make the experience far more enjoyable and successful.

Special issues

Who stays with it? Burnout and turnover during development stage

After a few meetings Mike has dropped out. Four women and two men have continued to meet regularly and are making plans to build their dream of community. This is generally the pattern. Few of the members of a cohousing core group were friends before they got involved in the group. This is not always the case, but it is a predominant pattern.

Another pattern is that more women are interested at first then men. My suggestion would be not to worry about the gender mix and simply let it unfold. The important thing is to encourage those who are genuinely interested to continue participating and work together to keep things going. Share in the creation of your dream.

Generally, it does take a "burning soul" to get things rolling. Someone must have the energy and fire to get everyone together, keep track of things, arrange for meeting locations and take care of all the little administrative details. Ideally, the burning soul will eventually melt into the rest of the group as the other participants catch fire too. Soon the new cohousing core group takes on a life of its own and no one member drives it. The group works together to keep records, plan for future meetings, and get things done.

Special Issues

There are several issues that all groups have to deal with. These are issues that can keep any one individual from feeling comfortable about joining the group. Some are immediately apparent, and some are more philosophical, but each has an impact on the way members or potential members feel about their relationship to the group. The following list may not be comprehensive, but it will give you an idea of the typical issues that come up and which must someday be addressed.

- Pets
- Parking
- Pesticides
- Firearms
- Wood stoves
- Smoking

Take the time to talk about these issues and others, but try to keep a perspective on which ones must be resolved now, and which can be resolved later. As the trust grows, concerns will diminish. As you begin to feel confident that "the community" cares about you as an individual, your concerns for security and other needs will become far less intense.

After a while, members who were concerned about their special concerns and their non-negotiable issues, were worried that their needs would not be met, begin to trust that the other members of the group care enough about them to see to it that their needs get met. They begin to trust in community, and what was once non-negotiable ultimately becomes a processing of identifying personal needs and preferences, and blending them with the other members of the group, refining their vision for community.

BY TOM MOENCH

Conflict and change

"Our lives are not dependent on whether or not we have conflict. It is what we do with conflict that makes a difference." — Thomas Crum

Sources of conflict

Creating a vision through working together is guaranteed to accomplish two things — conflict and change. Conflict is a call for creativity; it is something to resolve rather than avoid. Knowing in advance situations which often generate conflict can be helpful. Most people try to resolve conflict at the interpersonal level, but it is more effective to address conflict at the level of structure and processes. The following list gives some key areas of conflict and how they can be addressed:

Personality strengths or learning styles differ

It is important to understand the diversity that arises from internal structures — how people think, relate to one another, solve problems and learn new ideas and skills (visual, auditory, reading and movement). Understanding of internal differences lays the foundation for how well people work together in a group.

Hold a group workshop on Myers-Briggs Type Indicator (MBTI) Personal Strengths and Relational Power (Copyrighted workshop of Tom Moench, 290 Madison Avenue, N. Bainbridge Island, WA 98110), or some other exploration of learning styles or behavioral styles.

Values and priorities differ

If value and priorities differ, revisit the community vision statement, especially the core values, beliefs and shared commitments.

Communication is ineffective or non-existent

More people learn visually or through reading rather than hearing. In meetings, make sure that discussion items are written down in front of the group. Keep good records of decisions. Make sure every decision includes the rationale for why it was proposed and what it was supposed to accomplish. Create a decision log/database to easily reference prior decisions.

Outcomes do not meet expectations

A periodic review of your vision and goals document should reduce this conflict by identifying where to take on issues important to the members.

Power is inequitably distributed

Attend to group structure and processes when power differentials are causing conflict. Are certain members given special consideration and influence because they are female, male, older, younger, a minority? Are members with the same rights given the same standards of responsibility or are they given special treatment? Are the quiet members given equal opportunity to speak and be heard as the outgoing?

Perceptions of a situation differ

People's perceptions differ dramatically because of differences in values, personal strengths, learning styles, education and cultural beliefs. When there is a problem use the 3 Actuals – go to the actual place, talk to the actual people involved and get the actual facts. Then everyone is closer to talking about "the facts."

Capacity to handle complexity

Comfort with and the capacity to handle complexity differs greatly from person to person and is independent of education or general intelligence. Sometimes called complexity intelligence, it reflects the range and number of factors and variables a person can handle mentally to plan and execute goal-directed activities. How far into the future an individual can plan is called one's time horizon and reflects the individual's level of complexity intelligence. Cohousing is particularly prone to conflict from mismatches in the capacity to handle complexity. Mismatches are most evident when two people argue over the importance or necessity of task sequencing. Any association that approaches 50+ participants will become sufficiently complex that it will naturally begin to devolve into smaller groups in order to get things done.

Roles are unclear

Volunteer associations generate conflict by not clearly defining who is doing what and when. They also generate conflict by trying to define who is doing what by when. Words such as participative, egalitarian, fair, equitable and voluntary go undefined and are used without clarity. The group needs to struggle with the question,

"What do we do when others do not meet expectations?" Responsible members will generally try to define roles, expectations and logical consequences in order to see if they can trust others. The irresponsible will tend to avoid definitions and use shame to counter the efforts of the responsible.

Conflict resolution

"You have three choices: keep on fighting, ignore each other, or make up and be friends."
— John Knoblauch

The development and community forming phases of a cohousing project are full of intense conflict. The goal is to promote constructive conflict – conflict that results in co-creation and greater intimacy rather than destructive conflict – conflict that destroys the group.

The resolution of conflict begins with you. Begin with the end in mind – what is it that you care so much? The second question if the conflict seems to center upon a person is: Do you wish to have an ongoing relationship with that person and that person with you? Keep in mind that it takes two to say yes to a relationship and one to say no. If you wish to resolve differences and be friends or have a working relationship then a good place to start is working with "The Sentence" (see below). Using "I" messages and being clear about your own thoughts, feelings and wants can resolve some conflicts and help you to focus on the work you need to do. When the whole group is in conflict, round robin discussions give everyone a chance to be heard and are an excellent way for groups to work through their emotional issues and arrive at consensus. You can always use conflict mediation either by someone in the group who is trained in such skills or through a local dispute resolution center.

The sentence

"The Sentence" can help you to define your own boundaries and communicate them to another person to convert conflict into creative action. The Sentence is useful when emotions run high and interpersonal conflict is evident:

I feel _____ (emotion)

When you _____ (action or behavior)

Because I suspect that you _____ (assumption).

How I want you to treat me is _____ (action).

Just working through The Sentence by oneself is often a helpful process to determine what the conflict really is.

The greater good round robin, building consensus

In order to establish a "group consciousness" about a topic before the group makes a decision, try a "Greater Good Round Robin." In an attempt to build consensus make sure that each person is heard and understood, verbally and emotionally.

1. After a proposal and discussion has occurred, and before a decision a "greater good round robin" can be called.
2. Each person is allowed an opportunity to speak or pass in order around the circle. The first round is a sharing of both what you do and do not like (i.e., pros and cons) about a proposal or other suggested action. Request that people listen respectfully without comments or response.
3. During the second round each person answers the question "How might this action serve the best interests of the group?"

End notes:

Tom Moench

Tom Moench is a member of the Winslow Cohousing Group, one of the first cohousing villages in the United States. An organizational consultant who specializes in human capability, group dynamics and organization structure, he has participated, led, coached and done research on teams in athletic, academic, profit, and non-profit organizations. He has worked in the computer services, aerospace and food service industries. He is vice-president of Wired for Success, Inc., an on-line service provider creating on-line connections between people. He is also vice-president of Positive Sum Services, Inc., a consultancy with current focus on how innate personal strengths and multiple intelligences provide a basis for conflict and a foundation for success in human relationships. He is a certified creativity consultant and adjunct faculty at Antioch University, Seattle in the Masters of Psychology program and City University in the Masters in Leadership Studies and MBA programs.

3

The Development Process

Patterns for success • What is a developer? • Eight
major thresholds of a successful cohousing development • How
does a developer create cohousing? • Successful development
strategies • Take a developer to lunch

Patterns for success

Some think that the only way to build a cohousing community as a group is
to assume control at the beginning of the project and maintain that control
through to the end. Many groups assume that they will be their own developer, taking the responsibility and retaining control of the project. A few
groups have succeeded in following this path, but knowledge and some
caution are required to be successful. Establishing a relationship with an experienced developer can save you a lot of time, money and risk. In order to
improve your chance for success it is important that you understand what a
developer is, how they operate and what your development options are.

The development process is costly, complex and unpredictable. To be a success as a developer you must have money, and you must be able to borrow money. Successful, and therefore trustworthy, developers are able to convince someone to lend them money. Lenders prefer to lend money to those who don't really need it, those who already have money and who will use the money they borrow to make more money.

Successful developers are rare. Novice developers may successfully create a product once or twice, but they often don't make any money at it. Success requires knowledge, vision, intuition and cash. And only those developers who are prudent (and sometimes lucky) are ever really successful.

What is a developer?

Let's understand what I mean by a developer. I will compare the real developer to others in the development industry who might represent themselves as developers, or who might otherwise be confused with a developer.

Real developers have cash available to put into any project they choose – not borrowed money, but cash on hand. They are willing to take the risk required in development, and they have generally been successful doing so in the past, which is often where they made their money. They also have the capacity to borrow money, which means they have a track record with the money lenders. They often use the talents and services of promoters, consultants and building contractors. Sometimes they are licensed to do the construction themselves, but often they simply use the services of contractors in the area.

Promoters have knowledge and enthusiasm – developers without the cash. They often pretend to be developers but differ in that the only money they have available is that which they can borrow from you, or someone else. Promoters often set themselves up to be general partner in a limited partnership, where it is other people's money at risk. You might say they are good at spending other people's money, not taking the personal risk themselves because they don't have the money to do so. I would suggest that you stay away from promoters, or use them only as consultants.

Consultants simply have knowledge for sale. They generally do not offer financial support for the project and they ask to be paid for the services they provide, as they are provided. It sometimes happens that a well-established or very generous consultant will offer to delay payment for services, or take partial payment. This is unusual and not to be expected. Asking any consultant to delay receiving payment for services is asking them to become a partner in your project without giving them any control.

Contractors build buildings. Often called "licensed general contractors," if they have been successful in their business as well as prudent, they may have a modest amount of cash set aside. Some contractors have dreams of becoming developers, but be careful. Often they are cash poor (they may not have enough cash for the job that needs to be done) and have limited borrowing power. In addition they have very little experience with the risky business of evaluating, planning and designing a project.

Developers, promoters, consultants and contractors are different animals, different species in the development jungle. It is wise to know which species you are dealing with.

A few generalizations about developers

Developers are creative people, builders of dreams. Developers have a remarkable ability to pursue opportunities, while recognizing and accepting constraints. They are knowledgeable about how the complex development process works, and what is expected. They are able to define their dream, seeing not only what is, but what could be. And finally, they are able to build the pathways necessary to move from what is to what can be.

Developers tend to be politically conservative, seeking to maintain a system that is known, or perceived to work, however flawed it might be. They desire political and financial stability so that they can build their creative endeavors on a foundation that is known and dependable. Like most cohousing people, developers have a strong need to be in control. This is a common trait of successful and creative people. It is not something to run away from, simply something to understand and to manage.

For the developer, profit is usually a secondary goal. This may come as a surprise to you, but the typical developer would much rather create something beautiful or important than simply make money. It is important that they see the fruits of their risk taking. Money is a practical matter for them, necessary to continue their life's work.

Successfully developing cohousing requires the willingness to take a risk, and all developers are risk takers. Of the many developers I have known, all have been as thrilled by the risk as by the reward.

How does a developer create housing?

You probably don't want to be a developer, but understanding how developers successfully create housing will assist you in making better choices in your creative process.

Verify resources available

Before developers look for land, or evaluate market demand, before they dream of building buildings, they begin by making sure they have all the tools they need to successfully develop a project. They identify what resources are required and evaluate those resources immediately available to them: the skills, the time and the financial capacity (cash plus borrowing power). The successful developer must realistically evaluate his or her personal skills and then assemble a team of people with the skills necessary to supplement their own. Small developers can't afford to pay a large staff, so they provide most of the skill themselves. Large developers may be able to afford a staff and a lot of professional help, so their personal skills can be a little more specialized. One interesting thing about developers, however, is that they are generalists. They have a good understanding of real estate, finance, law, construction and marketing.

Select the right land

Developers are constantly looking for good land purchase opportunities. I think it comes as second nature to them, like breathing. If they have been in the business for awhile, many opportunities come their way from others who know of their success. They evaluate these opportunities carefully, always willing to let go, knowing something else will come along. For each site they consider, they do a quick feasibility review, evaluate the current zoning, the neighborhood plan, the potential to change the zoning, the local utility infrastructure, etc. They plug site-specific numbers into their standard pro forma (anticipated budget), and measure financial viability. This is generally done in-house, using their own experience and intuition. They review marketing feasibility, asking themselves practical questions, such as "What product will sell in this location?" and "How much could we get for it?"

Above all, successful developers know how to be selective, discarding potential sites that won't work, may not work, or which might be too risky. They only select sites they are certain will work well. They choose good locations, for a reasonable price, and they are always looking for the best purchase terms.

Quick, practical design

The design process for developers is short and to the point. They have built and sold many projects before, so they know what sells, they know what people want. The programming is automatic, based on what worked well on previous projects. Many of the design assumptions are made long before locating a site that works. Generally developers give the architect few instructions, since often the architect they use has worked with them before. They remain hands-off, trusting the architect to provide them with what they need. When they ask their architect to help with the initial feasibility review, they ask, "How many units can you get on this site?" and "What site plan options will work?" and "Can you give me an answer by tomorrow afternoon?"

In evaluating site plan options, they select a site plan that will sell, that is cost effective, and that is appealing to them personally. Schematic design and design development happen very quickly with brief, rough, to-the-point presentations. Decisions are just as quick, often happening on the spot. Since the working drawings (construction documents) are the most expensive part of the design process the developer puts this off for as long as possible, then turns the architects loose to complete the drawings quickly. Rarely do they have their architect provide more than the minimum necessary construction supervision to satisfy the architect insurance requirements. Post-occupancy evaluation amounts to asking the questions, "What worked?" and "What sold?"

Reduce liability, reduce tax burden

For developers the legal and accounting aspects of the development process are fairly straightforward. They explore ways to reduce their liability and their tax obligations. Often they simply set up a new (or numbered) company, separating other projects and other assets from the potential failure of this new project. Purchase and sale agreements, contracts with professionals, closing documents, are all standardized to lower cost, reduce time requirements, and add to predictability. For a developer, risk evaluation and risk management are very personal. They ask legal opinions from their lawyers, but they do what they feel is reasonable to do, sometimes, seemingly, without regard to what their lawyers say.

Financial planning

All developers have a standard project pro forma (anticipated budget used for planning) that meets their needs. They make a few informed guesses about what the project might cost, balancing unit pricing (the source of the income) with marketability (what will sell). After design and costing they complete a final budget for the bank. If things change after this point they change their internal budget, but the bank still sees only the original "Bank Budget."

Cash flow planning is usually informal, sometimes almost seat-of-the-pants. Developers are good at "robbing Peter to pay Paul." I think they invented the phrase. As they develop their borrowing strategies for a certain project they always look for ways to make their cash go further. They are always aware of who will lend, with what conditions, at what cost (interest rates and fees).

The most important part of the financial planning is tax reduction and avoidance. Developers hate to pay taxes. Politically right of center, they usually assume that all money paid to government has simply gone down the drain.

Selling the product

Since each project is only one of many, the marketing plan for a new project must fit into a long-term, multi-project marketing strategy. For smaller projects, 5% to 7% of project cost is spent on signs, advertising, promotion and sales. For a larger project, where the costs are amortized over a large number of units, the figures may be down around 3% to 4% of project cost.

Successful development strategies

There are a number of successful strategies for developing cohousing, eco-villages or sustainable communities. The following development strategies are described in terms of the "developers" and "buyers." By developer I mean the person or persons who put up the money and take the risk to get a project built. The buyer is the household or group of households that buy the finished product and move in.

Be your own developer

Many of you will assume that being your own developer is the only way to create cohousing for yourselves. Let's look at what it means. Being your own developer means identifying and assembling all the right assets and resources and then applying them appropriately to make your project happen. Implementing strategies for the cost-effective use of resources is one of the most important parts of this complex puzzle.

Eight major thresholds of a successful cohousing development

Development done by a community is very different from development by an individual, or a hierarchical organization. The group must form, put their money on the table, learn the language of development, learn to make decisions so they can speak with one voice, and so on.

I have noticed several stages in the successful development of cohousing. These are thresholds of commitment through which each group must pass, and with the group each of its members must make a personal choice to continue. The Eight Major Thresholds are:

- Commitment to form a group to create community.
  - Exploring goals and values.
  - Committing to one another.
- Commitment of time for building a community.
  - Meetings, meetings, and more meetings!!!
  - Taking the time to explore, the time to learn, and the time to feel trust.
- Commitment of money.
  - Incremental commitment of money.
  - $1,000 to $5,000 per household to achieve loss threshold.
- Commitment to a specific site.
  - Finding land, committing to a location. Spending money on feasibility studies, engineering, closing on the purchase.
- Commitment to hiring professionals.
  - Finding an architect, committing to a contract for services.
  - Programming commitments, design commitments.
- Commitment to construction financing.
  - Committing resources to assembling complex loan packages.
  - Committing to sign on the construction loan with all members.
- Construction start.
  - Committing to actually getting the buildings under construction.
  - Committing to pay to have the project built.
- Move in!
  - Committing to be there when it is time to move in.
  - Committing to pay for your unit, to sign for the mortgage.

Each of these thresholds or stages is a difficult time. Each forges community, but each separates those who are willing to make the commitment and take the risk from those who are not.

Being your own developer means taking all the risk. It means putting up all the money, knowing when to spend it and on what. For a group it also means being able to make quick, effective decisions, and it means speaking with one voice. Having a contract with a supplier of engineering services, for example, means giving clear, concise directions at the appropriate time. It means being in control and having the ability to exercise that control effectively. You will need substantial amounts of cash, sufficient credit at the right time, knowledge of the development and construction process, and the wisdom to know when to do what.

To many, it seems to be the only way or the "right" way to build a co-housing community, assuming control at the beginning and maintaining that control through to the end. Winslow Cohousing and Pioneer Valley Cohousing were developed exclusively by the members as a group.

Find a developer to be your partner

Another way to maintain some control while letting go of some of the risk is to find a developer to be your partner. Partnering with a developer has its positives and negatives. Certainly developers will want some compensation for spending their money and taking a risk, but they will also require some control, which means that the group will have to give up some control. The positive side of the equation is that your group will not have to come up with all the cash required, you won't be taking all the risk, and most importantly you will have a partner who knows what he or she is doing and can therefore get construction financing.

Typically, when a cohousing group establishes a partnership with a developer it begins as a loose understanding while the developer searches for an appropriate site. Once a site is located and the group is asked to make a decision the partnership is either forged, or it falls apart. If the group makes a commitment to the property, signing an agreement to participate in some way as well as indicating an intent to purchase the final product, the developer can move forward with the infrastructure planning, permit approvals and the design process.

If your group, or one member of the group, already has a piece of land you think will work, consider taking it to a developer. Ask if he or she will help you develop it, making it clear that you intend to make it worth their while financially. "Worth their while" varies from one developer to another, but generally the range would be 5% to 10% of total project cost.

If you can find an interested developer, he or she will assist you in evaluating the property and its development potential. When the feasibility evaluation is complete, the developer should make a presentation to the group. This is a good way to learn about each other before making any long-term agreements.

Working with a developer as a partner is one of the most effective ways to get your project built, but take care, and check out potential development partners carefully. Look at several projects they have built. Talk to the professionals they work with, including their banker. Ask other developers about them. Ask your lawyer about them. Take the time to get to know who you will be working with.

Work with a government housing agency

Many groups assume that since they can't afford to create cohousing on their own, or because they have or hope to have low-income members, that they should find and work with a government agency to create their cohousing dreams. Unfortunately, it is probably too early in the development of cohousing in North America to expect any direct financial support from a government agency.

In some areas government agencies are working with user groups and nonprofit associations or societies to improve housing stock, or even to build new housing. If you live in one of these areas you might look for a person at your local housing agency who could steer you in the right direction. Find out who is building affordable housing, or renovating existing housing stocks with government assistance. In some areas the best you should expect is that government-owned land might be made available to your group under special terms. When this does happen the government agency responsible for the property often is required by law to sell at a market price, to protect the public interest during the sale of a public asset. The special terms which might be made available could include a zero down or low down payment, low interest financing (either short term or long term) or a longer period of time before closing, giving you the time to prepare your group, your money and your project design.

Generally speaking, working with a government agency, however appealing it might seem, requires extreme patience and an abundance of time. The bureaucracy moves very slowly. It is big and cumbersome, and the right hand often doesn't know what the left hand is doing. If your expectations aren't excessive and you are willing to wait, working with a government agency might work for you.

Groups who have had some success working with government agencies in getting their projects built include the South Side Park Group in Sacramento and the Puget Ridge Group in Seattle.

Buy a completed project from a developer

Another approach is to buy a completed project from a developer. Retaining complete control, a developer moves ahead as he normally would, creating a "cohousing product" as quickly and efficiently as possible. At completion the developer turns to the group who has expressed interest in purchasing the project and offers to sell them private units at prices set by the developer.

There are obvious advantages and disadvantages to this way of creating cohousing. First, if a developer initiates and builds a cohousing project, you can assume the developer will retain complete control from beginning to end. The rule is, the one who spends the money has the control, and it is a rare individual, and an even more rare developer, who would relinquish control of a project where their money is at stake. On the other hand, the project will have been built quickly and efficiently. If the developer is sensitive to the needs of a cohousing community and really believes there are buyers to purchase the product when it is complete, the final product may provide a very satisfying place for your community to live.

The danger is that developers who say they believe in cohousing may prudently cover their bets by compromising the design, especially the site planning and the size of the common house, just in case they can't find enough "cohousing buyers." They know that if they have to sell the product as "market housing" there are features of a cohousing design, like the separation of the car from the private unit, that don't sit well with the "market housing" buyer who is looking for privacy and personal comfort. The compromise may be too much for your community, significantly reducing the chance that your group will be able to develop and maintain a real feeling of community.

Arrange for a "turnkey project" to be built by a developer

Another way to buy a completed product from a developer is to arrange for a "turnkey project," defining beforehand what product you wish to buy in the end. Your group might acquire the rights to a piece of land and go through the design process, paying for it yourselves. Then you go to a developer with a site and a set of plans, asking him or her to develop the project for you.

A developer who sees cohousing as a viable product can build a project with significant input by the cohousing group. By agreeing at the outset to purchase a finished project you significantly reduce the developer's risk, enabling the product to be built to your specifications.

One member acts as a developer

Sometimes the group comes up with a piece of land and then can't move forward for some reason. Difficulty in making decisions, unwillingness to meet often enough or to take the time necessary to work through the issues can result in a stalled project. Sometimes one or more members simply puts on the brakes and says "No, I am not ready yet." Frustration can lead to one member becoming the developer on his or her own.

This can also happen when an individual who is keen and ready to get going can't find enough people to join or make a commitment. The developer may just decide, "If I build it, they will come." When this happens the members of the group may feel left out. They may eventually harbor resentments. But there are examples where this development strategy has worked successfully.

In Sante Fe, New Mexico, a member of a new cohousing group was also a lawyer and an experienced developer. He wanted to live in cohousing and he didn't want to just talk about it. When the site became available and the group could not move quickly enough, he moved on his own. He consulted the group during the process, keeping them informed of progress, but he used his own money, took all the risk and retained control. He sold the final product to a few members of the original group and a lot of newcomers who simply liked what he had created. Some of the original members were grateful for what he had done. Others were not and went their own way, choosing not to participate. If you can live with the control issues, this can be an efficient and effective way of getting your cohousing project built.

Take a developer to lunch

How do you get the information you need about ownership structure, or financing, or land, etc? Call an experienced developer. Or, try a real estate lawyer or a mortgage broker who works with multi-family housing in your area. Explain to the developer that you have a group of people who wish to buy a multi-family project and you are looking for advice about shopping for such a product. Or tell the professionals you are shopping for services such as they provide. Whomever it is, invite them to lunch. They may try to pick up the tab, especially if you are talking to a developer. (Paying means being in control.) Stick to your guns, and pay for lunch. The few dollars it will cost will pay back many times over in the future.

Ask a lot of questions. Take good notes. If more than one member of your group wants to participate, keep the group very small, two or three at the most. Most people will be flattered to see you writing feverishly as they give you advice about how to make your project happen. Don't make any promises, of course, but leave the possibility of working with them open. They may continue to be a good source of information. You may grow to like them and even trust them. They may grow to like you and your project.

You probably don't want to be a developer yourself. If you thought you did, you may not think so after you have completed this process. There are times when it is tough, when you have to make difficult and expensive decisions. Bill Hancock, the developer partner with the WindSong project has more than once asked a meeting of WindSong members, "So, how do you like development now?"

Consider working with a developer who knows the game, who can get you through the rough spots, and keep you on track. With the knowledge you have gained here you will have a better understanding of how developers think, and what you can do to make your project go more smoothly, whatever development strategy you choose.

4

Working with Professionals

What professionals will you need? • Who (or what) is
an architect? • Selection process • Contracts • Using
professionals effectively • Summary

Consider the gardener who wants to build a simple garden shed. She knows
what she wants. She knows what it needs to do, how big it needs to be, and
where she wants it. She hears that she needs a building permit, so on Friday
before her week off, she goes down to the building department to pick up
the permit so she can start on Saturday morning. What does she find? The
zoning laws don't allow her to put the building where she wanted to put it.
The building code requires a foundation that meets certain safety requirements, making the project much more expensive than she expected. And
the process takes three weeks for review and approval, after submitting a set
of scale drawings on paper of a certain size. After all the visualization, the
planning, and the expectations, our gardener has to start over. She spends
her vacation, not building the garden shed, but figuring out where it will fit
legally, how to afford the expensive foundation, and how to get it drawn
properly. It may be next year before she will build her garden shed.

   If a cohousing group acts like that do-it-yourselfer it can strangle the development process by avoiding or delaying the professional help needed to make the project a success. You will be spending millions of dollars, building several buildings, for dozens of people. The process is complex and expensive and you will want to do it efficiently and effectively.

Don't avoid professionals. They will cost money, but part of getting your project built is learning to spend money wisely and appropriately.

What professionals will you need?

The lawyer

A lawyer or attorney will be necessary to advise you, as a group, on legal matters to do with organizing and incorporation, as well as contracts. They may also be of service in contract negotiations. Fees vary widely, and the legal budget you establish will depend heavily on how much you want to use the services of your lawyer. Using standard forms, self-help books and industry standard contracts, you can reduce the amount of time your lawyer spends, and hence the cost for legal services.

Lawyers usually work on a retainer basis with no written contract. This means you pay them a deposit and they start working for you. Then they bill you for their work plus their expenses. Often, lawyers bill irregularly, meaning they do not necessarily send you a bill once a month.

As with most professionals, it is best to find a lawyer by personal referral. I recommend that you look for a generalist who can handle contracts, real estate and business law. Don't try to do your project without talking to a lawyer.

The accountant

Consult an accountant about taxes. Your accountant can save you far more money than you will spend on accounting services if you consult them early, and throughout the planning stages of your project.

Your accountant can also assist you in setting up your bookkeeping and accounting system, and may have a bookkeeping service available if you don't have a member who is comfortable keeping the books.

Like lawyers, accountants usually work on a retainer basis with no written contract. Although they may not bill every month, they will bill for their work and their expenses more regularly than many lawyers do.

Real estate agents

In my experience realtors are of limited use to a cohousing group. They may be able to help you search for land, but most realtors have very little experience with raw land and especially multi-family projects.

Realtors work on commission and they get paid only when the sale is concluded, or closed. This means they may not be motivated to work on your behalf to get you a long closing period.

Some commercial realtors will work as consultants, charging you by the hour, or as a fixed fee. This can be a good way of securing their motivation and allegiance.

The mortgage broker

Mortgage brokers find loans. They are paid a fee, usually a small percentage of the loan amount, when the loan closes (when it is funded).

Consider using a mortgage broker. They can be a great help to you in assembling your loan package as well as getting that package in front of potential lenders.

The appraiser

The appraiser determines the value of your project and each private unit by comparing your project to actual sales in other comparable projects. In addition, they usually consider project costs and rental value. This provides the lending institution with assurance that they have reasonable security for the construction loan they are supplying. Since all future financing is based on the values established by the appraiser, it is important that your unit selling prices correspond closely to the values identified in the appraisal.

The appraiser is paid either by the financial institution, or sometimes directly by the developer. Since their future work is dependent on their credibility with the financial institutions, appraisers normally take their direction from the bank. Typical appraisal fees for a 30-unit project are in the range of $3,000 to $5,000.

The architect

The architect is the most important part of your professional team. Please don't try to do your project without one. Architects generally work on contract, or using a letter of agreement. Payment is hourly, by fixed fee, or as a predetermined percentage of the construction cost. They tend to bill monthly, although other arrangements can be made. (See Who (or what) is an architect? below, and Chapter 6, The Design Process.)

The landscape architect

A landscape architect specializes in the site planning phase of your design process. They are one of the most important, and one of the most overlooked of the professionals who can be of help to a cohousing group. Please don't leave site planning to an architect. (See also Chapter 6, The Design Process.)

Landscape architects generally work on contract, or using a letter of agreement. Payment is usually hourly or by fixed fee, and they tend to bill monthly.

The engineers

Several engineers will be involved in getting your project planned and built, but you won't necessarily even meet them. Usually the engineering team works for the architect (and landscape architect) to provide you with civil, structural, electrical and mechanical engineering.

Some groups have established relationships with civil engineers who are also licensed as landscape architects. I can think of no better combination when it comes to site planning than finding this blend of skills in one person or firm.

The engineers are often paid by the architects as a part of the architectural fees. They generally work on contract with the architect, or using a letter of agreement. Payment is usually hourly or by fixed fee.

The marketing professional

Consider using a marketing professional, especially if you can find someone with cohousing experience. They can help you plan and execute your marketing and membership program. Pay them hourly, or arrange a fixed fee if you feel you can clearly define the work you want them to do.

The surveyors

Often part of the engineering team, the surveyors are an important part of locating site features properly for site planning, and then locating buildings properly during construction.

Whether they work for you directly or as a part of the design team, they generally work on verbal agreement, or using a letter of agreement. Payment is usually hourly or by fixed fee, and they tend to bill monthly.

The contractor or builder

The largest and most important contract you will have is with a general contractor or builder who will build your buildings. There is always a carefully written contract between the builder and the client.

Generally builders are paid a fixed price for what they have agreed to build. Sometimes they will bill on a time and materials basis. Talk to your lawyer and other development professionals before signing a contract for construction.

The development consultant

The development consultant can assist you in evaluating the professionals you want to hire, they can provide a second opinion on your development strategy, or they can manage the entire development process. It depends on what you decide you need and what time and skills are available within your group.

Development consultants generally work on contract, or using a letter of agreement. Payment can be hourly, by fixed fee, or as a predetermined percentage of the project cost. They tend to bill monthly although other arrangements can be made.

Who (or what) is an architect?

Architects are a creative lot by nature, being attracted to the field by the desire to build things, to draw, and to be artistic. Often they are romantics as well, not well known for their practicality, or for staying within budget.

You need to work with an architect because you need to have someone pull all the complex pieces of your project together into a set of drawings that represent what you want to build. It might seem that you could hire a drafting person to simply draw what you need, but in fact much of the challenge comes from the process of interpreting what you say you want and turning it into something that really reflects your intentions.

The other benefit of using an architect relates to the difficult job of facilitating your group decision-making process. When the architect presents the designs, he or she will assist each member of the group in understanding that alternatives have been considered, helping them come to consensus as a community.

Architects do have limitations. Very often they have an unstated agenda, often unknown even to themselves. Such agendas include a pre-disposition toward certain building materials, certain design styles, and certain roof forms. So investigate their background and their references. View several projects they have done and see if you find any peculiarities. Ask other clients about them. If you like the design style, the materials selected, this is a plus. Don't expect architects to change the way they do things just because your group has asked them to do so.

Architecture training focuses on the process of designing buildings. They learn about structures, materials, and connections. They learn about space and form and the art of design. Often, an architectural education is weak in the following areas:

- Site planning
- Grading and drainage
- Building code requirements
- Zoning
- Financial planning and budgeting
- Cost control
- Group process and consensus building
- Business management (running their own office)

Architects are generally strong on building design, drafting and drawing, spatial relationships, and materials.

Watch out for young architects. They may be very talented, but they are not likely to have the life experience necessary to consider or even understand a number of basic human behavior issues. If they don't have children, they aren't likely to provide adequately for the children of your community. If they have never cooked, they are unlikely to really understand the kitchen experience, designing attractive but impractical kitchens. Good architecture comes from a combination of skill, talent and extensive life experience.

Selection process

When looking for professional help ask other professionals, and listen to their recommendations. Call several developers and ask what they think about a professional you are considering. Call an architect and ask about lawyers, and vice versa. The selection of good professional help is an art. In the end it requires intuition as much as anything else.

When you have a short list of people you are considering, take the time to get to know them. How do they think? What do they care about? What do they think of your dream of community?

The comments below focus most closely on the hiring of the architect. Many of these concepts and ideas will also be useful in hiring the other professionals you will need to work with. Take advantage of the growing number of skilled architects and professionals who have actually been involved in building cohousing. For example, consider hiring The CoHousing Company to come to your location to do the programming for your project. They can teach the local design team about the important cohousing design issues in the process. ("Programming" is the first phase of design. It is described in detail in Chapter 6, The Design Process.)

A strong warning is in order regarding hiring an architect with no *direct* cohousing experience. Some architects think they know all about it, having looked at the pictures of cohousing in a book. An architect without direct cohousing experience will need help to get a project to work well. Unfortunately, they may not recognize, or accept, that help is appropriate.

Requests for proposals

A Request for Proposal (RFP) is just that; it is a formal request that the intended professionals should make specific proposals regarding the provision of services for a fee. Professionals respond to specific items in the request, providing information that will help you make a good decision about who to hire.

The RFP is used in a variety of cases, selecting certain professionals, or selecting contractors. I will focus here on the selection of the design team.

HOW IS IT DONE?
- Write a Request for Proposal.
- Collect a list of qualified professionals.
- Submit the RFP to the qualified professionals.
- Accept their responses by an appropriate deadline.
- Have a committee review all responses and select a short list of three or four.
- *Important:* Call all respondents and notify them of your decision.

- Arrange to interview those on the short list.
- Have the committee select two finalists after the interviews.
- *Important:* Call all those short-listed and notify them of your decision.
- Invite the two finalists to make short presentations to the entire group. Ask them to present or demonstrate the following:
  1. Background and qualifications of all team members
  2. Project management and client response experience
  3. Group facilitation skills
  4. Post-Occupancy Evaluation of an existing cohousing community (a brief examination and evaluation of a completed community, including a look at resident satisfaction with community design)
  5. Sample of live programming and drawing (much like the "CoDesign Process," described in Chapter 6, The Design Process)
- After the second finalist has left (and you have had a good break) discuss the two finalists and come to consensus on one. Do not wait for another meeting to conclude this process.
- Call both finalists immediately and let them know what you have decided. Don't wait until the next day.

WHAT SHOULD A REQUEST FOR PROPOSAL INCLUDE?

Simply, it should ask for qualifications, a method of providing the services required, and a fee and payment schedule.

Typically, you would make a request for proposal when you knew you were going to need architectural services in about six weeks. This would give them sufficient time to respond without unnecessary rushing, and give you the time to review their responses.

I recommend including some material about your expectations on the six phases of design. (See Chapter 6, The Design Process.) Many architects don't think about these design phases (some do) and it is good for a group to use this language when asking for a specific set of services. Some architects think they can skip the programming phase. They seem to want to program while they design. In my experience with cohousing, this won't work.

In the RFP, stress the importance of the need for group process and facilitation skills. An architect must be able to help a group reach consensus. I have watched many good architects fall short when trying to "sell" their design work to a group. Don't let your group settle for bland, watered-down design compromises, in order to achieve consensus, as some early groups have done. A design team with good sales and presentation skills can sell good design to people who may not appreciate it.

You will receive questions about what is to be designed and where the focus should be. Keep in mind that you want your design team to help you design a community, and therefore it is important to focus on the community design issues, namely the common house and the site plan. This is what builds community, and what sustains community. Those group members, and their designers, who allow themselves to spend too much time and effort in private unit design do a disservice to the community, since no community benefit is derived. Customized private units are generally not affordable for those choosing to live in cohousing.

Post-occupancy evaluation

The Post-Occupancy Evaluation (POE) of a project is rarely ever performed. (See Chapter 6, The Design Process.) Architects don't like to look back at their mistakes, and clients don't like to pay for such an evaluation. They often assume that no benefit will come to them after their project is complete.

In your request for proposal, you can ask for a post-occupancy evaluation of a previous cohousing project. It could be a project designed by the architect you are considering, or it may be a project designed and built by someone else, even in another city. You can ask that an abbreviated POE be provided as a part of their submission in response to your RFP. During the contract negotiations you might ask for a more complete post-occupancy evaluation of another project as a part of the programming phase of your project. Both parties, the architect and the group, will benefit greatly.

References

Get references from the professionals you are considering. Call them. Spend time talking to them, or better still, visit in person. Tell them what you are trying to do and what kind of professional services you think you need. Ask about more than the individual professional you are considering. Have they worked with others? What kind of projects? Was there a group process involved? Is there someone else they would recommend you talk to who would know the professional you are considering? Keep notes about what you learn.

Members as professionals

Chances are there are members of your group who have professional skills which will be helpful in making your project a success. As you can imagine, the challenge is to use those professional skills for the benefit of the community without taking advantage of the individual, and without creating a difficult conflict-of-interest situation.

The most challenging professional role to have within the group is that of architect, since the architect is so important in the definition and implementation of your project. The design process is such that the architect will have a substantial amount of ego invested in the drawings he or she creates. In addition, they will need to sell those design "solutions" to other members of your group. It is probable that they will at times find themselves at odds with the wishes of the community. It will be difficult for them to let go.

Architects who are members of cohousing groups find themselves wearing a number of different hats. Sometimes it can be very difficult to determine which hat they should be wearing, or which hat they really are wearing. Are they acting as a member, just like any other member? Are they acting as a design committee member, part of a team doing a task for the benefit of the whole group? Or are they acting as an architect, as an employed professional working for a demanding and difficult client?

As an example, it can be challenging to have a talk with an architect/member who is not performing the expected duties effectively. It can be extremely difficult to replace the person. How do you tell a neighbor, and a friend, that you will have to find someone else?

I would suggest to those who are considering providing professional services to their group, and those who are considering using the professional services of a member of your group, please consider your decision carefully. Talk to someone who has done it before. Several professionals have successfully provided services to their group and would be happy to share their experiences and their advice.

Contracts

Standard contracts

Consider using standard contracts when possible, such as one of the various American Institute of Architects (AIA) documents available. (See the List of Resources in the appendix.) This can save time and money by reducing legal costs, reducing the negotiating time, and reducing stress in the hiring process. The design professional will have sample contracts for you to consider. If you have any questions or concerns, consult your lawyer.

There are a number of parties you may want to include in the agreements, and there are standard agreements covering most of these. These include, but aren't limited to:

- Architect–Owner
- Architect–Project Manager–Owner
- Architect–Contractor–Owner
- Architect–Contractor–Project Manager–Owner

Architectural fees

Most housing developers pay their architects between 1.5% and 3.5% of construction cost, often as a fixed fee, such as $750 to $1,000 per unit. For large projects the architect can live with this. The structural engineering is not included and is paid directly by the developer. In a conventional housing development there is no interaction with a group of residents, and therefore few design iterations, or cycles. A simple program, clear expectations, and lots of repetition makes this feasible for the design team. For a 100-unit project they may receive $75,000 to $100,000.

For the design of custom homes, architectural fees (including structural engineering) are often 7% to 12% of construction cost, depending on how much responsibility and control the architect has, and how involved they are during construction. Detailed programming, complete construction documents, supervision of the bidding process, and careful monitoring of construction, including owner-generated modifications, all add up to a large but well-deserved fee.

For cohousing the design team should theoretically get more like 15% or 20% of construction cost. They never do, and I doubt they ever will. Winslow Cohousing paid a total of about 7.5%. At Cardiff Place, the architect's fees were about 5%, but the group came in late and the architect worked for the developer most of the time. Seldom can a cohousing group pay an architect fully for the work required. Usually the architect underestimates the time required, thinking it can be done in X hours when it will really take them 2X hours.

Another option, of course, is off-the-shelf house plans (or even manufactured housing) where the design fees can be focused, quite literally, on the community design – the common house, and the site plan. Reasonable fees could be as low as 2% to 4%. But remember, you do get what you pay for.

BY KATIE MCCAMANT, THE COHOUSING COMPANY

Architectural fees

In estimating fees we have struggled to find ways to make our work as efficient as possible and still be realistic. Our goal is to set fees as low as we can hold to, and not lose our shirts. As a group and individually you play a critical role in how smoothly the process goes.

Consider the various ways that one can look at the role of the architect. A developer/builder would generally have an architect do a "builder set" of drawings to get building permits and minimal, if any, construction administration. The builder and/or developer will do most of the material selections using those they have found cost effective from previous projects. The developer may put together a set of upgrade options for buyers to select, such as a limited number of flooring types, countertop colors, exterior paint colors, etc. Anything but the most standard choices are extra costs and not part of basic fees. This is the way most "spec" developments are done and their architectural fees are very low at 4 to 5% of construction costs. These fees typically include structural engineering.

A non-profit developer or any developer whose company is not closely aligned with a builder will typically use an architect's full services through construction administration. In this case, the client is the developer and their project manager is the only person who has a say in details and aesthetic once you have planning approvals. Architectural fees are typically 6–10% of construction costs depending on the size and complexity of the project. These fees typically include engineering.

In custom house design, the architect works closely with the home buyer who is involved in every detail of the design and material selection. Architectural fees typically range from 9–15% of construction costs depending on the size and the ability of the client to make and stick to decisions. Construction costs are typically twice that of spec production houses (and can easily go up from there).

In CoHousing we are constantly struggling between the need to keep consulting fees and construction costs down and the complications of an opinionated "group client" made up of individuals who have a lot of design ideas. As architects, we enjoy working with clients to make the project really theirs and trying to satisfy their dreams for a home. On the other hand, we know how tight your budgets are and that to hold to a tight construction budget actually leaves very little room for much design input. We can spend a great deal of our time saying "great idea but not in your budget."

Architectural fees for CoHousing projects typically are in the middle realm in that you are a client who wants to make sure you get quality buildings and is usually looking for somethiµng a little different than the "developer special." It then becomes the group's decision as to how much input you want in the detail design and material decisions.

At The CoHousing Company we have found that the tighter the construction budget, the less difference resident input makes because there is actually very limited flexibility. And the more involved you get, the more you think about all the things you can't afford and therefore are more likely to end up disappointed. The more room there is in the construction budget, the more choices there are and therefore, the more sense it makes for people to be involved. Therefore, the first thing the group needs to consider is what is the construction budget you are aiming for and just how tight is it.

In negotiating the contract with your architect keep in mind that architects prefer to do the "real design" phases, the fun part. This is the schematic design and the design development. They will always provide the construction drawings, but only because they have to. In larger firms, the partners and the senior associates do the design, the young or new associates do the construction drawings. Construction details get boring, but they are actually the most important part of the design process. Talk with your design team about how they will allocate their efforts before you hire them.

The following table illustrates the typical distribution of architectural fees for each element of the design process, and my recommendation for the redistribution of fees. Clients and projects differ dramatically, so use this table only as a guide.

DISTRIBUTION OF ARCHITECTURAL FEES

Elements of Design	Typical	Recommended
1. Programming	2.0%	7.5%
2. Schematic Design	35.0%	15.0%
3. Design Development	30.0%	15.0%
4. Construction Drawings	30.0%	50.0%
5. Construction Supervision	3.0%	10.0%
6. Post-Occupancy Evaluation	0.0%	2.5%
TOTAL FEE	100.0%	100.0%

Using professionals effectively

Management

The key professional relationship is with the architect. Historically, the architect was a master builder, responsible for everything related to construction, from site selection to furnishing the interior.

In our day of specialization, the architect's role in the development and construction process is often reduced to that of a technician, trained to design a building to meet the specific requirements of the building codes. If they are good at design, they may be able to provide you with a building that is esthetically pleasing. If they are really good, they may be able to design a building that meets your needs, for the money you have available to spend.

Managing all of your professionals in today's world requires an understanding of the complex requirements and relationships which will affect each professional's work. It requires an understanding of their skills as well as seeing to it that all the required tasks are accomplished. This is where a development consultant or project manager may be helpful for your project.

Performance review

Don't hesitate to do a formal performance review. Indicate in your contract negotiations that you want to do this. Consider whether the services you have received are as you expected, and talk to your professionals about it. There is no need to make a performance review confrontational. An experienced professional will welcome the input and the feedback.

Summary

Don't let the do-it-yourselfers in your group keep your project from getting off the ground. A common challenge for many groups is the desire by some members to take on more than they can handle. Not wanting to spend money, they will attempt to do everything themselves. I have seen this kill several cohousing groups.

Experienced developers use professionals and there is no reason to believe that a group of amateurs could develop a multi-million-dollar project without the help of the same professionals.

Seek good professional help. Understand what they are doing for you. Monitor their work, pay them appropriately and expect good service.

5

Buying Land

Land is available • Defining expectations • Cutting and
pasting • Mapping reality • Site search checklist • The search
process • Talking to land owners • Making an offer • Trying
again • Feasibility analysis • Project feasibility checklist • Special
considerations • Forming an organization • Summary

Land is available

Land is always available. If you are open to remodeling or expanding an
older structure, they too are available. Whether you are interested in an urban or a rural location you can find the right property for creating your
cohousing community.

Think of this as a big treasure hunt. If you are successful, you will have
a place to build your community. If you are not, at the very least you will
have gotten to know your community a lot better. Your city or town may
seem built up, or developed to capacity, but look around at the number
of vacant lots. Watch for the special situations. Consider the older and
especially the vacant structures in transition neighborhoods. These areas
where land uses are changing might include old warehouse buildings
being converted to artists' studios, for instance. And most important,
compare your local zoning map to the real world. (See Chapter 13, Permits
and Approvals.) You will find old houses in multi-family zones, or an
old corner grocery in a newly designated neighborhood commercial zone

intended (by the city planners) for mixed use development or renewal (meaning demolition and replacement).

When you see a piece of property, remember, somebody owns it. That somebody may very well be interested in selling. They may even be interested in cohousing and may be open to helping your group in the development process.

In this chapter I will describe the search process used by many professional land acquisition people who don't even consider property that is already listed. If you choose to use a real estate agent, you will want to follow most of the same procedures. The only difference to you is that the real estate agent will do some of the work for you in return for a commission. (See Chapter 4, Working with Professionals.)

You do need money

You need money to buy land. The prospect of buying land is the first time your group has to deal with significant financial issues. How much cash do we need? Who can put in the money? How much risk are we taking? Do we still include those who can't put in money? How much am I willing to put in?

When you begin to look for land you need cash to make a down payment. It is a good idea to have a preliminary project budget by this time as well. (See Chapter 10, Finance and Budget.) As a community you could find someone who already has the resources to buy the land, such as a developer or a member of the group. Instead of giving up control to an individual or to a developer, consider raising the necessary money within your group. Start pooling your down payment money.

I recommend against seeking outside investors, especially since they will expect a profit (return on their investment). I strongly recommend against non-investor participation in the decision-making process. Those who say they want to participate but can't, or won't, put up any money can really bog down your decision process. Because they do not have a financial stake their attitudes and priorities will be very different. Make sure that future residents control the destiny of your community. And make sure all members carry their own weight, financially, so their stake in the decision-making process is balanced with all the other member/investors.

Throughout this book I refer to "member/investors" simply as "members." I assume that membership and decision control comes only with investment. In general, only those who can afford to own their own home can afford to invest and participate in creating cohousing. Until the day comes when government steps in to provide significant financial support for housing in North America, cohousing development is a process of creating home ownership.

Timing

How long does it take to locate suitable land for your group? The answer is not simple, but here are the principal factors:

- How solid, stable and committed is your group?
- Are you really ready to buy land?
- How rigid are your requirements for size and location?
- How much money do you have to spend?
- Are you willing to consider an existing building or project?
- Are you working with any experienced professionals who might give you a more objective view?

See the time line chart comparing Winslow, Cardiff Place and Wind-Song. Keep in mind that many groups have met for years before feeling as though they were ready to begin the land search process.

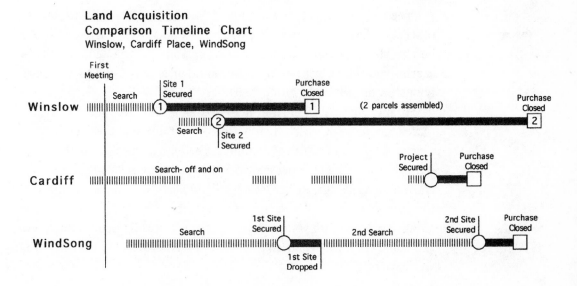

Land Acquisition
Comparison Timeline Chart
Winslow, Cardiff Place, WindSong

Defining expectations

Mapping preferences

Begin your search process by outlining preferred areas on an inexpensive road map. Use a map of sufficient size (approximately 1:50,000 scale) to cover all the possible search areas you would consider for your project. You can expect to need a number of copies of the same map and to do your drawing more than once. Use broad-tipped markers, preferably the translucent type used for highlighting. You will want to see the roads and names underneath your markings. Save the light yellow highlighting markers for the later maps. Find a darker, higher contrast color if possible. You can also color code areas by order of preference.

In my experience people often sit around a table and work on one map at the same time. Don't hesitate to change your mind and try again, and don't worry about mistakes. Keep copies that seem wrong, or out of date. They may be useful later. Try cutting and pasting the best parts of each map attempt together to form the ideal map. Allow this process to be messy at the start. And be sure you do it together as a group so that you own the results together as a group.

While drawing the possibilities, discuss the towns, neighborhoods or districts on the map that seem like good possibilities. There may be areas you need to go see together, a neighborhood that is not familiar to you, the other side of a river you rarely cross. If you wonder, "Will the freeway noise be a problem?" go out and listen. You are creating your new community by sharing your ideas, by listening to one another, and by forging and identifying a group will, and a group heart.

For most people, where they live is extremely important. Choosing the place together allows each member of your group to appreciate the feelings and opinions of other members. Feelings often don't make much sense, but working together provides the chance to build community together and respect the needs of each individual. When you have completed the process, compare the identified preference areas. Decide how you are going to proceed with your search. If the search area is discontinuous (not all in one place) you will need to rank your search areas. Decide where you will start.

Cutting and pasting

You may be lucky and have the primary search area fall in the middle of one map. Normally you will have to cut and paste your maps together to get your primary search area all on one page. Maps are not sacred like books. You can and should cut them up. Buy more than one copy if necessary. Often your search area will fall across the corner of four maps. When this happens it will require pasting together the four separate maps and then cutting off the areas not within your search area.

Begin with the top, or upper left map, cutting off the lower edge and the right edge if necessary. Paste or tape the lower map (from the back) to the upper map. If four maps are required, repeat this process for the two right maps before pasting or taping them to the two left maps.

After your maps are assembled and pasted together to cover the entire primary search area, lay them out and compare them to the road map showing your primary search area. Take time to get fully oriented, locating key features on each set of maps until you are familiar with the differences in scale and detail. (You may also find errors and omissions.) Using a light highlighting marker, like yellow or pink, outline the primary search area on each of the detail maps.

Using a different color, shade the areas on your search area zoning map which correspond to the zones you have selected to consider, such as all multi-family and neighborhood business zones. (See Chapter 13, Permits and Approvals.)

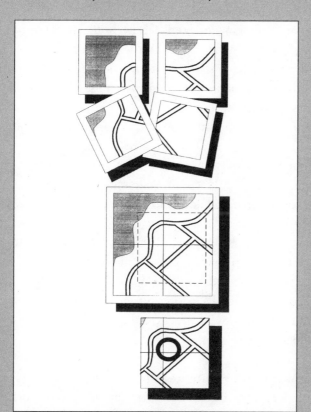

Urban vs. rural

Most people I talk to about cohousing imagine buying 40 acres together and building homes with a comfortable common house, gardens, and lots of room for all. This may still be possible in some parts of the world, but it is unlikely today. We are becoming more aware, as a society, that sprawling suburban development is socially and environmentally costly. Planners are writing and mapping comprehensive plans which limit development to designated urban growth areas. Open space is becoming more and more precious to all of us, so rural areas are being down-zoned to protect them from developers, and cohousing groups like you. Keep in mind that urban growth areas are not necessarily within the city. They tend to be defined by the capacity to extend existing infrastructure, which means they are often adjacent to small towns or along major roadways.

Close to schools, shopping, work and the video store

Many people go into the cohousing process with an ill-defined romantic notion of what they are looking for. Some feel as though they want an isolated retreat away from the urban areas where we normally live and work. Consider carefully the effect this will have on your lives. Consider also whether or not it is really practical when one of your goals is probably reduced dependency on your car.

For most people it is important to be close to good schools, shopping areas and other services, as well as within a reasonable commuting distance to work. Many rural locations simply don't meet these needs. What might sound romantic out in the countryside may become a shuttle bus nightmare, moving children and adults to where they need to be, when they need to be there.

Urban areas, while they may not sound like an ideal spot to create your community, certainly have their advantages – schools, shopping, work and the various cultural activities you have grown to enjoy. How far away is the nearest library? Consider carefully before you choose a piece of land. Does it fulfill a romantic notion, or is it a practical place for the community you are trying to build together?

How much land do you really need?

It's hard to identify property size as a need. A group may start off believing they need 80 acres, or more. When it comes to choosing a piece of land that works, they find that 20 or 10 or maybe only 2 acres works just fine.

If you know what type of housing you want to create (duplexes, town-houses, etc.) the following guidelines may be of assistance.

Housing Type	Dwelling Units
Single-Family Detached	1–8 per acre
Duplexes	6–12 per acre
Townhouses	8–20 per acre
Apartments	15–50+ per acre

What do you really want, or expect?

The fewer the expectations, the easier this process is. Try to identify your preferences for project size and location. Be sure to ask the following questions.

1. How many units is too many? When would it feel too big, or out of control?
2. How many is not enough? When would a community feel too small, or too intimate?
3. Will we need room for gardens? How much area will you really use? What do you plan to grow? Will the gardening be coopera-tive, or will it be done as individuals?
4. How far are we willing to commute to jobs? Where is the nearest employment center? Where does your current membership work?
5. Are there services you would prefer to have available? Where is the nearest bus line and where does it go? How far is the nearest fire hydrant, or fire station?
6. Can we afford to have views or access to water?

Be flexible

The more flexible your group can be, the more opportunities there are when identifying potential sites.

Mapping reality

Zoning and land use controls

If you are planning to build attached units, you will want to locate multi-family or commercially zoned property. This way, the development process is faster and less risky. In some cases it is possible to use single-family-zoned land to build cluster housing with attached units through a special review process. This is often called a Planned Unit Development (PUD) or

Site search checklist

Fill in as you can each time you have the opportunity to go by the site or pass through the area. (Use simple rating where possible: 1 = low 10 = high)

Location - address:
Owner (if known):

NEIGHBORHOOD

Name:
Character:
Nearest park(s):
Local bus routes:
Neighboring buildings:
Proximity to shopping, etc.:
Schools - location and quality:
Other properties in the area:

PHYSICAL CHARACTER OF LAND

Views:
Slopes:
Vegetation:
Solar access:
Roads and driveways:
Existing buildings, fences, paving:
Potential noise sources:
Noise rating:

SPECIAL NOTES/OBSERVATIONS:

(attach photos)

NOTE: Feel free to photocopy this sheet.

Planned Residential Development (PRD), where special permission is given to build attached or clustered units at an overall density similar to single-family detached dwellings. The risk is, however, if you don't buy your land subject to the basic land use approvals, the property may never receive the PUD approvals required to proceed with development. (See Chapter 13, Permits and Approvals.)

Pick of a copy of the local zoning map. Stand back and review the patterns of zoning designations. You might want to color code a few of the numerous zone designations. People that work for you (in your government) created this map. During the planning and mapping process they used, the planners assumed that zone boundaries should be logical transitions from one set of allowable uses to another. Generally, the more intensive uses are allowed in the zones nearer the main roads, and closer to the city center. In some cases there are neighborhood business districts that act like a mini town center, with more intense uses, such as retail, allowed near the intersection of two major roads. The zone density or intensity of use will diminish as you move away from that intersection.

Using specialized maps

After selecting the primary search area using road maps or large area maps, it is time to transfer this information to specialized, large-scale, more detailed maps. You may need more than one map of each type to cover the search area you have selected.

Area zoning map(s): Sometimes zoning maps are published in books with the local zoning code. They are available at the building department.

Large-scale topographic maps: Don't buy the cheap ones. You need accuracy and completeness. They are available at map shops, travel and outdoor equipment stores, or from your municipal engineering department.

Property ownership map(s): Available privately or at the tax assessor's office, sometimes available at the building department.

Optional: *Sewer and water district service area maps* are available from your city engineering department or your private utility district.

Optional: Use *comprehensive plan map(s)* to evaluate rezoning possibilities, etc.

Optional: Use *fire district service area map(s)* to determine available services and aid car response times for insurance and personal safety considerations.

Optional: *School district service area map(s)*.

Scales will vary, but try to find maps of approximately 1:1,000 to 1:40,000. Collect one copy each of the following types of maps covering all the primary search area. Don't cut corners to save a few dollars. You are creating your home for the rest of your life.

If more than one map of each type is necessary to cover your search area, make sure the scales match since they will need to be pasted or taped together (See illustration of Cutting and Pasting). Maps of different types do not have to be the same scale, although this will make the overlay process easier.

Identify areas on the topographic map within your search area where the slopes are very steep by marking them with a highlighter. (Construction on hillsides is difficult and often very expensive.) Using a different color highlighter, shade the areas where views might be expected. You may also want to identify south slopes for good solar access, which provides good light for gardens, heating, etc. The color coding you add to your maps is an aid to seeing the patterns of preferred development areas. Remember, we are defining expectations.

The ownership map will become very useful when you start looking at land. Most of the property lines shown on the ownership map will show up in the real world as fence lines, road or driveway edges, utility easements, etc. After identifying a promising parcel, the ownership map will be used to locate the owner through the assessor's records.

After transferring information to your specialized maps, overlay the three primary maps (the topographic, the zoning and the ownership) physically if you can. If the scales of any of your detailed maps match, you can physically overlay them for review. If the scales do not match, you will have to compare them visually. (It is possible to have a blueprint or reprographics shop help with this process. They can do amazing things with enlargements, reductions and transparencies.) The purpose here is to compare the expectations mapped on each detail map. You are looking for areas on your maps where expectations overlap. Create a final group map showing the areas which you all agree on.

The search process

Select an area

After your mapping process is complete, rank the various areas acceptable to members of your group. Don't try to look at everything at once. Select a specific area to start.

Listed and unlisted property

There are several ways to locate and buy property, whether you are looking for raw land or a property with existing buildings that will require demolition, renovation or substantial remodeling. The simplest, it seems, would be to go to a realtor with your maps in hand and ask what is for sale. Many of you will find your land this way through real estate agents, but there is an alternative that may save you time and money.

Experience shows that the best land values are not the properties already on the market. The sellers of listed properties have already established their expectations when going through the listing process. In my experience, the best value will be found in unlisted property where the owners either haven't considered selling, or haven't gotten around to listing if they considered selling. (See Making Contact, below, for ideas on getting in touch with land owners.)

Remember that the real estate broker who has a property listed has already done an evaluation of the market and has recommended to the sellers that the price be set as high as possible – the higher the better for the agent, who is paid by commission. And of course the sellers need to get enough to pay the realtor's commission over and above what they are expecting for themselves.

Looking at land

Prepare for your first trip in which you will actually drive out and look at land by creating a travel plan or route map before leaving. Whether or not you are using the services of a realtor, their offices often have area maps on legal-size paper. Mark a route on your map and make more than one copy. Clearly number the sites you plan to look at for cross-referencing with the data you will be collecting. I would suggest that you limit the number of sites you view each day. As an individual you may be able to handle six or eight sites. As a team you may be able to handle more.

Keep good notes. You might want to use a prepared data collection sheet, or a site search checklist. Before you leave, fill out the sheets with as much information as you can derive from the maps. Consider clipboards or notebooks to track and contain all your info sheets and maps.

The next step is getting out and looking at the land. No amount of mapping or paper research can substitute for being on site, getting a feeling for the land. Allow enough time to do this without hurrying. If you hurry, you may miss something important and cause long delays or course changes later. Take as many hours or days as necessary to look at all potential properties.

I find it easiest to have at least two people go together in one car, one to drive and one to navigate. A third also can be useful as note taker. When I am navigating on a land search drive I like to have all the maps out and available. For this reason, I sit in the back seat and spread everything out around me. A minivan would be ideal for this.

Don't hurry. If you are not familiar with the area, take the time to get to know it from the roads. Drive by the schools and the shopping areas, taking special note of the grocery locations. Note the type of vegetation, especially the trees, since they will have a big impact on site planning. Note views, if there are any, or special access areas, such as parks, riverbanks or beaches. Special site characteristics will play a part in how you plan the development of your community, and may significantly affect how you feel about a certain property.

When I reach a site I like to drive all the way around it, trying to see it from all sides while staying on the public roads. This may be very circuitous, but it is necessary to get an idea of accessibility. Notice the neighboring properties and how they are developed. When it seems right to stop and get out, plan to leave the car for at least a half hour. Something interesting may lead you off into the hinterlands, so don't stay tied to the car. Take a detailed map, such as the topographic, to keep yourself oriented with the neighboring properties and distant landmarks.

Avoid trespassing wherever possible. Be careful to respect the privacy and property rights of others. The next person you meet may be the property owner or a new neighbor and you will want to make a good impression. I follow a few simple rules. First, look for signs of life and go there first to introduce yourself. Second, if the property is marked "No Trespassing," don't. Third, if there is a driveway or partly improved road, and it is not marked "Keep Out," then wander down it. Stay on the driveway, following it to any buildings or signs of life.

Be ready to identify yourself clearly, and be ready to describe cohousing. Have a copy of McCamant and Durrett's book with you so you can illustrate cohousing with pictures. Most people will be happy to hear your story. You have an advantage here in that you do not represent a big developer and all the negative connotations that they might carry. You might also want to have hand-out sheets describing cohousing, and if possible, your group.

If there is a building on the property go there first and see if anyone is home. If you are shy about talking to strangers, bring along an extrovert.

If there are no buildings, no signs of life and no warning signs, and the neighbors know you are in the area, you can probably walk around on the property without upsetting anyone. Remember, though, that you are trespassing on private property. However, undeveloped or unused property is often used by the neighborhood for open space and recreational uses, such as kids' clubhouses. The trails will be evident if this is the case. Take care not to break new trails as this may be considered property damage.

Trees and site planning

Should you let the trees on your site drive your site planning? Trees are always a challenge – which ones do we save, which do we need to cut down? Can we afford to have them moved?

In an attempt to save you money, your contractor will tell you, "Trees always grow back. We'll just plant another one." Having experienced the cost of working around trees, the average developer or contractor looks at a site and sees it without vegetation which is the cheapest way to build anything.

Cohousing groups, on the other hand, look at a site and see the trees as a permanent part of the landscape. Cohousing people imagine fitting their homes snugly among the trees. Saving trees usually costs money and may cost in the quality of your overall design. Find a balance between your love of trees and the practical concerns for efficiency and make your choices wisely.

At Winslow we designed around several trees we wanted to save. Anticipating the costs involved, the construction superintendent instructed the bulldozer operator to remove these trees on the first day of construction. No apologies, just a simple "They were in the way. We'll put a few extra trees in when we get done."

We were upset but that superintendent was right about one thing – the cost of saving trees can be very high. If your trees are important enough to save, make them expensive to remove. Add a significant penalty clause in your construction contract.

Talking to neighbors

Be sure you take the time to talk to neighbors. Cohousing is generally well received as a grass-roots effort, people doing something for themselves. People respect this and will often ask questions about what you are planning. Be honest and let them know you are just beginning to plan. Ask for their help. There is no better way to win friends in the neighborhood than to ask for help and invite them to meetings.

Ask questions of anyone you find in the area. It is amazing what information you can learn just by talking to people. How are the schools in the area (even if you think you already know the answer)? Any complaints about water quality? Are there many children in the neighborhood?

Keeping records as you go

Use the prepared data collection sheet on a clipboard and add your subjective notes about how things feel. You will accumulate much information over the next few hours and days and you want to be able to sort it, compare it and relay it to others. I suggest using a Polaroid for one or two area photos for each site. You may want to shoot photos of distinctive vegetation, or the view across the street, whatever helps you remember what you experienced. Clearly mark photos on the back with the site number and specific information about the location and direction of the shot. Don't wait until later to do this. You likely won't be able to remember all the specifics, and you may get several sites confused.

If you look for standing or old fence lines and try to correlate them to the property lines on your property ownership map it will help you to get oriented. While on site, look for the information necessary to complete your data collection sheets. More importantly, make the time and find the space to stop talking, stop thinking, and simply listen to your feelings. Be quiet a minute. How is the energy of this place? Does it feel good? If anything comes to your mind that is identifiable, note it down.

As you return to the car, try to summarize in your mind what you have experienced here. How did it feel? Is this the place you want to live? Do you need more information? Sort through the data you have collected – drawings, maps, photos, notes – and file them away while you head for the next site.

Let go of the last site before you arrive at the next one. Clear your head and start again. Take a break to get a coffee, or a sandwich. Separate sites in your experience so you can separate them later in your mind. If they run together when you experience them, they will all run together in your mind, requiring trips back to confirm data or feelings.

At the end of the day, if you have kept good notes and your photos are all clearly marked, you can go back home and relax. I normally have a headache, feeling a little wiped out after a full day in the car, so I go home and take a nap before starting the next step.

Sorting data

When you are rested and ready to go again, take the time to review and compile the information you have gathered. It is better if you can get excited about what you are doing. Look over all your notes. Look carefully at the pictures.

Set aside sites that don't seem to work, and sites that don't feel right. You can come back to them later if need be. Don't throw anything away just yet. Quickly sift through the remaining sites. If there are still more than three, select the three sites that seem the most promising. This is a manageable number for your next round of research.

Schedule a trip to go out and look at the three selected sites again, this time with as many members of your group as possible. See if each site is still interesting. If you are not comfortable with the research you have done, consider hiring a landscape architect to help evaluate the property. (See Chapter 4, Working with Professionals.)

5.5 Sample Evaluation Matrix

Member Jane Smith   Rating 1 - 10
Date 5 April 1996   1 = not good
                           10 = great

	Site #1	Site #2	Site #3
Schools	6	9	5
Shopping	8	7	8
Neighborhood	5	9	8
Traffic	4	2	7
Average	5.75	6.75	7.00

Ask members to record their evaluation of each site. You might want to set up a matrix or table of these individual evaluations so that you can see how they stack up as a group. (See Sample Evaluation Matrix.)

Be sure to ask, and respect the answer to the question, "Could this site work for you?" These opinions may change later, but accept them for now and eliminate sites that don't work for some people. This is a process of building the trust that leads to community. For now, proceed only with the properties that you can all accept.

Talking to land owners

Making contact (properties not listed for sale)

You will want to locate the name, address and phone number of the owners of your selected properties. Go down to the property tax assessor's office (or often you can do this by phone) and ask for the records on the three properties you have selected. Your property ownership map will come in handy again, identifying the owner or the tax account number right on the map. Give this information to the clerk and ask for the records.

Generally the assessor's records are public and you have a right to see these records. You can review the history of the property and see what the assessor's office now thinks it's worth. You also can get a good idea of what improvements (buildings) are on the property and what special conditions, such as views, the assessor's office has already identified. Sometimes you can get copies of the property tax records to add to your file for the site.

Write a contact letter addressed to the owner(s) of each of the three properties. Make each letter personal by referring to identifying features of the property. Explain cohousing and what you are planning. Ask for their help in finding a piece of property. Be honest and forthcoming about who you are and what your intentions are. Then wait for a response. (See Sample Contact Letter.)

Prepare yourself to act quickly and decisively if you hear any positive response. If you don't hear anything within a week, contact owners with follow-up phone calls. Have the site file in front of you with a list of questions you might need to ask. Also keep a copy of the letter you sent in front of you.

Responding to the land owner

Once you have the land owner on the phone, start by asking if they have received your letter. Find out if they have any questions. Then ask bluntly,

Evergreen
Cohousing
Group

Street Address
City, State and Zip

Phone Number

(DATE)

(PROPERTY OWNER'S NAME)
(ADDRESS)
(CITY, STATE, ZIP)

RE: Your property located at (SPECIFIC SITE ADDRESS)

Dear Mr/s. (PROPERTY OWNER'S NAME);

We are a group of families in search of property suitable for creating a cohousing
community.

You may have heard about cohousing through the media, or in one of the several
books written about this new housing type. It is a concept imported a few years ago
from northern Europe, designed and developed by the residents who will live there.
It is market rate housing, not low income, or government subsidized. Most
cohousing groups choose the fee simple ownership structure. It is usually designed
as clustered housing where each home has a private living room, dining room,
kitchen, etc. Initial purchase prices depend on the size and location of the residence,
with unit types ranging from one to four bedrooms. All units are self sufficient and
usually owner occupied.

(EVERGREEN COHOUSING) is a group of families who are planning to create a
pedestrian oriented neighborhood of (25 to 30) clustered homes in the (NAME OF
NEIGHBORHOOD) area using the "cohousing" model.

If you would consider selling your property, or if you know of any other properties
in your neighborhood which might be appropriate for cohousing, please let us
know.   (MEMBER'S NAME) can be reached at (PHONE NUMBER). We look
forward to hearing from you.

Sincerely,

"Would you be interested in selling us your property?" You must be ready
to act, but unless you are confident and prepared to talk money and terms,
don't make offers or suggest terms at this time. If they ask you what you
would pay, plead ignorance and ask them what they think it is worth.
Record carefully any information that comes out of this phone call. Agree
to meet with them if they wish.

You can do a lot as a prospective buyer before making an offer. Talk to
the sellers about their needs. (Start thinking of them as sellers, and not as
the owners.) What would make them happy? What would they like to see

happen to their property? Informally gather as much information about the sellers' needs and expectations as you can. For the sellers to feel good after this process they must feel as though the terms of the deal meet their needs. What will the neighbors think? Many owners will be open to talking about how to make your project a success. Do they know anything about the permit process?

Learn about the timing that might influence your making an offer. Have the sellers thought of selling before? Have they ever listed the property? Are they talking to a realtor? Should you hurry? Remember, when sellers realize someone is considering giving them money for their property, the natural tendency is to imagine what they will do with all that money. Some sellers will even begin spending it, either mentally, or by running up charge accounts. People are people, not necessarily logical or rational. Take care not to build up the sellers' expectations unnecessarily.

Share your goals and objectives for the project, being realistic. Avoid suggesting a price yourself. The sellers may be able to tell you what they need or want for the land. Some sellers will even share information about large payments they may have coming due, which will help in forming your offer to them.

Ask about the history of the land, such as family traditions or unusual uses. Again, learn as much as you can about the sellers and what they need, want or expect. Do they have an idea of what should happen to the property if it is sold? Do they understand the zoning limitations or development restrictions? Are they aware of any wetlands problems, or environmentally sensitive areas on the site?

Respecting a seller's beliefs and expectations is the best way I know to begin a good relationship with a very important element of your project. Hopefully, this seller will be your first satisfied creditor, a partner in making your project a success.

Making an offer

Preparing an offer

This is where you will want some professional help or experience. If a member of the group is a realtor, or has some real estate experience, use it. Hire an attorney or real estate broker if you need one. (See Chapter 4, Working with Professionals.)

It's time to take all the information you have collected to your real estate broker or attorney to have them prepare an offer. The structure of the offer is critical to the later success of the project since the terms established for financing the purchase will become the driving force in financial management before construction financing. It is essential to understand what you will be able to afford to pay, and when, and how much risk you are taking in promising to do so. This must be balanced with the desire to have your offer accepted by meeting the seller's expectations of fairness.

Before making an offer you should have an acceptable pro forma in place. (See Chapter 10, Finance and Budget.) The expected land acquisition costs specified in the pro forma should be generous and yet practical. Carrying costs (interest payments on the purchase of the land) should be included since your hope is to have the seller carry the financing on the land purchase for the first few years, or until the start of construction.

Depending on the economic climate and level of real estate activity in your area, there are several rules of thumb for making an offer for raw land. Twenty percent down in cash is common and therefore generally expected. Sellers of raw land will rarely find an all-cash buyer since the buyer has very little chance of borrowing money from a financial institution secured only by the land. The sellers therefore will usually be in the position of needing to accept some type of short-term financing. This means they will sell you their land, transferring title to your name, for less than the agreed purchase price in cash at closing. They loan you the balance of the purchase price and you make payments to them until it can be paid off, or until you are ready to start construction.

At this stage it is good to keep your land costs in perspective. The terms of your deal can be more important than the cost. Often the land cost will be in the range of 10% to 15% of total project cost, sometimes higher, depending on the market where you live. Even at 20% of project cost, a 10% increase in land cost will be a 2% increase in project cost, and therefore a 2% increase in individual unit costs. In other words, with a 10% increase in land cost a $100,000 unit would go up $2,000. It might be well worth it, for instance, to pay a little more and take less risk by getting better terms.

Once your offer has been accepted, you are ready to begin a thorough site analysis. More often then not, your first offer will not be accepted. Either the seller doesn't respond in the specified period of time, turning down your offer, or responds with a counter offer.

Terms of the deal

Let's look at two sample offers and consider the various motivations of the buyer and the seller. Assume that you understand from your research and from talking with the seller that they might entertain an offer of $200,000 or more, and that if they listed the property they probably would list it at $300,000. Let's also assume you are confident that a fair value, the amount you are willing to pay, is somewhere in the neighborhood of $250,000.

SAMPLE TERMS – OFFER #1:

Aggressively priced, with somewhat high risk.
- $210,000 purchase price
- $25,000 earnest money (a promissory note due and non refundable on removal of all contingencies)
- 40% down payment at closing ($84,000 including the $25,000 earnest money)
- Closing within six months of acceptance of offer
- Seller carries contract on balance for two years after closing (secured by deed of trust)
- Interest only payments monthly at 10% APR (.00833 times the balance due, or $1,333.00 each month)
- Principal balance of $126,000 due within two years (normally paid off with construction financing)
- Contingencies (sometimes called "Subjects" or "Subject To's") to be removed within 90 days of acceptance of offer:
  - Satisfactory title report provided by seller

Cash now vs. cash later

Generally, cash talks. The more cash you can put up now, the lower the overall price, as in Offer #1. If a property is worth around $250,000 under "normal conditions" (meaning a six-month closing, financing, etc.), then you may be able to get it for around $210,000 if you have a lot of cash on hand ($84,000). You may even be able to get it for $200,000 or less if you can pay all cash and close tomorrow. If you want attractive terms, such as good financing, or a long closing period, you will need to pay more now (Offer #1), or pay more overall (Offer #2).

Cash vs. risk

Your risk is reduced if you have less money required up front, stronger contingencies (such as a clause that says, "subject to approval of toxic materials report"), or better financing (such as lower interest rate, delayed interest payments, etc.). If you offer more cash up front (as in Offer #1) you will increase the chances of negotiating terms that will reduce your risk long term. If you can pay more overall for the land (as in Offer #2) the seller is also likely to be sympathetic to terms that will reduce your risk.

SAMPLE TERMS – OFFER #2:

Generously priced, with somewhat reduced risk.
- $250,000 purchase price
- $10,000 earnest money (a promissory note due and non refundable on removal of contingency #1)
- 20% down payment at closing ($50,000 including the $10,000 earnest money)
- Closing within 12 months of acceptance of offer
- Seller carries contract on balance for three years after closing (secured by deed of trust)
- Interest accumulates monthly at 11% APR with no payments. (.00916 times the balance due each month)
- Principal and interest due as one lump sum within three years (normally paid off with construction financing)
- Contingencies to be removed within 120 days of acceptance of offer:
  · Satisfactory title report provided by seller
  · Satisfactory toxics report provided by seller
  · Satisfactory feasibility study by buyer
  · Planned Unit Development approved by municipality 6

Evidence of being serious now

Sellers are often very careful about who they sell to, especially when there are terms proposed such as financing. Substantial earnest money is the buyer's best evidence that you are serious. The seller will be more confident that the deal will work and that the buyer will complete, if the earnest money amount is larger, especially if some or all of it is non refundable. In

Offer #1 the $84,000 earnest money becomes non refundable after a satisfactory title report. The seller is more confident that you, the buyer, will be motivated to complete the deal with plenty of cash at risk and minimal contingencies (clauses in the agreement which protect the buyer from unknown conditions).

Evidence of being able to follow through

When considering an all-cash offer the seller does not need to worry about the ability of the buyer to perform, or complete the deal, especially if it is a short closing. Before considering a deal with non cash terms, a wise seller will want to know who the buyer is. Does the buyer have the financial capacity to complete on the proposed terms? How much risk are they taking tying up their land for a buyer who may not be able to perform?

Work with your project planning professionals to be ready to answer these kinds of questions from the sellers, especially if you are proposing to borrow money from them. I have found that a Group Financial Statement can look very impressive to a seller. Don't provide personal details and don't suggest personal guarantees, but compile a statement of your assets and liabilities all added together. Even you may be surprised. Your assets as a group will be pretty impressive when shown all together.

Specific needs of the sellers

Consider, if possible, the specific needs of the sellers. They may have a specific requirement for cash at some point in the future, such as when taxes come due, when a balloon payment on a loan is due, etc. The sale of the land may also have specific tax consequences for the seller which you as the buyer can influence. It is possible to pay for the land in installments, in different tax years, for instance. Again, consult with your professionals for advice here.

Cash flow management issues

Whatever you do, make sure your own cash requirements can be met. Consider carefully your cash flow planning and make the proposed land purchase arrangements in the offer fit. If they don't, you won't have a project.

Trying again

If you made offers and they were not accepted, try to find out why. What was the difference between your expectations and theirs? Does the seller view the situation in a completely different way?

If you have had no positive response from your inquiries, carefully review your expectations. Was your letter well received or did it sound silly? (Seek professional advice here from a lawyer or other project planning professional.) Should you follow up with more phone calls?

Check your mapping for consistency with your expectations. Have you overlooked something that prevents members from agreeing on a site?

Reconsider properties previously considered and set aside. Repeat any part of the process as necessary, identifying information that might be missing, or options that haven't been explored. A site that felt good may have been hard to see on your first visit. Maybe you need to contact this owner and ask for permission or assistance.

In doing the land search for the WindSong project, I found that we had to repeatedly reconsider the group's assumptions as we learned more about what land might be available, how much it might cost, or how long it might take to get the required approvals.

Feasibility analysis

The process of determining feasibility for a piece of land begins with your mapping process as you determine what basic zoning, utilities, and infrastructure requirements there will be. After you locate a piece of land that seems as if it might work, it is important to do a careful Feasibility Analysis to be sure it can meet your needs at a reasonable cost. Developers look at land and evaluate feasibility informally as they go, keeping most of the information in their heads. For a group of amateurs, inexperienced at development, it is best to formalize the process.

You wouldn't want to do a full Feasibility Analysis on land you have not yet tied up (completed an agreement to purchase) because it can be both time consuming and costly. If you do enough of them, and they don't result in land that works, it will also get frustrating.

The Feasibility Analysis is a way of reducing risk. The more you know about the land, and the sooner you know it, the lower the risk that you will waste your time and money, or that you will fail. Begin with the information you collected on your Site Search Checklist (see also The Search Process, and Keeping Records as You Go, above) and consider the Feasibility Checklist below. You may want to get some professional help, so gather your information. For the zoning and land-use issues regarding numbers or configuration of units on site, consult an architect or a landscape architect. For utilities and infrastructure feasibility, consult a civil engineer.

Development costs

A major part of determining site feasibility is determining the associated development costs, such as the cost of installing sewers. When you seek professional help to review feasibility be sure to provide them with your project pro forma (see Chapter 10, Finance and Budget) so that your professionals know what you expect to pay for the final product. They will be able to give you feedback on the appropriateness of a specific piece of land for your needs, as well as the practicality of your pro forma in general.

Project feasibility checklist

Land use and zoning

What do the comprehensive plan, the neighborhood plan and the current zoning allow?

- Zoning requirements
  - rezone requirements
- Specific allowable uses
  - housing density or floor areas
  - clustering, townhouse, or stacking units, etc.
  - setbacks and yard requirements
  - definition of family
  - kitchens
  - unrelated people sharing
  - accessory dwellings
  - guest facilities
  - common house definition/treatment
  - will it be counted as a separate unit?
  - parking requirements

- Subdivision requirements
  - ownership alternatives, such as condominium, strata title, air rights, transfer of development rights, etc.
- Conditional use requirements
  - daycare, for instance
- Development permit requirements
  - site plan review
  - design review

Utilities

If we expect to use local utilities, what utilities are available at what cost and what schedule?

- Sewer
- Municipal system timing and/or requirements
- Individual or site specific system requirements
- Potential for neighborhood collaboration
- Water
- Municipal system timing and/or requirements
- Individual or site specific system requirements
- Power
- Local system
- Off grid
- Communications
- TV options
- Telephone options

Road and access

What are the requirements for vehicle access?

- On-site road or driveway requirements
- Curb cut and driveway locations at public right of ways
- Emergency vehicle access requirements

Surface water management requirements

What requirements are there for managing surface water runoff?

- Storm water drainage control

- Special detention requirements
- Effects on or by neighboring properties

Fire and life safety requirements
What fire and life safety considerations will affect our project?
- Building codes and structural requirements
- Building locations and required distances between buildings
- Common kitchen treatment
- Special seismic requirements
- Fire department access
- Fire hydrant special requirements or location

Permits and approvals required
What approvals are required, when, and how much will they cost?
- List of required approvals
- Special requirements
- Timing
- Cost

Off-site improvements, soon or in future
What off-site improvements might be required, and when?
- Road upgrade requirements
  · curbs
  · gutters
  · sidewalks
- Sewer upgrade and participation
- Water upgrade and participation
- Parks and recreation contribution

Project costs and pro forma development
What will all this cost?
- Land cost
- Portion of unit cost
- Carrying costs

- Overall cost
- Soft costs (any extraordinary or unusual conditions)
- Construction costs (any extraordinary or unusual conditions)

Estimated unit pricing

What will we have to charge for these units to break even?
- Affordability evaluation
  - minimum unit costs
  - alternative affordable unit design options
  - alternative financing opportunities
- Unit pricing requirements for existing members

Financing

How will we finance our project?
- Seller financing of land purchase
- Available construction financing
- Available take-out financing
- Mortgage insurance conditions

Membership, sales and marketability

Will we find other members to buy units in our proposed project?
- Local market conditions
- Comparable unit prices in neighborhood
- Other cohousing?
- Does this site meet the needs of our group?
- Size and location
- Allowable uses (businesses, animals, crops, etc.)
- Number of housing units allowed
- Are there other sites that might be better for us?
- Is the group stable enough at this point to move forward together?
- Group finances and cash reserves
- Group process and decision making
- Development skills or professional resources
- Our attitudes and beliefs about success

Special considerations

Buying more land than you really need

Consider buying more land than you need. Sometimes it makes sense to sell off excess land later when your actual needs and budget are confirmed rather than limiting yourself within a site that turns out to be too constraining for your group. The only challenge to this strategy might come from members who may believe that this represents "land speculation." Some might think this is inappropriate for your group. Certainly, if your purpose was to make a profit, buying extra land would represent land speculation. But, in my opinion, if your purpose is to create community, then the purchase and resale of surplus land is appropriate to achieve both design goals (through spatial flexibility) and affordability (through income earned from the sale of land).

Keeping the group in control

It is important to keep in mind that, with very few exceptions, the owner of the land is and always will be in control of its development. So keep the group in control. Buy your land as a group if possible. If you want to work with a developer, try to buy your land first as a group and take it to your developer.

Some groups who have worked with developers allowed the developer to buy the land for them, thus reducing the financial burden and the apparent risk to the group members. Some groups have had success with this, and some have not. If you choose to work with a developer and let the developer buy the land, your group will lose some control of the development process, and many key decisions may be out of your hands. The choices made during the development process, such as energy efficiency, environmentally appropriate materials, seismic design, heating system quality and material selection, will be made quickly and efficiently, based primarily on financial considerations, by a developer who isn't going to be living there.

Working with a developer can be both beneficial and challenging. See Chapter 3, The Development Process, for a more complete discussion.

Forming an organization

Now that you have a group with a single voice, I recommend organizing as a cooperative corporation, but take some time to investigate the alternatives. Ideally, you will want to establish your cooperative corporation and raise some money before making an offer on land. (See also Chapter 9, Legal Issues.)

In order to buy land you need a legal entity to own it. Again, the owner of the land will be in control of developing it, so if possible, buy your land in the name of the community. Forming a corporation will facilitate identification of the community as something different and separate from any of the individual members. It allows the community to establish an identifiable "self" independent of the individual leaders and promoters within the community.

A lawyer may tell you that you should be incorporated prior to making an offer on land. However, with an accommodating seller and a trustworthy buyer/representative, you may not need the final incorporation papers filed until you are ready to close the sale. This may be three to six months after acceptance of the offer, as in the case of the Winslow project. Group members trusted me to make offers and sign purchase agreements in my own name, adding the phrase "and or assigns" to my name as purchaser. This allowed the group to consider ownership formats while we raised the money to make the earnest money and option payments. (See Winslow Purchase Timeline for an example of a relatively complex purchase.)

Summary

It is worth repeating that land is available. So are projects ready to be taken over, or buildings ready for renovation. If you remain open to the possibilities, and if you can contain your romantic visions, you will find something that will work for you and your group.

Do your research. Use the maps and see what works before you go driving around, getting frustrated. Check it out before you make an offer. Knowledge is your most valuable tool.

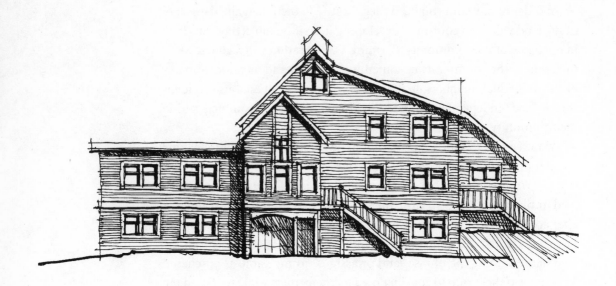

6

The Design Process

The language of design • Working with your design team •
Architectural fees • Design development • Parallel design tracks
• Programming • Goals for the site plan • Consider CoDesign
• What if we need to change the program? • Schematic design •
Design development • Construction documents • Construction
supervision • Post-occupancy evaluation • Summary

The language of design

The language of design varies somewhat. Architects don't always agree on the terminology describing the process. In this section I will share with you a common, if not universal, terminology which will help you when working with your design team. I suggest asking them to use this terminology.

It is convenient to consider the design process in terms of the following elements:

PROGRAMMING

Most of the design process is drawing-based, whereas the program section is primarily a written description of your expectations for the completed project. The program should include such abstract elements as "feel" and "quality," as well as room sizes, price expectations, etc. For instance, if you want your common house to feel warm and welcoming, you must specify this, or you may end up with a building that feels too institutional.

SCHEMATIC DESIGN

Schematic design is the initial stage of drawing. "Bubble diagrams" or rough sketches are often used at this point to evaluate spatial relationships, etc. At this stage drawings are done on layers of tracing paper, or even on napkins in a restaurant during brainstorm sessions.

DESIGN DEVELOPMENT

Design development takes the design process to a level of practicality. Drawings are done to scale. Room sizes and door locations are worked out.

CONSTRUCTION DOCUMENTS (WORKING DRAWINGS)

Construction documents, often called working drawings, are the completed plans ready for construction. Every construction detail has been worked out. All materials are specified.

CONSTRUCTION SUPERVISION

Construction supervision ensures that the construction is accomplished in the way it was intended. During construction supervision, the designer assists the builder in working out unanticipated problems or issues.

POST-OCCUPANCY EVALUATION

The complete design process (very seldom accomplished) includes post-occupancy evaluation. The purpose for the designer is to evaluate the first five elements of the design process and learn from mistakes, and from successes. But it is also useful to the client in learning to use the newly constructed project. It is often possible to make adjustments and modifications that improve the project.

Working with your design team

You will want to give your design team (architects, engineers and planners) input as a group. Your design team will want to make presentations to the group, hoping to have the group accept their work. At each meeting you should ask the design team to summarize the outcome of the previous design meeting and then have them present their revised work which responds to specific decisions made by the group at the previous meeting.

It is important to use a good meeting facilitator during design meetings. It can be someone within your group, or you can choose to hire someone outside the group. A good facilitator is able to manage your meetings and see that everyone is heard. They tend to be well-organized extroverts with good listening skills. The facilitator should assist all members in being heard, ensuring that members are listening to one another and understanding the implications of what is being presented by the design team.

Make sure that all design decisions made by the group as a whole are recorded, and that copies are provided to the design team. Only written decisions of your group should be considered as directions to the design team. This will prevent the louder or more articulate voices of individual members from being the only voices heard by the design team.

Meetings and presentations

The following is a useful schedule of meetings and presentations during the design process. If your group is small or makes decisions very quickly, some meetings may be combined with others. However, leave yourselves enough time on each meeting agenda to actually deal with each step. It is possible that your group will need more time or more meetings to make your design decisions. Don't expect your design team to continue working for free.

- Programming Workshop
  - Several regular evening or weekend discussions by group members.
- Programming Workshop with a design professional (3 to 9 days)
  - Review and approval of the final written design program as a group.
- Schematic Design
  - Initial presentation of ideas by the architect, with discussion.
  - Presentation of specific plans by architect for evaluation and input.
  - Second presentation (optional) by architect for evaluation and input.
  - Final presentation and approval of schematic design with architect.
- Design Development
  - Initial presentation of drawings by architect for evaluation and input.

· Second presentation of drawings by architect for evaluation and input.

· Third presentation (optional) for evaluation and input.

· Final presentation and approval of design development with architect.

• Construction Documents (Working Drawings)

  · Building Permit set presented by architect for approval by group.

  · Completed construction documents presented for approval by group.

• Construction Supervision

  · Weekly meetings on site between architect, project manager, and builder.

  · Periodic presentation by architect to the group to review progress.

• Post-Occupancy Evaluation

Before you start: get an abbreviated POE report of a previously completed cohousing project presented and explained to group before selection process is completed.

After you move in: Evening meeting (accessible by those who work during the day) with your architect on site six months after completion for review and evaluation of your project.

Parallel design tracks

Early in the design process, often during programming, it becomes necessary to split the design process into several parallel tracks. (See also the examples in Chapter 12, Scheduling and Planning.) The cohousing design process consists of three elements: site planning, common house design, and private unit design. These are not necessarily sequential processes.

Site planning is the process of identifying where buildings will go on your site. It will include such mundane things as making sure the sewage systems works (usually it will flow downhill). It also includes such esoteric concepts as "creating a sense of entry." The sense of entry you feel as you arrive will have an impact on how you feel about your community. It separates you from the outside world, defining the edge of your community. When does the outside world stop, and when have you arrived? Doorways, gateways, pathways, archways, all contribute to a sense of entry.

Site planning, especially for the development of vacant land, is best done by a design team with extensive raw land site planning experience. I recommend using a licensed landscape architect for your site planning. It is only an exceptional architect who can do a really good job of site planning. Their training and their attention are usually focused on the design of the buildings.

In addition to the special challenges of providing for the infrastructure (sewers, water, roads, etc.) designing for a cohousing community has special demands. Chapter 7, Design Considerations, addresses a number of the larger issues. See also *Cohousing, A Contemporary Approach to Housing Ourselves* by McCamant & Durrett, Ten Speed Press © 1988, 1994. As with this book, they also have a very good chapter called Design Considerations. Read it carefully and talk about the various suggestions with your design team to make sure the designers understand the content as well as you do. Remember, they are graphics people, not words people.

Site planning is the first priority and will normally proceed very quickly since you will be in a hurry to apply for planning approvals. The application(s) for approval from your local government can often be made with design development drawings of the site and schematic design drawings of the buildings. This is true if you are making a rezoning application, a Planned Unit Development (PUD) application or any one of several other specific government approvals. (See also Chapter 13, Permits and Approvals.)

It is important to bring the divergent design tracks back together periodically. Take the time to consciously and intentionally review all design work whenever you sit down to compare your design program to the work that has been completed.

Programming

Design begins with programming, writing down what it is you want. For an individual, this may be a simple task, like a shopping list. Bread, bananas, ice cream – two bedrooms, one bathroom, large open living room. For a cohousing group, or any group of individuals, it's a different story. Not only is it more complex and more difficult to arrive at a common decision, but you will have to deal with the divergent interests of the site, the common use areas, and the private areas. Keep in mind the need to constantly balance the needs of the community with the needs of the individual.

A design program is a written account of what you want to create. It is an instruction to your design team, and later in the design process it will act as a measuring tool for evaluating various drawings and models. Generally the program is a list of requirements. It includes things like numbers of housing units, numbers of rooms or required room sizes. It also includes feelings and relationships, like warm and cozy, visually connected or acoustically isolated. Creating a program requires some commitment, and some discipline. It is not enough to say, "I just want one that looks like Trudeslund." (See Chapters 1–3 of *Cohousing, A Contemporary Approach to Housing Ourselves.*)

When working with your architect, or other design professionals, remember you are dealing with people who generally don't think with words. Architects think graphically, and often spatially. Some architects will suggest beginning the design process by drawing. They might say that they like to program while they draw. This may work for an architect designing a house for a graphic designer who is single. It doesn't work for a group or a community of independent people. Many members will relate to the written design program, but all will benefit from combining sketches and illustrations with the written program elements. (See also Chapter 2, Forming a Group.)

A sample page from a programming document created by The CoHousing Company with the WindSong community.

Goals for the site plan

GENERAL FEEL

- Facilitates a sense of community
- Feels like home
- Facilitates privacy as well as community
- Shows reverence and respect for our part of the world
- Sense of nature all around
- Feeling of warmth and physical comfort

SUSTAINABILITY

- Facilitates sustainability
- Conserves natural resources – save energy
- Provides access to organic food
- Allows for opportunity to add appropriate technology later (as new technology evolves)
- Encourages saving money
- Allows for expansion of some homes
- Reduces need for driving and commuting

PEOPLE/RELATIONSHIPS

- Age and child friendly and safe

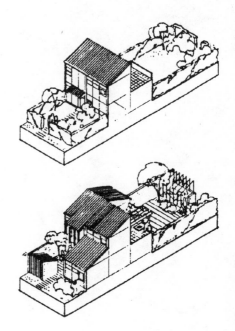

- Encourages flexibility in lifestyles (i.e. opportunities for working at home, adapting through the lifecycle)
- Encourages a diversity of people
- Facilitates opportunities for spontaneous and frequent interaction
- Facilitates communication between residents
- Facilitates friendly interface with neighbors outside community
- Facilitates high quality friendships
- Allows for peace and quiet when desired
- Facilitates convenience

PHYSICAL QUALITIES

- Balances individuality and harmony in the architecture
- Allows for individual expression
- Attractive
- Neat and tidy
- Maximizes natural light to building interiors
- Encourages affordability
- Facilitates use during wet weather
- Encourages diversity of unit types
- Allows for a hierarchy of spaces

Initial Programming Checklist

SITE CONSIDERATIONS

- location
- schools
- shopping
- work
- transportation
- size requirements
- uses intended
- gathering
- retreating
- parking
- gardening
- storage
- sense of entry or arrival

COMMON HOUSE ELEMENTS

- sense of entry or arrival
- kitchen
- dining
- lounge or library
- children's play area
- workshop
- guest rooms
- storage
- specialty rooms

PRIVATE UNITS

- number of units
- unit mix (how many 2 bedrooms, 3 bedrooms, etc.)
- unit sizes (for each type of unit)
- flexibility, expandability, adaptability
- common elements for cost savings

Use the initial programming checklist above as a group and discuss what each element of the checklist means to you. Ask questions of one another about relative importance. What items have the biggest effect on community? What items are strictly individual in nature? Individuals or households should then take their lists and fill in their programming ideas. Leave items blank if you don't know or don't care about them. Take time with the elements that mean something to you. Assume that others will have an interest where you might not, such as in the programming of the garden requirements.

This is not about control. This is about definition. If your vision is clear and beautiful in one area, do your best to define it in words. If you need visual images, don't hesitate to cut photos out of magazines. Make sketches. Write poetry. However you think, get it out the best you can so you can share it with your group.

Bring all your lists together. Look at your visions, your ideas and your questions. Take the time as a group again to move through the checklist point by point. Compile the words and ideas, the clippings, the sketches, etc. Try not to judge one another's efforts. First try to understand them.

After all your work is compiled, it may be possible to come to a consensus about your program, but don't expect this. Depending on group size, it can be very difficult to reconcile some very divergent visions. Defining your individual visions well enough that others will understand and appreciate your ideas sometimes seems impossible. You will probably want to seek professional help from an architect at this point.

Consider CoDesign

You might want to consider CoDesign as a programming process. Developed by Stanley King while at the University of Calgary, CoDesign is a special process of design participation which puts artists and users/residents into small groups. As the users brainstorm about their visions for the design, the artist tries to capture the ideas in sketches, such as bicycles in a rack near the front door, under a small roof overhang. Later the small groups of participants share their ideas with the larger group. As individuals, everyone rates each image based on three categories:

1.   I love it – go for it.
2.   O.K. but it needs more designing.
3.   O.K. but it belongs somewhere else.

The process also works well for children, so if you want to get them involved, try CoDesign. For more information on CoDesign, look for the book by the same name (currently out of print) or contact Stanley King Architects, 738 Millyard Street, Vancouver, B.C., V5Z 4A1. He can be reached at (604)873-3547.

Receptionists greet participants, hand out information, and guide latecomers into the proceedings (two).

The workshop conductor lists the time line of all activities and introduces the artists (co-design).

Photographers record the event, as well as the drawings and diagrams created during the workshop, for the report (two).

The report group writes and assembles the report (four to five).

The organization committee plans the event and supervises the production of the report (four to five).

The setup and cleanup group puts up paper on the walls and afterward rolls and labels the drawings, arranges chairs and the reception table, and cleans up the hall at the end of the event (four to five).

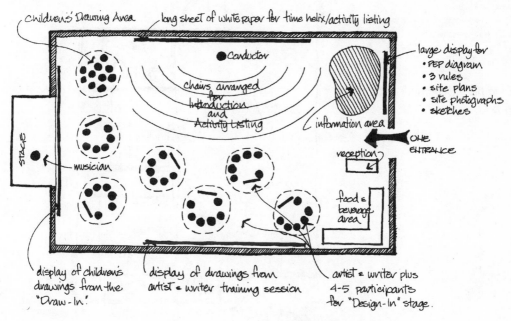

Typical hall layout for a workshop.

From CoDesign, by Stanley King

What if we need to change the program?

As you proceed through the design and development process you will probably want to make a few changes to your design program. As new members join your group, as you learn more about what you want, what you can afford, and what it means to the growth and maintenance of your community, you will probably want to modify or improve your program to reflect your refined vision for the community. You may add a guest room, a community hot tub, or even shrink your private unit sizes. Don't hesitate to make changes when necessary, but it is important to inform new members of the need to review and accept each completed stage of your design process.

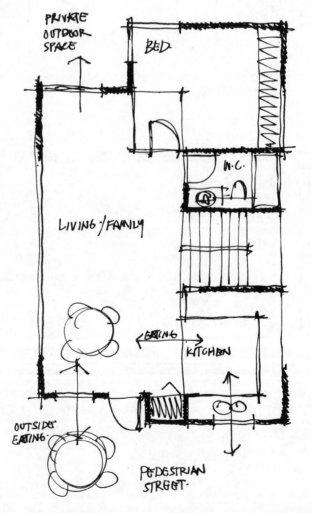

Example of schematic design drawing

Schematic design

The second phase of the design process is schematic design. This is what most people think of when they hear the word "design." During schematic design, the design team begins to draw bubble diagrams or thumbnail sketches on envelopes, magic markers on newsprint. It is a search process, a creative evaluation of forms and concepts, bringing together the dreams and visions defined in the program. It is a process of forming two – and three-dimensional images that represent approximate solutions to the complex problem of implementing your program for building community.

Schematic design is fun for architects. This is what they love, and this is often why they do architecture. If you are working with an architect who is willing to draw in public, encourage him or her to do so. Suggest alternatives that they might draw during a presentation. Ask them to suggest alternatives and show you what works or doesn't work. Making the process exciting helps keep you going. It also keeps your architect inspired to work hard for you.

This is a process of learning for yourselves as a group what works for you, what you like and what you want. It is also a process of learning to read two-dimensional drawings. The more you watch the drawing process, the more you will understand how to use it, and how it gets used.

Build a working site model

Consider using a rough site model for evaluating various site layouts. The most successful design processes I've seen take advantage of a large-scale model of the site, including major trees and features. The group works together, interactively, trying out various site plans. If you use roughly scaled wooden blocks to represent the buildings, you can take turns pushing them around to see what works. Photograph each alternative so you have a record.

After the design has evolved, it makes sense to create a simple "working" model of the buildings. This helps members who have trouble visualizing from the drawings, but it also forces the designers to face three dimensional challenges they may not yet have recognized. It is possible that members of your group can help in constructing the model to save on professional fees. It is also fun, and a good way for members to become intimately familiar with the design as it evolves.

Design development

During design development the design process is taken to a level of practicality. All drawings are done to scale. Room sizes, as well as window and door locations, are carefully worked out. This is when the kitchens are designed, when door swings are determined, and when the practicalities of the recently approved schematic design are evaluated.

When moving into design development, the design team begins to look at structural systems. They evaluate structural loads, seismic and wind design requirements, and spatial needs for the mechanical systems. They will also evaluate energy conservation strategies, roofing types and limitations, and appropriate heating systems.

Example of design development drawing

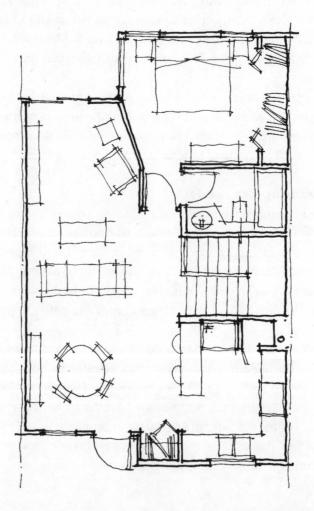

BY KATIE MCCAMANT, THE COHOUSING COMPANY

Design development

The most important part of the Design Development phase is working out all the systems (structural, heating, plumbing – working with the consultants) and getting a handle on costs (value engineering) which in this case means working closely with the builder to get input on what they see as the most cost effective way to carry out the design. The drawings done during this phase are typically incomplete and difficult to read. The most time efficient process would be to have residents write up and/or draw their comments on the Schematic Designs including ideas about heating systems and materials. Let us do the best we can with it given that there are many other factors to consider in addition to your input. We would not try to build consensus within the group, however, it would be useful to have a clearly defined set of prioritized criteria (cost, low toxic materials, energy efficient, aesthetics, etc.) – although without more specific direction we would try to optimize the considerations we know are important to the group within the given budget.

The way we often work with CoHousing groups is to have weekly meetings with a resident design committee. This is especially helpful when working on material selections. At the end of the Design Development phase we would present the revised design, suggest upgrade options, and answer questions. The group can veto whatever they can't live with.

During design development it helps to build a model of the common house, and possibly the private units as well. Many people will understand much more clearly if they see what's planned in three dimensions. Ideally, if the design doesn't change too much, it's nice to have a model that represents the final design which you can then use for membership and outreach.

During design development your design team will be implementing your approved schematic design. This is a time when you should be evaluating the designs based on your carefully developed design program.

Construction documents

Construction documents, often called working drawings, are the completed plans ready for construction. Once you have approved the design development drawings, your design team will begin the long, arduous process of carefully drafting a set of plans and specifications (often called "specs") from which a contractor can accurately build your project. The specifications manual supplements information provided on the plans. It is a written document with detailed material, equipment, performance and installation specifications.

Early in the process of creating construction documents, one set of prints might go out for preliminary cost estimates. This is a good time to check and see if your budget expectations correlate with the design assumptions. (See also Chapter 10, Finance and Budget, and Chapter 4, Using Professionals: Contractors.)

Near the end of the process of creating the construction documents, it is possible to apply for your building permits. The building department only needs a part of the construction documentation and you can speed up the approvals process by completing the information they need first. (See also Chapter 13, Permits and Approvals: Speeding up the Process.)

By the time the construction documents are complete, every construction detail has been worked out. The plans and specifications are ready for submission to the contractor and subtrades for final costing.

Specifying "environmentally appropriate" building materials and construction practices can be a real challenge. Chapter 8 provides information about dealing with this issue in a practical way.

Construction supervision

Construction supervision ensures that the construction is accomplished in the way it was intended. During construction the designer assists the builder in working out unanticipated problems or issues. Change orders requested by the builder are evaluated for appropriateness. Sometimes a specified material or procedure is not available and alternates must be considered. When it affects quality, or when it might have an effect on the community later, the design team will consult with the group to apprise members of the situation.

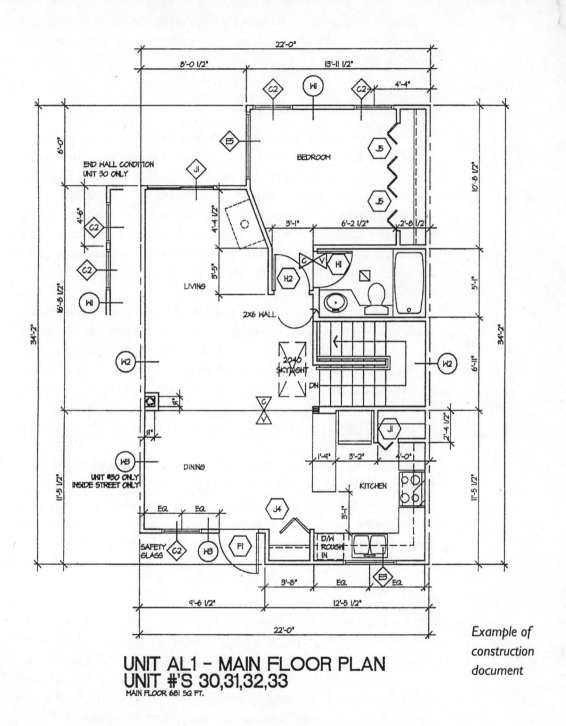

UNIT AL1 - MAIN FLOOR PLAN
UNIT #'S 30,31,32,33
MAIN FLOOR 681 SQ FT.

Example of construction document

Finally, and possibly most importantly, during construction the design team will also monitor quality, verifying that the correct materials and procedures are used.

Post-occupancy evaluation

The complete design process (which is very seldom accomplished) includes post-occupancy evaluation. The obvious purpose for the designer is to evaluate the first five elements of the design process, including the construction, and to learn from mistakes. But surprisingly, post-occupancy evaluation can be very useful to you as the client in learning to use your newly constructed project. By reviewing the programming and design goals after completion of your project, it is possible to make adjustments and modifications that will result in significant improvements.

When interviewing architects, I recommend you ask each design team to provide you with a post-occupancy evaluation of a previously built cohousing project (either of their own design, or another's) before completing the selection process. This is an opportunity for you and your design team to learn from the experience of another cohousing project, allowing each of you to avoid making any number of mistakes. It also allows you to judge the architect's understanding and appreciation of the cohousing concept.

About six months after your project is complete, have your design team spend at least one day doing a post-occupancy evaluation of your project. Ask them to spend an evening with you a week or so later at a meeting on site for review and evaluation. If you negotiate this with the contract and fees up front it won't cost very much and you will benefit greatly.

Summary

The design process should be fun. For many it will be the only time in their lives when they will get to participate in the design process. It can also be the most exciting part of building your community, socially and physically. If you can minimize or let go of the private dwelling design issues and try to focus on the design of your site plan and common house, you will go a long way toward creating the community you are seeking.

7
Design Considerations

Purposeful separation of the car • Pedestrian pathways • Kitchens facing the pedestrian pathways • Centrally located common house • Optimum community size • Learning from the past • Affordability • Design alternatives and housing types • Site considerations • Evolution of a site plan • The common house • Private unit design • Summary

This chapter is about the actual design product rather than the process of design. (See Chapter 6, The Design Process.) It will identify several areas which you might want to learn about so you can improve the design of your community.

There are a number of key design issues which will have a significant effect on sustaining community after you move in. These include the purposeful separation of the car from the private dwellings, pedestrian pathways connecting the dwellings, private kitchens facing the pedestrian pathways, and a well-designed, centrally located common house.

There are three distinct but interconnected parts in the design of a cohousing community. Most groups begin with a focus on the site plan, then work together as a community to design a common house. Eventually you will need to agree on the design of the private dwellings. Along the way you will come upon significant questions about how to achieve affordability. You will want to discuss the possibility of standardizing private units, and the inclination to customize them, either before construction begins or during the construction process.

Let's look at each of these issues in a little more detail. When you hire an architect, you might want to go through this chapter point by point, discussing each concept and considering each recommendation. Working with your architect, having discussed each of the following issues together, you will be able to make informed decisions about the design of your community. You will choose the type of community in which you want to live.

Purposeful separation of the car

We have a powerful relationship to our cars. Some would say it is a love-hate relationship. It is responsible for many of the evils in modern society, from pollution to social alienation. And yet, it not only symbolically represents individual freedom, but it affords each of us a true freedom of movement not available before the advent of the car. But what does the car cost us, socially and environmentally? We look to government to protect us from increasing smog and jammed highways, but we can also answer these question for ourselves as individuals. Consider your true needs and evaluate the alternatives you have to owning and using a car.

In their book, McCamant and Durrett indicate that one of the common characteristics of Danish cohousing is the intentional neighborhood design. In addition to intentional neighborhood design, I would add that separation of the car from the dwellings is a key feature in the design of successful cohousing communities. Encouraging people to interact with other people requires that the cars be parked away from the private residences.

Consider what it means to sacrifice that physical closeness to your parked car. Are you willing to walk a few more feet when you need to use your car? I would suggest that the following opportunities arise when you separate the cars from the private dwellings:

1. Greater opportunity to interact with other residents while walking through the community.
2. Less space required on your site for cars, allowing more space for gardens and gathering places, as well as open space and the natural environment.

3. Less pavement required for driveways, parking and turn-around areas.
4. Increased security due to the increased presence of people on site.

Pedestrian pathways

When the car is separated from the private dwellings you have the opportunity to create smaller scale pedestrian pathways connecting each residence, instead of the massive streets and driveways of the typical suburban neighborhood. You have an opportunity to create a wonderful place for children to play. Adults will have the opportunity to experience spontaneous interactions with neighbors as they bump into one another on the way to or from their cars.

A number of groups who have chosen to adopt the other principals of cohousing have retained their old relationship with their car, choosing to park at their private unit in a garage or carport. This requires more land and depreciates the opportunities afforded by the pedestrian pathways. However, the main risk is that this will lower the chances of sustaining an ongoing community in the years down the road. What will happen in five or ten years when a new person buys one of those houses with private parking at the door? Will they make the effort to integrate into the community? Will you ever get to know them? Will you continue to feel that your children are safe among strangers?

Kitchens facing the pedestrian pathways

Another, less obvious aspect to intentional neighborhood design is locating the kitchens of the private units so that they look out on the pedestrian pathway. As the highest activity area of the house, this increases oversight and supervision of the public pathways, providing security and safety for the children, as well as a sense of connection.

While this issue may not be as important as the choice about where to park your cars, some would say it is nearly as significant. Kitchen location seems to have a significant effect on how the community functions, and long-term effects on social sustainability.

Centrally located common house

It seems that you can't have cohousing without having a common house located centrally within the community, which is easily accessed by all members. This all-important point of focus for the community will vary in size, depending on the number of dwellings and the resources dedicated to its construction.

Early communities in Denmark had smaller common houses of 1,500 to 2,000 square feet. Later communities have chosen to build much larger common houses, often supplementing them with other shared amenity buildings around the site. This seems to be a result of the increased trust by members in the benefits of this significant investment. These range from 3,500 square feet to as much as 10,000 square feet of common house and shared amenities. For example, the WindSong community of 34 dwelling units has a total of 5,980 square feet of heated common house, plus an additional 2,230 square feet of unheated but enclosed bicycle storage, workshop areas and pedestrian nodes. They also have more than 10,000 square feet of enclosed glass-covered pedestrian walkways connecting the private dwellings to one another and the common house.

Optimum community size

Cohousing seem to work best when the community is between 12 and 36 dwelling units. Smaller or larger groups can work, but they have special challenges and seem to work best under special conditions.

It seems that if the community is smaller than about 12 units it may feel too intimate, or have limited funds for creating and maintaining common facilities. The smaller communities of 6 to 12 units tend to work best in an urban area where there is less dependence on the personal relationships within the community, and greater likelihood of participation by non-residents in community meals and other activities.

If a community is too large it can be very difficult to get to know everybody, or it may become too administratively complex. Communities larger than 36 units tend to work best in suburban or rural areas where the residents will be more insular.

Learning from the past

Since the first cohousing projects were built back in the early 1970s, certain planning, spatial and building size patterns have emerged. Jan Gudmand-Høyer, considered the father of the cohousing movement in Denmark, observes that cohousing designs have evolved considerably. He identifies four distinct generations:

First-generation cohousing

The early projects included private units averaging about 1,500 square feet with a common house of a similar size, about 1,500 square feet. People still didn't know for sure how well this idea might work, or how often they might benefit from the use of the common house. Private units remained large in case the community idea didn't work. The early community of Skråplanet where Jan Gudmand-Høyer still lives is an example of first-generation bofællesskaber (cohousing).

Second-generation cohousing

As confidence grew, the next generation of cohousing evolved, including smaller private units and larger common facilities. Private unit sizes came down to an average of about 1,000 square feet, while the common house increased to about 5,000 square feet. In second-generation cohousing the pedestrian street became more well defined. As well as becoming larger, the centralized location of the common house and its relationship to the private units became very important. The Trudeslund community in Denmark and the Winslow Cohousing community in the U.S. are examples of second-generation cohousing.

Third-generation cohousing

In third-generation cohousing the common house continues to get larger and the private units continue to get smaller. More and more resources are dedicated to the expansion and enhancement of the common facilities, with the common house size increasing to nearly 10,000 square feet. The average size of the private unit may shrink to 750 or 800 square feet, just enough to accommodate the necessary private areas for personal privacy, retreat and sleep.

More significantly, the common house and the private units are brought together into a single building, often connected with a glass-covered street.

Access to the common house is easier and more and more specific uses are included in the common house, such as darkroom facilities, or a music room. Although the private units are somewhat larger, the WindSong community in Vancouver, B.C. is an example of third-generation cohousing.

Fourth-generation cohousing

In fourth-generation cohousing, clusters of second- and third-generation cohousing are brought together into a larger neighborhood or village. Jan Gudmand-Høyer designed a new neighborhood of 48 cohousing communities, including shops and other commercial services. Located in the village of Ballerup, a suburb of Copenhagen, Denmark, much of it is now complete. A number of groups are planning fourth generation cohousing communities in North America. The first of five neighborhoods at "Eco-Village at Ithaca" in New York State is scheduled to be completed in December of 1996.

Affordability

How do you achieve affordability through design, and what is affordability to you? Everyone has a different idea about what it is and how it can be achieved. You can make your project more affordable by considering your design choices carefully. (See also Chapter 10, Finance and Budget, for a discussion of affordability issues.)

Affordability depends significantly on your expectations. The more modest and more flexible your expectations are, the easier it will be to achieve something you regard as affordable. If you want something large and cheap, you may not achieve affordability. If you're willing to consider smaller and higher quality, you may be pleasantly surprised.

The following design strategies will contribute significantly to making your project more affordable:
- Increase the number of private units. The more units you create, the less each one will cost, because fixed costs are distributed over more units.
- Reduce the size of each private unit (many units) and increase the size of the common house (just one common house). Obviously, smaller is less expensive, and making the common house larger makes it easier to live in a small unit.

- Keep things simple. Corners cost money and complexity of all types is expensive. This has a lot to do with why developers often build ugly buildings, although simple does not need to be ugly.
- Don't fight the building codes, try to work with them. The more you try to make things different from what is normal and expected, the more likely you will be to experience costly delays, etc.
- Include rental units within owned units. Many people just can't afford to buy.
- When choosing materials and equipment, consider life cycle costing. What does it cost over the life of your project to put in a cheap heating system? While the capital costs may be greater, lower operating and maintenance costs will make your project more affordable in the long term.
- Consider clustering tightly to save money. Lower infrastructure costs, shared walls and reduced heat loss will save you money. (It will also save the natural environment and improve your access to it.)
- Consider stacking units, saving construction costs as well as long-term energy costs.
- Simplify your utility and infrastructure plan by taking requirements into consideration during the initial site planning process. Reduce roads, driveways and paving wherever possible, and simplify alignments.
- Consider unusual unit types, such as shared units. (See Design Alternatives and Housing Types, below.) A large three- or four-bedroom private unit with one kitchen might be shared by several single people, for instance.
- Building a few larger units will reduce the cost of the smaller units. If you have members who can afford a larger unit, or if several members would consider sharing a unit, that can make sense.
- A major way to achieve affordability is through standardization. Reduce the number of unique buildings and floor plans. Do your best to agree on standardized bathroom and kitchen designs. Standardize siding, roofing and windows wherever possible. (See Standardization of Private Units, below.)
- Do not allow any customization during the initial construction process. (See Customized Private Units, below.)

How design affects affordability

Everything outside of the ordinary you want to include in cohousing from more durable, less toxic materials to an extended design process will add cost to your project above and beyond the cost of a "conventional project."

You have not been in the development business very long and you probably know very little about it. Although you are not working with a profit assumption, you may add well over 20% to the cost of your project by learning about development as you go along, by adding things which are not in "conventional" developments and by engaging in a complex and extended design process. (You cannot avoid this entirely. You are a group, and you must listen to yourselves and your consultants. Developers know what they want and simply instruct the consultants.)

It gets worse. Developers have fine-tuned the art of building in the cheapest way to make the most appealing (marketable) project. They are appealing to the broadest possible demographic group. The point is that when you depart from the cheapest methods, which you must surely do to make your project special, then you also make it more expensive.

Suppose for instance, you discover that cardboard is cheaper than plywood. You make the decision that you will therefore save money by sheathing your project in cardboard. You will encounter extra costs from:
- your engineer or architect who will now have to figure out how to use this new, cheaper material,
- the building department who will want to know that this new, cheaper material is the equivalent of plywood,
- your supplier who has never heard of this new, cheaper material,
- your subtrade who has never installed this new, cheaper material,
- your insurance agent . . . you get the idea.

Even if you overcame all the obstacles and had a new home that cost less than "conventional," there is the small matter of the value of the house at resale. In the end, you will own a house built out of cardboard!

"This is a very fine house, it is built out of cardboard but we can show you all these certificates . . . you say you might want to look at the other one hundred thousand houses on the market which are not built out of cardboard . . . ?"

No matter how hard you try, your project is going to cost more than a "conventional" project. If you really are smarter than the developers and can build more efficiently, stop what you are doing immediately and get into development. Humanity needs you!

Design alternatives and housing types

What physical form should your project take? Should it be townhouses like the Winslow community, or should it be apartments in the city, like Cardiff Place? The form of the housing you want will have a significant impact on the development method you choose, as well as the cost of the final product.

Developers normally build a limited range of housing types, products the banks will finance, and that they know will sell. They don't often consider the wide range of housing needs, and the alternatives which are available. Consider the following types of housing for your project, individually, or in some mix of housing types:

- Townhouses and cluster housing, where every family owns their own home and a small piece of ground, with no one living above or below them. These are sometimes referred to as "garden apartments" and can be combined to form row houses.
- Row houses are on individual lots, and are usually three or four stories tall. They share common side walls along a public street with private yards at the back. This is a common housing form in Europe, and in older North American cities.
- Apartments or condominiums, where units are stacked more efficiently and access is by stair or elevator. This form can be low-rise, up to about four stories, or it can be high-rise. More than one cohousing project can share a high rise-building.
- Shared homes within cohousing, such as pod housing, where families or singles have their own private space and share a kitchen and living area.
- Single-room occupancy, where an individual might simply have one or two rooms with a bath and no kitchen.
- Dormitory, where youths or visitors might be able to share a room, without private kitchens.
- Renovations and adaptive reuse of commercial buildings in which large open spaces can be creatively reused for housing.
- Live-aboard boats and houseboat (floating home) facilities are sometimes considered the nearest thing to cohousing. If you have waterfront land, this may be an option.
- Individual lots for the private construction of single-family homes are more expensive, but they can be used exclusively, or in combination with other housing types.

- Single-family dwellings are more expensive but they can be a part of a larger cohousing project.

Although I advocate exploration of alternative housing types, I do have a few words of caution. The financing required for construction, and to some extent for the private mortgages, will have a significant impact on your design choices. Banks lend money based on what they understand. You may be required, for instance, to include more bathrooms than you think are necessary just to get a construction loan.

Talk to local builders and developers early and find out what the lenders expect. This is not to suggest that you should only design and build based on what is expected by lenders; however, it is wise to know how far you are stretching the envelope before you do so.

Site considerations

There is no right or wrong way to develop your site. Each site has both opportunities and constraints which will effect the design and planning choices you will make. If environmental concerns are important to you please have a look at the discussion and recommendations in Chapter 8.

Consider the various site planning options available to you. Ideally, before you start your site planning you will have completed a programming workshop with experienced professional help. (See Chapter 6, The Design Process.) As a way of getting started, before you have done the actual programming, ask yourselves the following simple questions:

- How important will the car be in your site plan? Will the cars occupy the best parts of the site?
- How much paving do you want on site?
- How will you access the site? Where will the pedestrian access be, and is there a different place for cars to enter?
- What will you do with your car when you don't need it? How far away from it are you willing to be when you leave it parked?
- How important is the pedestrian walkway concept and will it be a prominent part of your site plan?
- Is solar access important? Do all private units need solar access, and what about the common house? Does solar energy design make sense in your climate?
- Where are the utilities coming from and how will they affect your site plan?

• What will the infrastructure costs be, and are there ways of reducing these costs?

As you plan your site for development try to remain flexible. The WindSong group learned this lesson as they had to redesign their site plan several times before finding something that was both acceptable to the Ministry of Environment, and practical to build. (See the sidebar, Evolution of a Site Plan, for a description of how the WindSong site plan evolved over time. Also, for a good discussion of design considerations related to site planning, see Chapter 14 in McCamant and Durrett's book, *Cohousing.*)

BY TERRY LYSTER

Evolution of the WindSong site plan

Cohousing design is the search for an organizing principle which satisfies the needs of the group within their resources. Remember the design will have to serve future needs.

The Winslow Cohousing site plan emerged in its final form when the members saw that their schematic design didn't create an organized pattern. They came to this realization when the architect presented sketches of several cohousing projects, comparing them with their own design. (See Comparative Cohousing Site Plans in Chapter 8, Environment.)

The WindSong design process is illustrated by these selected sketches which show the evolution of the design. The site is nearly six acres. Historically, it had been created by pre-emption of a larger farm lot in the 1800s. In 1912 the site had been subdivided as part of a subsistence farm development. Small-lot, single-family homes had grown up around the site in the '70s and '80s. A townhouse and apartment complex had been built along the west boundary in the early '90s. The site itself had remained undeveloped because about two-thirds of it was environmentally sensitive. An upland area contained a large family home with a horse barn on a lower bench. There was a fish-bearing stream with well-defined banks in the lowland.

Old air photos and the previous owner indicated that the lowland area had been a pasture for horses in the '50s and '60s. When the previous owners arrived, the horses were removed and the pasture was allowed to grow as a deciduous forest. In the late '70s, a colony of beavers flooded the lowland, drowning the forest. Most of the trees were gone by the time the cohousing project was being designed. Environmental assessment indicated that the beavers were in marginal habitat, having been displaced by surrounding development, and would consume their food supply faster than it would be replenished. A review of old aerial photos revealed the natural history of the site. The design was influenced by the knowledge that the site was in a rebound from the effects of glaciation, farming, beavers and surrounding settlement. WindSong resolved to leave the lowland undeveloped and to cluster the project on the upland. Municipal contour maps provided rough contours for early designs. They were supplemented

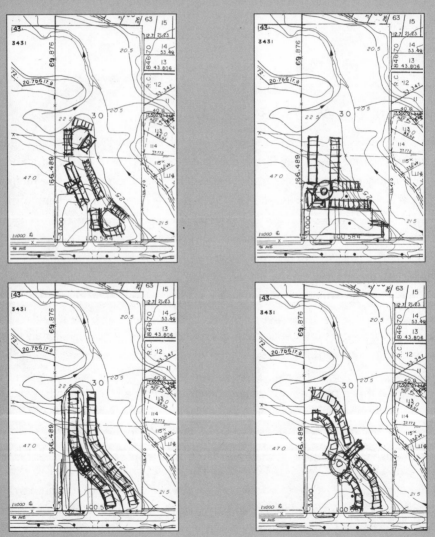

with surveys of land form, location of major trees, creek banks and soil tests. The first sketches showed a townhouse form on the upland area. The overall density proposed was equivalent to single-family density. The next sketches tried a variety of dwelling and parking arrangements. Finding space for both on the upland area proved to be difficult. The group's rating noted on the sketches guided the architect. Stepping the east units one story down into the bank allowed the upper floor of the westerly units to see the view, if the easterly units had a flat roof.

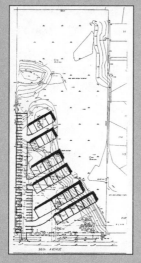

−10: This is a fragmented plan. Inequitable relationship between dwellings and common house.

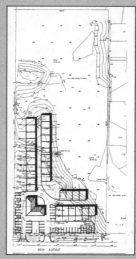

+2: "Classic" second-generation co-housing layout. Entry dominated by parking. Common house did not enjoy views of lowland and mountains to the north.

+4: This design is getting there. The common house is cantilevered over lowland making it structurally expensive.

+5: Best early alternative. Move common house out to share enjoyment of lowland and views. Dish-shaped arrangement of dwellings conformed to land.

A design crisis resulted when the Ministry of Environment insisted on greater setbacks from the creek. The sketch shows the challenge. Instead of building on a third of the site, WindSong had less than a quarter of the site available. After all the attempts to design surface parking, it was forced underground. This change added more than half a million dollars to the cost of the project. As the revised design was squeezed, the central space between units decreased to a convenient span. The enclosed atrium was born. Eventually it evolved to the section illustrated, which included a downstairs gallery. The atrium added significantly to both cost and amenity. Code requirements were met with equivalences: sprinklers instead of fire walls, openings instead of ventilation.

The group had agreed on the overall design. During working drawing production, the architect referred several questions to the group to determine their preference. As the budget was firmed up, cost-saving measures, such as leaving spare rooms unfinished, were implemented. The result of the WindSong design process was a unique solution for a special site.

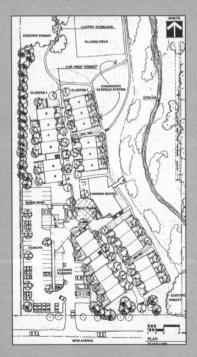

First site plan approved by WindSong

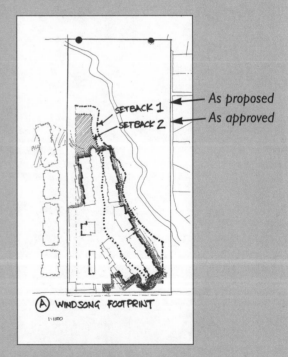

The setback challenge: the approved site plan didn't work

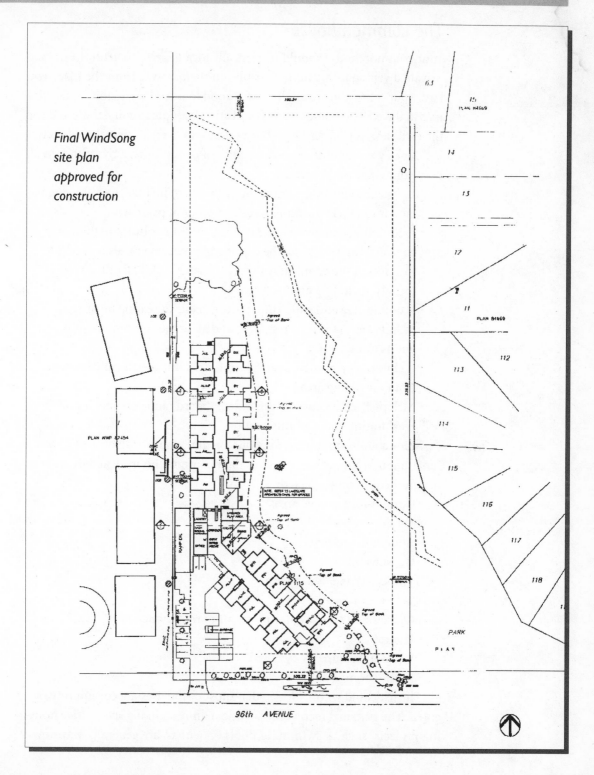

*Final WindSong
site plan
approved for
construction*

96th AVENUE

The common house

Your common house should be centrally located, easy to get to from each private dwelling unit, and if possible, on the pathway from the place you park your car to your front door. It is good to include functions and activities in the common house which will attract people to come there and use the facilities. As Charles Durrett says over and over, "Activity breeds activity." Make your common house a center of community activity and it will keep your community alive.

Almost all cohousing communities choose to include the following basic functions in their common house, in order of priority:

- A common kitchen which is convenient for use by more than one cook at a time. It should be capable of preparing meals regularly for most of the community and, infrequently, for all of the community, including guests.
- A dining area and gathering space, capable of seating most community (60% to 70%) regularly, and all of the community plus guests infrequently.
- A children's play area, visually connected but acoustically isolated from the dining area.
- Mail pick-up location, with bulletin boards and personal "cubbies" for internal communication.

Many cohousing communities also include some or all of the following functions and special use spaces in their common house, listed in order of the most commonly selected:

- Community storage areas
- Laundry room
- Adult lounge area
- Guest rooms
- Workshop and craft spaces
- Teen room
- Office space for the community, or to rent to members
- Hot tub
- Work-out room
- Music room

The list could go on. Notice that most of the uses are community oriented. The personal recreation facilities common in big speculative housing projects, such as swimming pools or saunas, are generally way down the list for cohousing communities. As common houses get larger more opportunities exist to include special uses, such as a dark room, or a home theater installation. Your community will want to consider all the possible options, evaluate potential costs, and rank them based on what is important to your group.

When it comes to designing your common house, make sure you get good professional help. The common house is the heart of your community. Designed well, it will bring life into your community for many years to come.

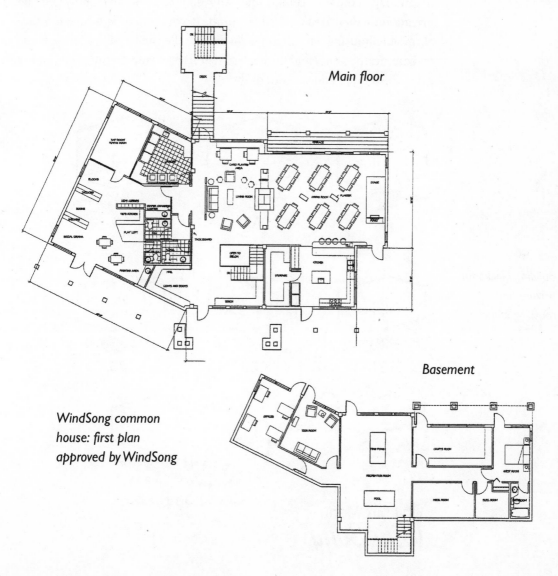

Main floor

Basement

WindSong common house: first plan approved by WindSong

Private unit design

Let the architect design the private dwellings

Unless you can each afford the luxury of custom-designed private units, or you plan to build single-family detached homes, I recommend that you leave the private unit design to the professionals.

In my experience the cost of participatory private unit design is high, and the result is often less exciting than what can be designed independently by a experienced architect. One of the costs, besides the time and the money, is the bad feelings that can result when no one family gets the private unit they actually had in mind. If your intent is to create more affordable housing, and if you want to take the time and money to focus on community issues and the common house, let your architect design the private dwellings and stay out of the way.

Building blocks for private unit massing study

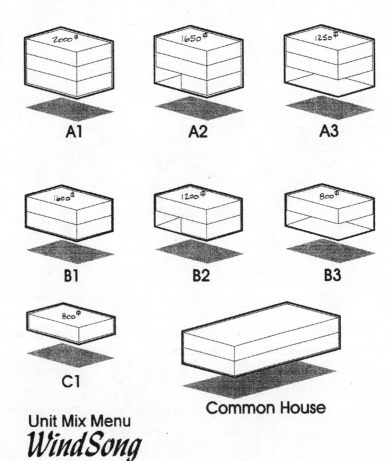

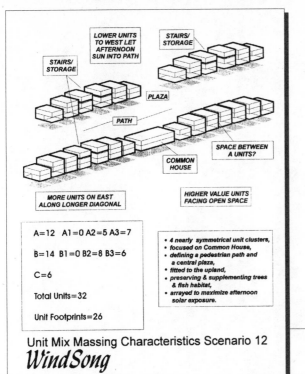

A=12   A1=0 A2=5 A3=7

B=14 B1=0 B2=8 B3=6

C=6

Total Units=32

Unit Footprints=26

- 4 nearly symmetrical unit clusters,
- focused on Common House,
- defining a pedestrian path and
  a central plaza,
- fitted to the upland,
- preserving & supplementing trees
  & fish habitat,
- arrayed to maximize afternoon
  solar exposure.

Unit Mix Massing Characteristics Scenario 12
WindSong

A=12   A1=0 A2=5 A3=7

B=14 B1=0 B2=8 B3=6

C=6

Total Units=32

Unit Footprints=26

Unit Mix Scenario 13
WindSong

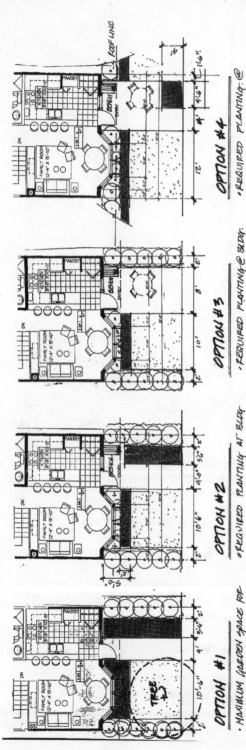

OPTION #1

- MAXIMUM GARDEN SPACE PER RESIDENCE.
- MINIMUM WALKWAY/ PAVING.
- NO REQUIRED PLANTING @ BLDG. EDGE OR ALONG WALK.
- NO BENCH/ BOOT KICK-OFF AREA.
- POTENTIAL FOR PAVING UPGRADE.
- NO ROOM FOR OUTDOOR TABLE.
- TREE SHOWN HERE FOR SCALE & LOCATION.

OPTION #2

- REQUIRED PLANTING AT BLDG. FACE.
- BENCH ON PAVED LANDING @ DOOR.
- POTENTIAL FOR PAVING UPGRADE.
- NO ROOM FOR OUTDOOR TABLE.

OPTION #3

- REQUIRED PLANTING @ BLDG. FACE.
- MAXIMUM PAVING.
- BENCH (18" DEEP x 3' WIDE).
- ROOM FOR OUTDOOR ACTIVITIES ON PAVED AREA.
- MINIMUM PERSONAL PLANTING AREA, MAXIMUM AREA UNDER COMMUNITY CONTROL.

OPTION #4

- REQUIRED PLANTING @ BLDG. FACE.
- HEDGES GONE. OPEN GRASS AREAS FULL LENGTH OF STREETS.
- PERSONAL PLANTING SPACE @ CORNER OF PAVED AREA FOR UNIT "IDENTIFICATION."
- POTENTIAL PAVING UPGRADE.
- BENCH.

LEGEND.   SCALE: ⅛" = 1'-0"

- LAWN AREAS (STAYS SAME).
- PERSONAL GARDEN SPACE
- SHRUBS / GROUND COVER (PUBLIC)

* NOTE: ① AVERAGE DISTANCE FROM DOOR TO PEDESTRIAN STREET IS ± 15'-0".
② "REQUIRED PLANTING" = MINIMUM REQUIRED AS PER APPROVED PLANS SUBMITTED TO LANGLEY MUNICIPAL HALL. THESE PLANTS IN GROUND AT MOVE-IN.

PERSONAL/ PUBLIC LANDSCAPE AREAS.

Early WindSong private unit entry studies, by David Wright

UNIT TYPE A MAIN FLOOR (A)

UNIT TYPE A UPPER FLOOR (U)

UNIT TYPE A LOWER FLOOR (L)

*WindSong four
bedroom unit*

Standardization of private units

Standardization of private units is cost effective, whereas customization of private units is very expensive. This may be disappointing news, but let me explain why standardization makes economic sense.

Custom (designed with user input) single-family housing normally costs at least $75 to $100 per square foot for construction, not including soft costs (see glossary) or land costs. It can cost more than $200 per square foot for very high quality construction or when exotic materials and equipment are used. Multi-family housing, on the other hand, can cost as little as $25 per square foot, and rarely more than $75 per square foot, again depending on quality, but affected mostly by the number of units being constructed. These costs vary, depending on your location, but the numbers are correct relative to one another. In other words, all the numbers may be lower or higher in your area, depending on the price of labor and the availability of materials.

Standardizing your private unit means that as many things as possible are the same from one unit to the next. The kitchens and bathrooms are the same, or at least very similar from one unit to another. There are a small number of different floor plans. In a 30-unit townhouse project built by a developer for the "normal market" there would typically be only two or three standardized floor plans. These would include a couple of two-bedroom plans, one a little larger and more expensive than the other, and a

UNIT TYPE B MAIN FLOOR (B)

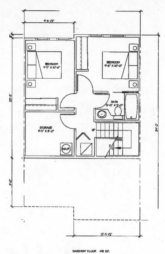

UNIT TYPE B LOWER LOWER (Y)

Over parking

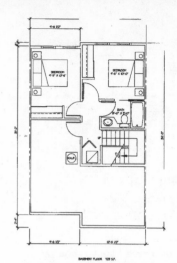

UNIT TYPE B LOWER FLOOR (Y1)

Not over parking

WindSong three bedroom unit

UNIT TYPE C MAIN FLOOR (C)

WindSong one bedroom unit

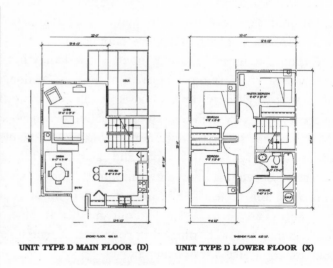

UNIT TYPE D MAIN FLOOR (D)   **UNIT TYPE D LOWER FLOOR (X)**

WindSong two bedroom unit

single one-bedroom "economy" plan. If the project includes three bedroom units, one-bedroom units are often not available.

The reason for the limited selection is economic. The more repetition in your project, the more your construction costs come down. You can buy whole truckloads of kitchen cabinets that match and they cost less. You can successfully employ young construction workers with less skill because they can learn how to install it once, and then do it over and over again.

Multi-family projects that cost a little more are projects that have fewer standard features from one unit to the next. Kitchens may vary, there may be more floor plans, fixtures may not be "builder basic." Instead of paying $75 each for plain white normal toilets, a higher grade of fixture may cost $250 or $300 each. Multiplied by 30 units, two per unit, you might have a project cost increase from $4,500 to $18,000 just for toilets. Imagine what happens when you do this for heating systems, roofing, carpeting, and so on. A unit that might have cost $50,000 to build can quickly increase to $100,000 or more.

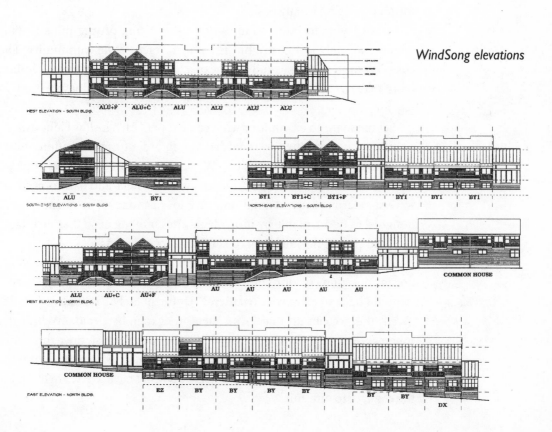

WindSong elevations

Customized private units

We all imagine designing our own home and making it exactly what we want. Some of us can afford this luxury, but most of us can't. It is tempting when we get involved in the design process, paying our hired architects and other design professionals, to believe we have a right to a custom-designed personal residence. The reason that most people never use the services of an architect is because most people can't afford to build a custom house. There is no reason to assume, just because you are using an architect to help you design your community, that this is the time to design a custom home. Not only is it expensive for you, it will have other costs to the community.

If our goal is to create a community, sometimes we have to let go of our unrealistic dreams, or our wishes for personal luxuries we can't afford. For many the sacrifice is easy. Look to the common house to make up the difference. Choose to put energy and resources into creating wonderful common facilities where you will feel at home, a place you will feel comfortable using on a daily basis.

When trying to build community, customizing private units is dangerous. Not only is it costly, but is tends to fracture the community. The customization process is full of unexpected divisive situations, including costs that weren't foreseen, costs the individual family doesn't want to pay for.

Let me share an example of what can happen. At Winslow Cohousing a number of us "preached" standardization in order to achieve affordability for as many members as possible. We agreed to standardization, and we completed very good designs – designs with kitchens and bathrooms that were standardized, and would save us a lot of money. The kitchens were designed to be adaptable by individuals after moving in so that each family could change the kitchen to meet their specific needs.

As we were ready to start construction, well-meaning people asked innocent questions of our contractor: "Can I make a slight change here?" "Could I have an extra window there?" Unfortunately, the contractor said, "Well sure, we can do that." And then other members said, "Well, if the Joneses are going to have an extra window, why can't I just move this closet a foot to the left – it makes the floor plan we chose work so much better for us?" "I will pay for the changes." "The group won't have to pay anything for the changes to our unit."

In the end, more than 20 units out of 30 were customized, some with minor cosmetic alterations, some with really major structural changes. The identified costs for these changes, costs that were supposed to be carried entirely by each member making the changes, ranged from a few hundred dollars up to nearly $10,000. Calculated by the contractor and billed to individual members, these changes totaled approximately $75,000. These fees were supposed to cover the entire cost of customizing private units. Theoretically, the bill for each customized unit was marked up enough to include all overhead and administrative costs associated the changes requested.

However, these were only the costs as they were calculated before the changes were completed. They did represent the construction costs experienced by the contractor; however, the real costs were actually much higher because of the mistakes, the headaches and the hassles. As far as I know, the contractor never tried to figure out what the changes had actually cost them, they simply decided never to do another cohousing project.

What about the costs to the community of private unit customization? Several months after completion I made another cost calculation. Using the benefit of hindsight I looked at the unattributed professional costs for architects and project managers. I added in the sizable amount of interest accrued during the several months of delay. The complexities caused by the customization process had added somewhere in the neighborhood of $90,000 to the entire community's cost. This was $90,000 which wasn't being paid for by the people who did the customization. This was $90,000 that could have gone toward a guest house, a workshop and a barn. It could have gone toward affordable housing for a previous member who couldn't stay in because of cost. This was a cost to the community, a cost on top of the costs already paid by individual members for their individual changes.

Standardizing units may sound awful, and sticking with standardization, even when you agree to it, will be hard. But there are great benefits to the community. Develop reasonable and practical design alternatives during the design process. Design for flexibility and adaptability. Show individuals how to change their private units after they have moved in. Live with your private unit design and then customize your unit after you take possession. Believe it or not, it will cost all of you less. And it won't damage the community.

Options and design alternates

In a normal townhouse development, the developer will offer design alternates or options to those people buying before the completion of construction. These options include such items as paint and carpet colors, and sometimes they include special cabinet upgrades, floor coverings or even skylights. In any event, the options are specific, and they have each been designed to fit into the existing building plans without structural, electrical or mechanical modification. The prices for these upgrades are set beforehand by the developer. He has figured out what the extra costs will be.

Sometimes these alternates don't have to cost anything. For instance, if you establish a small set of color options using the same brand and quality of materials, there may be no difference in cost from one option to the next. The number of options is limited. Obviously, if everyone chose to do something that wasn't standard, the standard was inappropriate. It should also be noted that these options or design alternates are only available before construction is completed. After a unit is complete, it is purchased as is, unless you want to pay for remodeling. If you are going to remodel, wait until the project is complete and everyone has begun moving in, the general contractor has been paid, the bank has been paid, and you have now taken individual responsibility for your private unit.

Before and during construction the challenge is to keep the project affordable so as many members as possible can successfully move in. As costs climb, some members are priced out, which can be devastating to any new community.

Cohousing groups find it practical to standardize private unit designs as much as possible, and convenient to then establish design alternates, or options. This allows individual members to have features of their preference, paid for by themselves and not by the group as a whole. It allows some units to remain affordable, while others might add several expensive design options.

Summary

Consider your priorities carefully before beginning the design process. Do the required programming and learn from what groups before yours have done. Review carefully the plans for other communities that have been built. Visit them if possible.

As you design your project, I recommend that you separate the cars from the private dwellings. Create pedestrian pathways connecting each dwelling. Place the kitchen in your private dwellings so that it is facing the pedestrian pathways. Spend the time and money to design a wonderful, centrally located common house. Consider more than just the normal housing forms, especially where other forms might make your project more affordable. Consider the quality issues first, including the quality of the construction materials, the quality of the spaces you create, or the quality of life you will experience.

Consider the quantity issues second, in terms of size of units, or numbers of fixtures, especially as they relate to building and sustaining community.

Standardize the private units and let an architect design them for you, after you have done the programming. Do not allow customization of private units, either before construction begins or during the construction process. And see McCamant and Durrett's book *Cohousing, a Contemporary Approach to Housing Ourselves* for great illustrations and an architectural look at design considerations for cohousing.

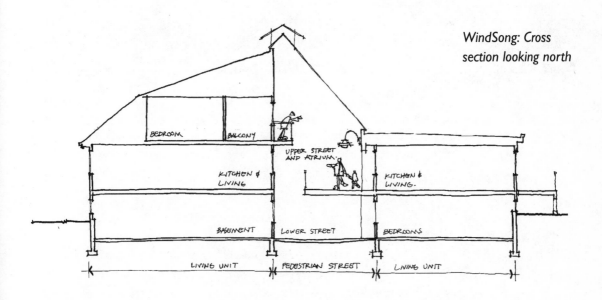

WindSong: Cross section looking north

8

Environment

Use of the car • Site selection • Site planning • Housing
types • Materials selection • Reduce, reuse, recycle •
Managing costs • Summary

Most of us are interested in being environmentally aware. We say we want
to live lightly on the land. We don't want to damage the natural environment, and where possible we would like to enhance it. "Civilization" has
done some pretty dreadful things in the name of progress, and most of us
feel some responsibility to turn that around. Environmental concerns are
often overlooked during the construction process, and housing developers
are not famous for their environmental sensitivity. As you consider under-
taking housing development yourself, you may want to understand why
this is so.

In this chapter I will briefly identify several significant environmental
factors in community planning and development.

Cost, of course, is always the big factor when considering what you can
do to be more environmentally appropriate in the development of your
project. The cost of nonstandard materials and methods can be very high
when compared to "normal" or traditional construction materials and
methods.

As a community you have the opportunity to work together to establish goals and set budgets which will allow you to go beyond what's normally acceptable. An individual often feels overwhelmed by the magnitude
of the environmental problem and may give in to the contractor's constant

harangue about saving money. As a community you can make your decisions about what's important and stand by them, together.

Use of the car

The single biggest environmental impact we have in North America is the car. It takes up land which could otherwise be left in a natural state. It consumes nonrenewable fossil fuels at an alarming rate. It discharges toxic and other harmful substances into our environment. The vast amounts of personal effort required to purchase and support a car could be better used in many other ways.

In planning for your community you have the opportunity to rethink the way you want to relate to the car. What transportation is really required, individually and as a community? How can the car be used more wisely? Typically we dream of the private retreat of a single-family detached home. The current model of suburban living developed rapidly after the Second World War. Architect and urban planning visionary Paolo Soleri calculates that over 70% of the land in the Los Angeles metropolitan area is devoted to the car. This includes streets and right-of-ways, but it also includes parking lots, driveways, garages, car dealerships, car factories, car repair facilities, filling stations, etc. How much of our natural environment is given over to our addiction to the car?

There are a number of simple things we can do to change our habits and reduce our dependence on the car. Creating a well-designed and well-situated community can be a major contribution. We can reduce our need to commute, and we can share rides and vehicles. Consider your need to be near "civilization." How will you and the other members of your community actually behave, versus how you wish you would? How often do you get in your car to go shopping, to schools, or the video store? Consider carefully before you select a site for your community.

Site selection

Possibly the largest single environmental decision you will make as a community is your selection of a site. Most of us dream of a pastoral setting, hundreds of acres of meadows and forest, bubbling brooks, wildlife and a wonderful view. We want a quiet, serene place, away from the hubbub of the city, a place to go when we need to recharge. But we also want civilization. We want electricity, water, sewer and communication systems. We want schools, shopping and after-school activities nearby. And we don't want to commute long distances to work. For most of us our dreams of living in seclusion and solitude do not match our practical need to live within society. You can't have civilization and escape from it, too.

When you consider where you want to be and where you want to create your community, you need to be practical. You need to consider the true behavior of the members of your group. Who will be commuting? How far will the kids have to go to school? How many members of your group rent videos regularly and can you expect them to change?

When it comes to choosing your site you will want to be environmentally aware of the consequences of your choices. How dependent will your members be on their cars? Will the local roads need to be extended or improved? Does the existing sewer system serve your area? And what environmental impact will you have as a community in the short term, as well as the long term?

The decision between a rural or urban location is a difficult one. If everyone chose to move out into the country and build new, what we would have would be more urban sprawl. With the sprawl we have suburbia, and the complete destruction of the natural environment. It seems to me that true environmentalists would choose to live in the high density of the city, doing their part to protect the natural environment from further development.

It is possible for your community to choose an urban location, even a tiny site, or a few of floors in a high-rise, and then buy some rural agricultural land to be owned and managed by the community. Your rural land might have a regular farmhouse on it, with barns and other agricultural buildings. You could add a bunkhouse and and a camp kitchen for community retreats to the country. It seems to me that this is a much more sustainable approach to owning rural land.

Before you choose your site, consider your options carefully. Consider the small town, or the urban village within the city where you live. Do you want to pay the environmental and social price of moving to the country? Is it your right? Do you want to accept the responsibility?

Site planning

Site planning is another area where your decisions will have a significant environmental impact. Balancing privacy and community is important,

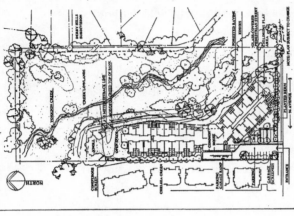

AS THIRD GENERATION CoHOUSING SITE:

As cohousing site, 72 percent of land remains undeveloped by restrictive covenants and future residents' desires to preserve ecology of Yorkson Creek and ravine uplands

34 townhouse units under single roof on less than 2 Acres of land, leaving nearly 4 acres undeveloped

Design fosters sense of community interaction and connection

No net loss of tree or shrub cover due to careful site planning and minimal regrading

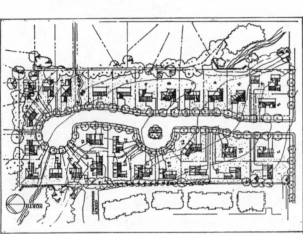

AS A TYPICAL SUBDIVISION:

Assuming no planning and environmental controls on site development, we have the following scenario:

29 single family homes on 7,000 square foot lots on 60-foot road right of way which consumes roughly one fourth of site.

Loss of community as neighbourhood is governed by auto-mobiles, lack of "eyes on the street"

Environmental loss: stream culverted, woodland and shrub habitat destroyed as 100 percent of site is utilized, denuded, regraded and filled

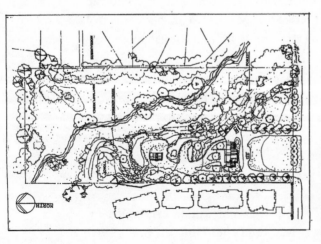

EXISTING CONDITIONS:

5.89 Acre site with single family home and old house barn

Ecology: successional upland forest and lowlands, migrating beavers are transforming lowlands into wetland habitat. Yorkson Creek is a high-quality salmon rearing stream

Wildlife: salmon, fox, coyote, rabbit, deer, hawk, eagle, owls, beaverherons songbirds, raccons, muskrats.

SCALE

CoHOUSING: A SITE AS IF LAND AND PEOPLE MATTERED

but consider the environmental effects of building a community of single-family detached houses. The length and depth of the sewer installation is multiplied. The urge to be near your car is increased, and the temptation to build parking next to the detached house is compelling. The energy usage of detached dwellings is huge when compared to attached, and especially stacked dwellings. More materials are required to build additional roofs, walls and footings. More land is covered, and less natural area will remain. In every way, the single-family detached house has significant environmental costs. (See Chapter 7, Design Considerations.)

In an ideal situation, where human expectations were not an issue, we would build our communities three-dimensionally. The environmental costs are minimized, and the opportunities for social interaction are maximized. (See Paolo Soleri's work for a complete description of the "miniaturized," three-dimensional community.)

For most cohousing groups choosing to build new construction, the site planning compromise is the townhouse form, reducing environmental costs (the spread across the land, the consumption of energy, etc.) to acceptable levels. Most members eventually feel comfortable with the acoustic isolation measures available with shared walls, especially with no one living over or under them. The environmental impacts are reduced but certainly not eliminated.

Utilities and infrastructure costs are always high, both financially and environmentally. At Winslow Cohousing the first site plan included townhouses, but they were spread in a disorganized way across most of the site. When new architects were hired (Edward Weinstein and Associates) they evaluated what had already been done and came to the group with a suggestion that would save nearly $100,000 in utility and infrastructure costs. The group became quite experienced with the design process and the idea of living in cohousing. They spent more than a year visualizing the new community, how to use the common house, where each wanted to live, etc. When the new architects suggested "reorganizing" the site plan and making it more compact to save money on infrastructure costs, the group readily agreed. The illustration of *Comparative Cohousing Site Plans* was presented as a means of seeing how "disorganized" the original, "organic" site plan was, compared, for example, with other cohousing site plans from Denmark. This is not to say that organic design is necessarily more costly. In this case, the cost savings was mostly due to reduction of the required sewer lengths and depths.

Energy consumption, especially of fossil fuels, also has considerable environmental impact. The orientation of your site plan to take advantage of solar gain in appropriate climates can significantly reduce your energy consumption. In most climates, it is the conservation of energy that will contribute most considerably to independence from external energy sources.

Comparative Cohousing site plans

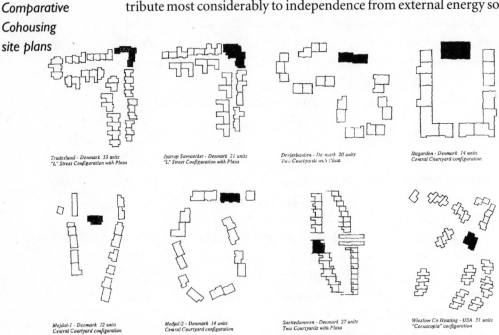

Trudeslund - Denmark 33 units
"L" Street Configuration with Plaza

Jystrup Savvaerket - Denmark 21 units
"L" Street Configuration with Plaza

Drejerbanken - Denmark 20 units
Two Courtyards with Plaza

Ibsgarden - Denmark 14 units
Central Courtyard configuration

Mejdal-1 - Denmark 12 units
Central Courtyard configuration

Medjal-2 - Denmark 14 units
Central Courtyard configuration

Saettedammen - Denmark 27 units
Two Courtyards with Plaza

Winslow Co Housing - USA 31 units
"Cornucopia" configuration

Housing types

Your selection of a housing type or form will have a huge impact on the environment. For example, by choosing the single-family detached dwelling you would be choosing to spread your community across land that might otherwise be used as gardens, or left in a natural state. You may also jeopardize the ongoing health of the community by reducing the opportunity for social interaction.

As a society, we have allowed ourselves to be programmed with the belief that we need "space" to be happy, and that we need a single-family detached dwelling to have privacy. We can choose to deprogram ourselves, evaluating our real needs as individuals, as partners and families and communities.

The following list of housing types is arranged in order of environmental friendliness, from best to worst. (Notice that the order would be different if it were organized by personal expectations, or socially determined "appropriateness.")

- Dormitories
- Single room occupancy (the classic SRO hotel)
- High-rise apartments (more than four stories)
- Low-rise apartments
- Attached townhouses
- Semi-detached townhouses (e.g., a triplex)
- Duplexes
- Single-family detached houses

Your group will have to decide which options strike the right balance between social and environmental appropriateness.

Materials selection

Specification of the materials for the construction of your project will have significant environmental impact in both the short term and the long term. Nontoxic materials which are not standard in the construction industry are more expensive to purchase and to install. Due to cost you will be tempted to use standard materials so you can afford a larger house.

Often standard construction processes and installation methods are not environmentally friendly. There are a number of relatively toxic substances used during the construction process, and there is a lot of waste. Again, nonstandard methods are more costly and you will be tempted to look the other way and use only standard construction techniques.

Reduce, reuse, recycle

In order to have the resources available to afford environmentally sound materials and methods, I suggest a realistic look at simply reducing personal expectations. Consider reducing the size of your private dwelling. As you become confident with your group, and your belief in the community increases, you may find that your private house no longer has to be quite as big as you once thought. The common house will provide a great deal of space for your personal use, even though that space is shared with others.

Reducing personal expectations has more to do with simplifying life, rather than material deprivation. It can be the means of implementing your commitment to the environment. It costs less and requires fewer materials to create smaller private spaces and a larger common house, which may increase your level of satisfaction with staying "on site." This reduces transportation requirements and the associated environmental costs while increasing quality of life. The third- and fourth-generation cohousing communities of northern Europe, with smaller private units and larger common facilities, are very successful. (See Chapter 7, Design Considerations.)

Consider reusing an existing housing development and adapting it to your specific needs. The Monterey Cohousing Community in St. Louis Park, Minnesota purchased and adapted an old nursing home for their reuse. With sufficient property they have been able to add townhouses to expand the community to meet their needs.

Or look for a building that can be recycled, in an area where the infrastructure is already in place. The Doyle Street Cohousing Community in Emeryville, California started with an old warehouse building and rebuilt it into 12 beautiful loft apartments. The environmental impact of their development was minimal compared with new construction on undeveloped land.

When you are confronted with these environmental issues, how are you going to feel? Maybe quality could be more important to you than quantity (size) so that you can afford the environmentally appropriate building materials and practices. I suggest reading, or rereading, Duane Elgin's *Voluntary Simplicity: Toward a Way of Life That is Outwardly Simple, and Inwardly Rich.* (New York: William Morrow, 1981.)

Managing costs

Since the costs for nonstandard materials and construction methods are significantly higher than "industry standard" techniques, it takes a substantial level of commitment to accomplish your environmental goals. I would suggest that early in your financial planning process, you should identify a dollar amount you are willing to commit to spending over and above standard construction costs. Keep this budget line item separate until construction documents are being prepared and construction costs are being calculated. You will then have money set aside in your budget to spend on those nonstandard materials and construction methods.

Consider using the services of a consultant who specializes in environmentally appropriate construction. You will certainly be interested in the indoor air quality of the new homes you plan to build for yourselves. Likely, you will want to consider the use of environmentally appropriate building materials and construction methods. You may also want to consider alternative energy sources, or nontraditional water and sewer systems. These consultants can help you consider the long-term costs and benefits, providing you with such detailed information as energy used in manufacture and transport for certain materials. They can also help you look at environmentally appropriate construction methods, evaluating special considerations for debris removal, burning, and recycling opportunities, as well as energy used during assembly.

Summary

I recently attended a conference at the Findhorn Community in northern Scotland entitled "Eco-Villages and Sustainable Communities: Models for Twenty-first Century Living." One of 370 participants from 45 nations who attended the conference in October 1995, I made a brief presentation on co-housing early in the conference. As the conference proceeded, I realized that much more needs to be said about land use issues and about our tendency to design our communities based on our expectations for our use of the car.

The conference was a real opportunity for all the participants to look at the bigger issues. What is sustainable development? Is sustainability enough, or do we need to start putting back, or enhancing the natural environment we have been destroying? How can we reduce the devastating impact of the car on our biosphere? It was an opportunity for each participant to think globally and to evaluate our individual efforts in a larger context.

In the words of the conference organizers, "There is an urgent need for positive models of human settlements that demonstrate a viable and sustainable future for people and this planet. Eco-villages represent 'human ecologies' that are sustainable: spiritually, culturally, economically and ecologically. To promote the consciousness of living in balance with the natural world, we must also be in balance with ourselves. The transformation of fundamental human attitudes underlying our destructive impact on Nature requires a deeper look at their causes. In order to solve the environmental crises we must also look at the social and cultural crises: we must look at sustainable economics and sustainable social systems, as much as ecological technologies."

I can't help but think that we have a special burden and a special opportunity here in North America. Much of the world looks to us as a pattern for the growth and development of their economy, resulting in land use and consumption patterns that mimic what we have done here. The ecosystems of this planet can't handle what we are doing to it now, much less the growing tendency for suburban sprawl and consumption.

For me, the questions are: What are we doing to this planet, and what can I do to make a difference? I choose to create cohousing.

9
Legal Issues

Legal advice • Ownership structure • Setting up
your corporation • Summary

In this chapter we will be talking about ownership structure, both before completion of the project and after moving in, as well as contracts and other legal matters.

The first thing to keep in mind when considering legal forms for your group is your purpose. What are your goals? What legal form is most flexible and best suited to the purposes of your group? What are the banks accustomed to seeing?

Legal advice

Do we need legal advice as a group?
Yes. The information in this chapter is a guide to the legal issues from a practical and businesslike perspective. It does not replace professional legal advice, but it should assist you in knowing when to get advice, what kind of advice you might need, and how to use the advice you get.

Do I need to get legal advice as an individual?
Again, the answer is yes. Each individual member of the group is affected in a way that is completely different from the group as a whole. The best examples are tax implications and risk management. What may be "smart" for the group may be too risky for the individual, or vice versa.

Ownership structure

Why form a legal entity?

The one-word answer is credibility. In addition, once your group has formed a legal entity you will have the right, as a group, to enter into legal agreements, such as signing a contract with an architect. You will be able to borrow money. You will be treated with respect as a serious organization.

When evaluating legal forms for your group, keep in mind that your group will exist in two distinctly different phases. First your purpose will be to create cohousing, to build the physical form, the container for you to live in later. When you have succeeded in creating your project, when you are ready to move in, your purpose will be to live in community. Your legal requirements may be completely different. After choosing one legal form for the development process, you may need to completely change legal forms at the point of moving in.

What forms of ownership are possible?

Several forms of ownership may work very well for you during the creative development phase. No matter where you are in North America, these generally include the association, the partnership or the corporation. Let's examine each of these alternatives in general terms so that you will have an overview of your options. (For a detailed and very readable description of this topic, see Don Lindemann's article "Understanding Community Ownership Structures" in the Winter 1996 issue of the journal *CoHousing*. It is available from the Cohousing Network.)

THE ASSOCIATION

Generally, it is safe to start off as an association, registered or unregistered. Most states and provinces recognize associations of people with a common purpose without requiring the filing of special documents and organizational papers. If you already meet regularly, work together to define your common goals and document your decisions, you are probably already an unregistered association. You could make it official by registering with the local government.

PARTNERSHIP

Another form of ownership is the partnership. In a partnership, each partner is an owner, sharing in the risks and benefits of the enterprise you undertake together. Some places allow for a "limited partnership" which has a general partner in control, and a set of investor partners who invest but have no control, and who must stay out of the way. As the name implies, the limited partners have limited liability, and limited risk as a result of their limited control.

With some exceptions, in a normal partnership each person is equal. Like a marriage, a partnership requires trust. Each partner has equal responsibility, which means equal control and equal risk. Generally, partnerships work best when each individual partner is equally capable, with the skill and the financial capacity necessary to hold up their end of the bargain.

A final word about partnerships. In my opinion this is the most complicated form of legal ownership for a group of people trying to build community. People aren't equal; situations change. As an example, partnerships have a tendency to work best when partners are equal in terms of financial capability (income and assets), their ability to take risks, and their knowledge of business conditions. This is rarely the case in the membership of a cohousing group. Older and younger members, in particular, vary in terms of their financial ability and approach. This can lead to increased risk to older members, as well as resentment and fear.

You must have a good buy-out or dissolution agreement in place before you engage in a partnership. If you are seriously considering a partnership as the legal structure for your group, please, I can't stress this enough, please get good legal advice personally, and as a group.

WHAT ABOUT A CORPORATION?

Corporations are simple and old fashioned, but they work. If you form a corporation you have the flexibility to have differing levels of investment by owning different amounts of stock. Financial risk is similar to other ownership models, but the liability for other potential hazards, such as accidents, mistakes, etc., is reduced.

Except for nonprofits, a corporation is simply a collection of people who each own stock, or shares, in the corporation. As individuals, they may or may not be actively involved in the management of the corporation's affairs. There are several different types of corporations which might be appropriate for your group.

NONPROFITS, OR NOT-FOR-PROFIT CORPORATIONS

States and provinces typically allow you to set up a nonprofit, or not-for-profit corporation. While your group probably is not in this for a profit, don't be fooled by the terminology. A nonprofit is more strictly controlled then a standard corporation. Technically, a nonprofit is not owned by anyone, and therefore, no shares are issued. When a nonprofit dissolves, or quits business, the assets must be transferred to another nonprofit.

The federal government allows some nonprofits to accept tax deductible gifts and donations, but you probably won't be able to qualify for nonprofit status under the federal guidelines. If you're intending to be a cohousing advocate (sometimes known as an umbrella group), not intending to actually build a community, you may qualify, but generally, not if you are creating a place for yourselves to live.

Choosing to form as a nonprofit may make sense, but consider carefully, and get good legal advice.

STANDARD (FOR-PROFIT) CORPORATION

The "standard" corporation is the most flexible, the most easily recognized by a lending institution, and in many ways the simplest to set up and run. While corporations are generally competitive, for the purpose of cohousing development they can operate very cooperatively.

You can retain a lawyer to set up a corporation for you, or you can do it yourself using one of the many self-help books available. Cost is generally a few hundred dollars at the most. Ownership of a standard corporation is by shares or stock. Each member of your group buys shares in the corporation proportional to the investment they are making in the project. Typically, cohousing groups write into their bylaws, or their policies and procedures if they use a standard set of bylaws, that each shareholder will automatically become a member of the board of directors. This way you keep the corporation from accidentally becoming hierarchical with a small group of people running it, something not desired by most cohousing groups.

You will have to elect officers as required by traditional corporate law, and the elected president will have special rights and responsibilities. To maintain a nonhierarchical management structure you may want to rotate the "job" of president, making it a figurehead position. For instance, select the person who has the next birthday after the date of incorporation, and then each year transfer it to the person with the next birthday in rotation. Obviously, if there are 40 people in your community, it will be 40 years before any one person has to be (or gets to be) president again.

The other two officers generally required are the secretary and treasurer. These are practical responsibilities you will need to find someone to do anyway. Many groups try to share these positions, electing two people as co-treasurers, for example.

THE LIMITED LIABILITY COMPANY

In recent years a number of cohousing groups have adopted this new legal structure. The Limited Liability Company (LLC) is a relatively new form of ownership which may suit your purposes during the development process. Often described as a cross between the corporation and a partnership, the LLC is only available in certain locations. Ask your lawyer if this would work for you.

COOPERATIVE CORPORATION

Another form of corporation is the cooperative. It can be seen as a cross between a nonprofit and a standard corporation. Each member owns shares and the shares can be sold as with a standard corporation. The stated goals of the organization are not to compete but to cooperate.

Many people think that the cooperative is the ideal or classic ownership model for cohousing. Some consider cohousing to be cooperative living in its ideal form, because there is actual sharing and cooperation within the community, in contrast to the lack of cooperation seen in some co-ops.

The cooperative corporation is far less common than the standard corporation and therefore you may have difficulty finding a bank to finance your project. Most banks have never heard of co-ops, and cooperative ownership is usually not something a lending institution understands.

WHAT ABOUT A LIMITED EQUITY COOPERATIVE?

Generally there are two forms of cooperative. One is called the "equity cooperative" where the shares can be sold for any price based on market value, the other is the "limited equity cooperative" where the value of the shares is determined by a set formula. Generally speaking, the equity cooperative is enough like a standard corporation that your investment in your home is pretty secure and you can reasonably expect it to grow (with inflation and other factors).

The limited equity cooperative is a subsidized housing format in which someone has to pay for the control of the future value of the shares. As a buyer you would be agreeing to give up any future increase in value, subsidizing the purchase of your shares by the next buyer. While this is socially laudable, lending institutions often don't appreciate this form of ownership. They lend money based on having a tangible asset as security. To them, shares in a limited equity cooperative have too many restrictions on their redeemable value.

WHAT ABOUT CONDOMINIUM OWNERSHIP?
(SOMETIMES CALLED STRATA TITLE)

If you are just getting started and you are thinking about establishing an ownership structure, don't consider condominium or strata title ownership now. The condominium or strata title ownership structure is a means of separating legal ownership of a building (or a piece of land in some cases) into smaller parts. It is commonly used for townhouse projects, or buildings where individual units are above one another, as in an apartment building.

The condominium ownership structure works well after you complete your project, but don't consider setting up a condominium until after you have constructed the buildings. Generally you can't file the documents to create a condominium until after the project has been substantially completed. The condominium documents are based on real, three-dimensional spaces which don't exist until the buildings are constructed. Normally the documents aren't approved until after the buildings are almost ready for occupancy.

What form of ownership would be best for your group?

When you seek legal advice, personally, or as a group, ask specifically about the comments I have made here. Don't assume this is all you need to know. The lending institutions and state or provincial laws will have a significant influence on your choice of legal structure. In California, for instance, all cooperatives are limited equity as defined by a state law. As a result, cohousing groups in California are not using the cooperative ownership structure because they either can't find financing for a limited equity project, or they don't want to have limited equity.

What legal forms are the banks accustomed to seeing?

This is perhaps the most important question when considering ownership structure for your group. Start by considering what banks you may approach for financing – what they expect, and what kind of projects are getting financed. Unless you already have deep pockets in your group and don't need any outside financing you need to listen carefully to the answer.

What ownership structure do we need to get this built?

Many groups spend a significant amount of time trying to figure out whether they want to be a "condo" or a "co-op," imagining what it will be like to live there, and which form of ownership might be preferred. When you are getting started the real question is what ownership structure do you need in order to get your project built.

There is a difference between the ownership structure you need for living there, and the ownership structure required to get your project built. For example, the condominium ownership structure cannot be used during the development of your project. You will want to choose a simple ownership structure, such as a corporation, which will allow you to manage your project and get the financing you need for development and construction. Later, you will select a structure, such as a condominium or cooperative, that will allow individual members to finance the ownership of their private unit, as well as supporting your need to manage the affairs of the ongoing community. You should make your choice of ownership structure based on what is traditional in your area, and how much you are willing to fight that tradition.

Risk management

A major part of the ownership structure decision may come down to managing risk. This is particularly true if your group has (or expects to have) members with different financial conditions. The biggest concern will arise when some members have significant assets and other members do not. If your group is attracting a broad age range, especially if some members are at or near retirement age, you will have members with significant assets to protect. When you borrow money as a group, your lender takes into account both the income and assets of the borrower. If there is a default on the loan, they will first come after the members who have assets.

A partnership in this case can be very risky to the members with assets. I have found over the years that the simple corporation provides the necessary risk management for those members who have assets, while allowing all members to join and participate at the level of their financial capability.

Tax questions

Perhaps the second most important question is how the ownership structure will affect when and how much tax you will be required to pay. Watch out for "taxable events." These are situations when you may have done something, such as transfer ownership of property, which triggers an automatic tax payment requirement, whether you realize an actual cash profit or not. Avoid transferring property more often than you absolutely have to. Each time you transfer the ownership of land you may be subject to certain taxes. Get up-to-date advice. I can't stress enough that your choice of legal ownership structure will depend on good information. Talk to your tax advisor and your lawyer.

Setting up your corporation

Where do I get sample documents?

Sample documents are available from a good bookstore in the legal self-help section, or ask your lawyer for samples so you can review various options. Many cohousing groups make their legal documents available to new groups, but consider a couple of things before making a request. First, most early cohousing groups started from scratch and paid significant fees to get legal advice and to have their documents drafted. Second, documents drafted by a lawyer for one group were designed to meet that group's specific needs as understood by the lawyer and the group at the time they were being drafted. Situations change, or your situation may be completely different. If you are in a different state or province, you may be subject to entirely different laws.

Sample documents are also available from many of the professionals who work with cohousing groups. The CoHousing Company in Berkeley, California (510) 549-9980, and the CoHousing Center in Boston, Massachusetts (617) 923-1300 are two examples. Give them a call.

Initial organizing agreement

When you get started you may want to define your common purpose and expectations in writing. This can be done with an initial organizing agreement signed by all members. As with everything, keep this agreement simple. Have a look at the sample included here. Notice that it is on one page, it is simple, to the point, and it is in English, not legalese.

It may be overly simplistic for your needs. You will have to be the judge.

Winslow Cohousing Group of Bainbridge Island

INITIAL ORGANIZING AGREEMENT

PURPOSE OF THE WINSLOW COHOUSING CORE GROUP: The undersigned hereby form the Winslow Cohousing Group of Bainbridge Island to develop a Cohousing project in Winslow, Washington. The functions of this group include but are not necessarily limited to:

1. Making an offer on all or part of the property known as the Landmark Plat.
2. Exploring the development potential at this and other comparable sites.
3. Recruiting and orienting new members to the Winslow Cohousing Core Group.
4. Preparing a detailed development program.
5. Securing the services of professionals as necessary to facilitate the above.

MEMBERSHIP: Interested persons become active members of the Winslow Cohousing Group by attending three meetings, paying a non-refundable membership fee and monthly organizing fees and signing both the Statement of Purpose and this Organizing Agreement.

TO LEAVE THE CORE GROUP: Members will provide written indication of intent to withdraw from the group if at all possible. Members who have not attended three consecutive meetings and have not paid their monthly organizing fee will be dropped from the membership list.

MEETINGS: Minutes of discussions and decisions made will be available to attending and absent members at the next scheduled meeting. A notebook record of all receipts, memos, correspondence, research materials and other records will be available to all members at each meeting.

DECISION MAKING: In order to promote a feeling of community, caring and trust among all members of the group a consensus-seeking process will be used. A formal decision-making vote of three quarters of those present will be used only to avoid an impasse. All decisions are to be discussed thoroughly before a decision is made. Decisions can be brought up by members who were absent in the next meeting only.

FINANCIAL OBLIGATIONS: The finances of the group shall be the respective obligation of all individual members. The undersigned agree to pay a one time non-refundable fee of $100.00 plus an organizing fee of $25.00 each month beginning 1 May 1989 for costs which are limited to paper, mailing, photocopying, professional assistance (architectural, legal, engineering, surveying, etc.) and the rental of meeting rooms. For other purchases, or to incur any cost above $50.00, authorization must be given at a scheduled meeting. No deficit may be incurred.

Payments for refundable earnest money deposits shall be shared by all members on a prorata basis. Depositors shall individually approve conversion of their earnest money funds to non-refundable status when exercising the removal of contingencies from an offer. Those not approving such removal of contingencies shall be refunded their earnest money and shall not sign legal documents or organizing agreements as appropriate for the purchase of the site approved by the remainder of the group.

If the group dissolves, any surplus monies will be donated to the Bainbridge Foundation.

THE NEXT STEP: Within 60 days after acceptance of an offer on the Landmark Short Plat (or other property as approved) this group shall incorporate itself, forming a business entity such as a partnership or corporation with ownership, a buy-sell agreements, and liability specified. As that incorporated entity it shall make the decision whether or not to remove the contingencies of the offer to purchase and proceed with the purchase. If that incorporation does not occur, the contingencies shall not be removed and the property will not be purchased under the offer to purchase authorized by this agreement.

ONCE INCORPORATED: Members reserve a residence in the cohousing community by joining the Winslow Core Group and then investing in the corporation (or partnership) at the point of it's creation, or by later investing in the corporation (or partnership) if space is available. Persons not able or ready to invest in the corporation (or partnership) may continue to follow the project as members of this Winslow Core Group with the potential of buying in later if units remain available.

Agreed this 11th day of March 1989:

NAME _____ PHONE _____

ADDRESS _____

Who and what is your initial organizing agreement for, and why? Is it to make sure everyone is on the same wavelength, or does it need to stand up in court when someone sues someone else?

Articles of incorporation

Required by traditional corporate law, Articles of Incorporation are necessary when you first form a company. They are sometimes known as Articles of Association or a Memorandum of Association. Ask your lawyer or use a self-help guide and file an absolutely standard document. Make sure to observe traditions here. Where possible, leave as much flexibility as you can by not being too specific about the purpose of your incorporation. Indicate, for instance, that your purpose is to "conduct any business allowed by law."

Bylaws

Use a simple, standard set of bylaws to file with your state or province. Again, they are required by traditional corporate law. You could spend a lot of time and legal fees crafting an ideal set of bylaws, debating all the fine points of decision making, election of officers, and job descriptions. Or you can divide your administrative policies and procedures into a document separate from the "official" bylaws.

The WindSong group spent over a year and about $8,000 Canadian to have their bylaws carefully crafted by a very good lawyer. The Comox Valley group later adopted those bylaws with minor modifications, using the same lawyer, and paid only about $1,200 Canadian. The Cardiff Place group needed to be incorporated quickly so they went to an experienced real estate and development lawyer to ask for help. When they arrived for their first meeting with him he had already drafted standard documents which he reviewed with them in his office. The group asked to have the proposed name changed slightly, signed everything, and the lawyer simply filed them later that day. Total cost was about $400 Canadian and they were incorporated within a week, ready to sign a purchase and sale agreement with the developer.

Administrative policies and procedures

I suggest developing a set of written administrative policies and procedures that are separate from your bylaws. This internal document can evolve as required without being refiled with a government agency. In it you should cover such basics as decision-making procedures. If you choose to use consensus, what is it, and how does it work? What if it doesn't work when you absolutely must have a decision? How do you decide what is a necessary decision?

The sample that follows is simplified to address all the major cohousing issues, without getting into a lot of detail. You might use this sample in one of two ways. It can be adopted as is, assuming that you will, as a group, discover things along the way that you want to change, knowing that you can always make those changes. Or, you might use it as a starting point for discussion. Address each issue as a group, finding consensus when you can and modifying the sample document to reflect your goals and objectives as a group.

Summary

Get legal advice, but use it wisely. Follow the legal advice you receive, but only if you feel it will work for you and your group. As a part of the development process, you must be prepared to take more risk than your lawyer might otherwise recommend.

Keep things simple. Use English language (as opposed to legalese) agreements if at all possible. And don't reinvent the wheel. Seriously consider modeling your legal structure after someone else's.

Expect to change your policies and procedures regularly. Don't cast them in stone and then struggle to make the necessary changes later, or worse, ignore your bylaws or organizing agreements because they have become out of date.

10

Finance and Budget

It takes money • Language of development financing • Budgets
and pro formas • Borrowing money • Mortgage qualification
assistance sheet • Mortgage financing qualification analysis •
Other issues • Establishing preliminary unit pricing • Summary

---

It takes money

It takes money to create a physical community. Capital is required to build
the structures, and operational money is necessary to manage and promote the organization. The relatively permanent things, such as a common house or a dwelling unit, will last for a long time and are perceived to
have value by lenders. You will be able to borrow against that value to raise
some of the capital needed to create them.

Initially, a little operating money is all that is necessary to cover the
costs for photocopying, or to rent space for meetings and presentations.
Most groups collect a small amount each month in dues to cover these
costs, ranging from $5 to $20 per month. Some groups have simplified this
process by collecting a one-time fee of $100 to $200 per household. As you
can imagine, this simplifies the accounting.

Substantial capital contributions from members will be necessary before you can actually buy land or pay for professional assistance. Most groups start out small and gradually increase their financial requirements.

Incremental investment and commitment

Gradually, as individuals become more involved in the cohousing process, they make commitments of time and money. Their belief that the project will come to fruition increases as they see more evidence – money, incorporation, drawings, etc. Trust increases and the willingness to contribute money gradually increases as well. In the early stages of group development it is important to structure the financial requirements incrementally.

Later, after the initial members have passed the financial threshold and invested more money than they are willing to lose, the incremental investment is no longer necessary. (See Eight Major Thresholds of Commitment, in Chapter 3.) With evidence of the group's viability, new members will be willing to put up all the money necessary to become peers with the original members. This can be an important issue in planning your group's cash flow. (See What is a Cash Flow Plan?, below.)

What does it cost to create cohousing?

Does cohousing cost less than similar "market rate housing"? The simple answer is – no, it doesn't. There are several opportunities to save money in the cohousing process, but the projects that have been successful in North America were built at normal housing costs, except for those that were externally subsidized. To illustrate why, we will look at the numbers for two project budgets, below. (For a discussion on subsidies and affordability, see Other Issues: Affordability, below. See also Chapter 7, Design Considerations.)

Language of development financing

There is a language of development financing which you will want to be understand. Knowing the terms, what they mean and how they relate to one another, will assist you in maintaining some control as a community during the development process.

Cash Flow: The balance of incoming cash and outgoing expenses, perceived as a flow of money.

Cash Flow Plan: A schedule of income and expenses by month, used for managing cash flow.

Collateral:	Something of value, normally a tangible asset such as a home or car, used to guarantee a loan.
Construction Loan:	The loan required by the group to complete construction, prior to individual families securing mortgages on their private units.
Cost:	Actual cost to purchase land, materials, equipment or services.
Draw Requests:	After the construction loan has been funded the contractor will make regular formal requests to draw on those funds as construction proceeds. Sometimes called "progress draws."
Liquid Assets:	Those assets which can easily be turned into cash. Does not include assets tied up in real estate, for instance.
Loan Commitment:	A written commitment from a financial institution to provide loan money for a specific project or other purchase.
Loan Proceeds:	The amount of the loan. Points and fees are taken out of this amount, leaving you with loan amount less points and/or fees.
Mark-Up:	The amount that is added to the cost of something to cover the overhead (and possibly profit).
Overhead:	The expenses necessary to supply a product at a given price.
Permanent Financing:	Take-out loans, or private mortgages, used by individuals to purchase the private residences after construction is complete.
Points (on a loan):	A percentage of the loan amount in addition to the interest charged. Normally paid out of loan proceeds.
Price:	The total cost of the project or individual unit including overhead (plus profit, if any).
Pricing:	The price set for a product such as a dwelling unit in your community.
Pro forma:	The preliminary budget used for planning and evaluation before real costs are known; the anticipated project budget prior to verification or approval.
Project Budget:	The schedule of costs expected for your project, used in contracts with professionals, etc.

Soft Costs:	Those project costs which are not used for land or construction. Includes such items as architect's fees, interest charges, etc. Usually runs 40% to 50% of total project cost.
Take-out Loan:	Private mortgages used by individuals to purchase the private residences after construction is complete.
Unit Pricing:	The prices established for each dwelling unit in your community, adding up to the total project cost.
Value:	What someone else is willing to pay for a finished product or services.
Vendor Financing:	Financing provided by the seller, typically of land.

Banking

Set up a relationship with a bank early in the development process. A good relationship with a bank can have long-term benefits to your group when it comes time to borrow money later. A bank with records of your group's income and cash flow over a period of time is more likely to lend you money when you need it. Also, a good relationship with one bank will help you get a construction loan with another bank if that is necessary.

In the early stages, individuals should begin thinking about arranging for their "take-out" mortgages, or permanent financing. It is never too early to prequalify for a mortgage. As your group becomes increasingly committed, all members will eventually need to prequalify as a part of maintaining their status as a member. Members who need financing but can't qualify for a mortgage are not viable members. However, they may be supportive to buyer members as potential renters who will provide income.

Budgets and pro formas

The pro forma

A pro forma is a detailed estimate of what your project will cost. Typically, developers take the budget from their last project and put in the numbers they think will apply to the next project, such as new land costs, different number of units, etc. At first the numbers in the pro forma are rough estimates used for evaluation of the property, or consideration of project concept alternatives. Are townhouses financially viable on this site, or do we have to go to low-rise condos?

Once a project is underway, the line items indicating anticipated costs in the pro forma are refined and updated as more information about the project becomes available. Prior to completing the construction drawings, for instance, the construction costs in a pro forma are based on general cost-per-square-foot numbers derived from calculating recent construction costs on other projects. Once you have settled on the costs and are making agreements with your design professionals, your pro forma becomes your project budget.

The project budget

The project budget is a refinement of the earlier pro forma, containing more accurate information and a more complete picture of what the project will cost to build. The project budget is used as the basis for managing

Sample budget: Summary page

Assumptions:			Results:		
# of Units	30	units	TOTAL COST	$5,192,545	
Aver Unit Size	1050	SF	Aver Unit Cost	$173,085	
Units Cost / SF	$60.00		Aver Unit Price	$181,739	w/GST
Common House Size	4500	SF	Res SF Total	31,500	SF
CH Cost / SF	$75.00		Total SF	36,000	SF

Evergreen Cohousing Budget

DRAFT 1.0

Category #					
			$2,227,500		
01-16	Construction				
17.000	Consultants	$636,205			
18.000	Land	$1,061,504			
19.000	Muni Levies	$523,072			
20.000	Financing	$256,000			
21.000	Sales	$120,000			
22.000	Contingencies	$121,000			
	Subtotal Development		$2,717,781		
	Subtotal Dev + Const			$4,945,281	
	Mark up to Development Partner at 5%				$247,264
	TOTAL PROJECT COST				$5,192,545
	Sales Taxes at 5%			$259,627	
	GRAND TOTAL, with Sales Taxes			$5,452,172	

the development of the project. It is normally used, for instance, as a part of the contract with the architect who is expected to design a project to fit within the construction cost limitations of your budget.

Comparing two project budgets

Let's compare a market rate 30-unit clustered townhouse project and a 30-unit cohousing project in a similar clustered townhouse format. By comparing budget line items we will better understand the differences in budgeting for cohousing versus 'standard' housing and discover what choices have a large impact on unit pricing for the completed project. For our comparison we will use two projects with essentially the same specifications for materials and equipment. (See, Where could we go over budget?, below.)

Our townhouse project will be a mix of two- and three-bedroom units, with an average unit size of 1,150 square feet. This will include 10 three-bedroom units at 1,500 square feet, and 20 two-bedrooms at 975 square feet. There will be a clubhouse of 5,000 square feet containing a party room with a kitchen, dance floor, lounge and pool table. Total heated floor area for the project is 35,000 square feet. There will be 31 kitchens (one per unit and one in the clubhouse) and 62 bathrooms (two per unit and two in the clubhouse.) This would be a fairly standard townhouse project, generally considered to be market rate.

Across the street we will be building a cohousing project with a mix of one-, two-, three- and four-bedroom units. Our unit mix will be five one-bedrooms at 600 square feet, 10 two-bedroom units at 850 square feet, 10 three-bedroom units at 1100 square feet, and 5 four-bedroom units at 1,500 square feet for a total of 30,000 square feet. This gives us an average unit size of 1,000 square feet. We will be including a common house of 5,000 square feet, which is generous but not overly large by cohousing standards. It will include the standard features most groups choose to include: large kitchen, dining area, children's play area, guest rooms, workshop, laundry, and so forth. Our cohousing project will include 31 kitchens (one per unit and one in the common house) and 57 bathrooms (two per unit, except one bedrooms, and two in the common house).

Reviewing our pro forma, under category numbers 01.000 to 16.000 (Construction costs), we find that building 35,000 square feet of heated living area with 31 kitchens and about 60 bathrooms should be similar for each project, assuming the same specifications for materials and equip-

Comparing Two Project Budgets
Standard Townhouse vs. Cohousing

Townhouse Assumptions:		Cohousing Assumptions:	
# of Units	30 units	# of Units	30 units
Average Unit Size	1150 SF	Average Unit Size	1000 SF
Total Private Units	34,500 SF	Total Private Units	30,000 SF
Club House Size	500 SF	Common House Size	5000 SF
Gross Project Size	35,000 SF	Gross Project Size	35,000 SF

Category #	Townhouse	Cohousing	Cohousing higher (lower)
1.000 - 16.000 Construction	$1,925,000	$2,000,000	$75,000
17.000 Consultants	$60,000	$180,000	$120,000
18.000 Land	$375,000	$450,000	$75,000
19.000 Muni Levies	$150,000	$150,000	$0
20.000 Financing	$200,000	$250,000	$50,000
21.000 Sales, Membership	$170,000	$85,000	($85,000)
22.000 Contingencies	$80,000	$200,000	$120,000
Project Totals	$2,960,000	$3,315,000	$355,000
Developer's Mark Up	$444,000	$265,200	($178,800)
Grand Total	$3,404,000	$3,580,200	$176,200

ment. A few thousand dollars in savings can be realized for the cohousing project with 57 bathrooms instead of the 62 bathrooms across the street.

Let's move on to budget line item Consultants (17.000). The only thing we know will differ between the market townhouse project and the cohousing project is the participation by the cohousing group members in the design process. In a normal market project, the developer hands the design team a piece of land and a rough idea of what he expects to see built there. Most often, the design team has already done other projects for this developer and nothing more needs to be said. They just go to work designing the project they know the developer wants – as many units as possible, designed so that people will want to buy them. Generally, there will be a pricing point established, so the design team knows how much these units are going to have to sell for.

Reviewing the list of consultants, it would seem that only the design team, primarily the architects and the landscape architects, will be influenced by the desire of the future residents for significant design input. This should add to design costs.

Most groups, however, find it necessary to also engage the services of a development manager or development consultant, to assist them in dealing with all the complexities of the development process. So our costs for consultants on the cohousing project will increase a bit due to the special needs of a cohousing group.

The market townhouses will be designed to have minimum landscaping. The developer and the architect worked out the site plans based on construction efficiencies, driveway locations and parking lot design limitations. The landscape architect had no input into the site design; instead, her job was to specify the plant materials and any required irrigation system to meet the basic requirements of the municipality. The architect for the market townhouses has worked for this developer before and has several sets of floor plans that might work for this project. The architect works more quickly for the developer, with fewer interruptions and fewer changes then they would with a cohousing group. (See also Chapter 3, The Development Process: How does a developer create housing?)

The design team for the market townhouses will cost about $60,000 including the landscape architect's single sheet drawing. The design team for the cohousing project has agreed to a fee of $120,000. (If the fee truly reflected the work you want them to do for you it should be closer to $200,000.) In addition to the design fees, there is another $60,000 for the development consultant (project manager) bringing the total consultant fees for the cohousing project to $120,000 more than the fees for the market townhouse.

Looking at the next line item, Land (18.000), it would seem that land should cost the same whether it were being used for cohousing or for market townhouses. However, there are a few factors that can change this. (See also Chapter 3, Buying Land.) The most significant factor that increases the cost of land selected for cohousing is the fact that with a cohousing group involved the piece of land selected must be more easily visualized in its raw, undeveloped state than would be necessary for a developer. Developers are used to seeing "raw" land and visualizing a final product on it. As a result, land selected for cohousing is often more expensive. It looks good, and so it commands a higher price. Another factor is that most groups visualizing their dream of cohousing imagine a site out in the country – large, remote and pastoral. As a result, they take on the special challenges of developing such a site, which include higher costs and higher risks. They may include such costs as providing the required utilities and services, or the risk of having to get the property rezoned to allow for the development.

On average, land selected by groups who have actually created cohousing has cost a little more than land which a normal developer would choose for market townhouses.

Municipal Fees and Levies (19.000) should not vary from one project to the other.

Financing (20.000) will be greater on the project that takes longer. Normally cohousing projects take longer for several reasons. The decision making is slower, design process is longer, and the land chosen is often more difficult to develop.

Sales and Marketing (21.000) should be lower for a cohousing project, since the members can contribute significantly to the membership and marketing effort.

Contingencies (22.000) will generally be higher for a cohousing project since there are more possibilities for things to go wrong. This money is not always lost, however, since it can be used later to complete common facilities, etc., if it is not needed during construction.

Where could you save money?

There are a few simple things you can do to save money on your project. These are choices that will have long-term effects on your community as well as the environment. Keep in mind that the last two items, especially, will need to be balanced with your desire to be environmentally friendly. They include:

- Reduce the number of bathrooms where possible.
- Simplify everything – the design, the structure, etc.
- Standardize kitchen designs.
- Standardize specified equipment, such as refrigerators.
- Make private spaces smaller.
- Resist the temptation to spend money on things a developer would not spend money on, such as expensive heating or roofing.
- Limit use of nonstandard materials and construction methods.

Where could you go over budget?

Since the cohousing project will be designed with substantial input from people who plan to live there, a significant temptation exists to spend more money upgrading construction materials and equipment specifications. Some cost tradeoffs are possible, such as reducing the number of bathrooms, which will allow for upgrading elsewhere. However, it should be noted that the bank and its appraiser will have a significant impact on such things as whether you include two bathrooms in every unit. (Remember that they are looking for security and want a project that they can sell to someone else if you fail to meet your payment obligations.)

Another danger is pushing your budget and not leaving enough in the contingency fund. Be a little conservative by not cutting your budget too close.

What is a cash flow plan?

The developer's business is to reduce the amount of financial risk while maximizing the return on investment. Reducing the amount of risk means not spending money until absolutely necessary. To manage what cash is needed, what is available and when it is spent you create a cash flow plan.

If you imagine a budget listing items and their expected cost, and then spread those costs over time, you have created the basis for a cash flow plan. When will you need to pay the taxes? How will you spread your advertising budget out so it lasts for the duration of the project? Use the cash flow plan to anticipate your need for cash. Will the required cash come

Actual budget and cash flow plan for Cardiff Place

Victoria Cohousing Development Society

Cardiff Place Budget and Cash Flow Plan

Project Budget: $3,121,034 (with price increases, 18 May)
8 June 1994

Cat. #	Budget Item	4 Feb 94 Budget	Adjusted Budget	Paid to Date	June	July	August	TOTALS
1.000	Construction, new + reno	2,856,000	2,856,000	170,000	0	0	2,686,000	2,856,000
	Add: Sound Transmission	20,000	20,000	6,667	6,667		6,666	20,000
	Add: Sprinkle Existing	10,000	10,000	3,334	3,333		3,333	10,000
	Add: Sundry Add Ons	14,241	14,241	4,747	4,747		4,747	14,241
	Change Order: Surveyor	0	425	425				425
	Change Order: Blasting	0	12,000	12,000				12,000
	Change Order: round 1	0	6,679	1,670			5,009	6,679
	Change Order: round 2 est.	0	16,790	0		4,200	12,590	16,790
17.050	Architects: M&D, Deitz	10,000	15,000	14,549	200		251	15,000
17.120	Legal	10,000	10,000	3,362		2,500	4,138	10,000
17.200	Accountant	2,000	2,000	0		1,000	1,000	2,000
17.300	Cohousing Consultants	17,000	35,000	23,934	3,600	3,600	3,866	35,000
21.010	Advertising	25,000	25,000	15,090	3,300	3,300	3,310	25,000
21.011	Group Logo & Identity	500	500	0			500	500
21.012	Small Brochure	400	400	153			247	400
21.013	Invester Package	700	700	0	700			700
21.014	Poster	120	120	75	15	15	15	120
21.015	New Member Package	100	100	100				100
21.016	Site Plans and Graphics	1,000	1,000	250		200	550	1,000
21.017	Mailouts	750	750	0	250	250	250	750
21.020	Site Sign	300	300	171			129	300
21.030	Information Meetings	1,000	1,000	300	100	350	250	1,000
21.031	Special Events	1,100	1,100	0		1,000	100	1,100
21.040	Booth Rental and Display	1,500	1,500	0		750	750	1,500
21.050	Commissions	2,000	2,000	0		1,000	1,000	2,000
21.060	Misc.+ Admin.	3,500	3,500	1,479	500	1,000	521	3,500
21.070	Coordination, FRITZ	14,000	9,680	9,320	360			9,680
22.010	General Contingency	107,500	34,749	0			34,749	34,749
22.020	Carry Unsold Units	8,500	8,500	0			8,500	8,500
22.020	Guest Room Purchase	0	32,000	0			32,000	32,000
	TOTALS	3,107,211	3,121,034	267,626	23,772	19,165	2,810,471	3,121,034

from existing members, or will it come from new members joining? Do you have enough saved, or will you be borrowing money?

It is important to keep in mind that the cash flow plan is not fixed or permanent. Update it regularly. It will evolve significantly as conditions change and your project progresses.

Borrowing money

Financing the land purchase

Vendor financing is the most common way of financing the purchase of raw land. Only very rarely will a bank or other financial institution get involved in the financing of undeveloped land. If a bank is willing to lend you money, it will likely be less than 50% of purchase price, or value. They will want you to come up with the rest in cash.

If your group is looking at purchasing a piece of land which includes a habitable building you should be able to get traditional mortgage financing on the property. Often this is the most ideal land purchase arrangement as it allows you to rent the property and generate some cash flow which can help cover the cost of carrying the land during the planning and design phase of the development process.

Many groups have found that they needed to pay for the land themselves in cash, or arrange financing with the vendor (seller of the land) in such a way as to not make payments on the balance due until the project was ready to start construction. (See Chapter 5, Buying Land.)

Cash requirements

There are costs that occur throughout the early stages of development, prior to getting a loan. The land purchase is only one of them. Others include the soft costs, such as professional fees, which must usually be paid for with cash in order to meet the requirements of today's construction lending.

In the late '80s it was not uncommon to build a project with 10% cash and 90% financing, based on project cost. In today's world a developer is generally expected to put up 30% to 50% of project cost before a construction lender will provide any loan money. This means that if you want to create a $2,000,000 project (20 units at $100,000 each) someone has to provide, and spend, the first $1,000,000. This may be the best reason to consider working with a developer. (Remember, a real developer has cash to invest in a project.)

Obviously, there are front-end soft costs for everything from surveying to hiring a biologist to determine where the wetlands are. Today, the controlling factor in determining how much cash you will need is not how much the soft costs are. The real determining factor is how much cash you have to invest prior to getting your construction loan.

Construction financing

The construction loan is a short-term, relatively high-risk proposition when compared to a regular home loan, or a car loan. Construction can be risky, especially if the product being constructed is not already 100% sold. If you don't have the product sold when the construction is complete then you have no way to repay the construction loan.

As a result of the risk, interest rates on construction loans are somewhat higher than conventional mortgage rates, often 2% to 5% higher. In addition, there will be points added. These are taken as a cost of setting up the loan. Each point is 1% of the amount of the loan and is usually deducted from the proceeds of the loan. If you borrow $1,000,000 from a bank you may pay 2 to 4 points (or more) in loan fees. That's $20,000 deducted from the amount they actually provide to you, leaving you with $980,000 in borrowed money and $1,000,000 in debt.

When seeking a lender to finance the construction of your project, if you are not working with a developer then consider working with a mortgage broker. A mortgage broker will help you look in the right place, as well as prepare your package for presentation to the financial institutions.

The track record of the developer and the contractor plays a substantial part in the analysis of risk when banks evaluate your construction loan. When they look at the package they will ask, "Has the developer done this before? Has the contractor done this before? Have they always been successful? Are these units really sold? How much risk are we taking here?"

Also, consider the following:

- The loan package you assemble should be comprehensive and professional looking. It should answer all the questions a lender might have about your project.
- Banks need to make loans. It is what they are in business to do. Your loan will be an asset to the bank.
- Try not to think of the bank as doing you a favor by giving you a loan. Try to turn it around so that you think of yourselves as providing them with what they are looking for in a secure, money-making investment. Act that way when you meet with them.

One of the things you should make clear to a lender is the fact that many of the units in your project will be presold. If your project is substantially presold it reduces the lender's risk considerably.

You will want to start shopping for a construction loan several months before you have a package ready to present formally. By the time you have a package you should have a good idea who will be interested. In my experience, most banks will not be interested if your proposal sounds different from a normal development proposal. I suggest that you do everything you can to make it not sound different.

Don't go just to the primary, full-service banks. Talk to a broad cross-section of the lending community when you're seeking a construction loan. Construction lending institutions include banks, mortgage companies, conglomerates, partnerships, insurance companies and all kinds of different institutions that lend money on construction. Many will lend money on the take-out mortgages as well.

Permanent financing

Early in the formation of your group you will want to begin talking about the money necessary to pay for the finished product you hope to move into. Can everyone in your group afford to buy a home in the community you plan to create? Do they each have a way of making the down payment? Will they each qualify for a mortgage?

For most groups the permanent financing will be in the form of private mortgages. Members will borrow money from a bank to pay for their own homes. As your group becomes more serious and businesslike, your membership requirements may include prequalifying for a mortgage, or evidence of the ability to do so. (See the Loan Prequalification Worksheet for an example.)

In some cases, you may be able to arrange a group mortgage. This may happen if you decide to finance the common house separately, as some groups have done. It will certainly happen if you decide to be a cooperative. As a cooperative the community will own everything and the principal financing will be undertaken as a community. Individual members will only then have to get financing to buy their share of the cooperative.

There is always a possibility that you can get a financial institution to combine both the construction loan and the take-out loans in one package. This is how the Winslow project was financed. The advantage to the bank is that they know how the construction loan will be paid off. The advantage to the community is that you may be able to negotiate lower financing costs. A half a point (0.5%) on a $4 million loan is $20,000. That's enough money to furnish much of the common house, for instance.

Other issues

Affordability

Affordability is a mysterious thing. Everybody has a different idea about what it means and how to achieve it. For instance, it can be achieved by finding someone else to pay some of the cost of building your project. This is possible, but I don't recommend planning your project based on this expectation. (See also Chapter 7, Design Considerations.)

In my opinion, affordability is a relative term and depends significantly on your expectations. The more modest and more flexible your expectations, the easier it will be to achieve something you regard as affordable.

Consider the following methods of achieving a more affordable community.

LIFE CYCLE COSTING

Consider life cycle costing. Choosing materials and equipment with lower operating and maintenance costs will probably have higher initial capital costs, but they usually pay for themselves over time. An example is compact fluorescent lighting. The Winslow group spent about $15,000 to upgrade the lighting from incandescent to compact fluorescent. At an annual energy cost savings of about $5,000 per year the new lighting started saving money in the fourth year.

CLUSTERING TIGHTLY

Consider clustering tightly to save money. Fewer materials, smaller footprint on the land and lower energy consumption all add up to huge cost savings in capital costs as well as ongoing living costs. At Winslow when the second architect suggested reorganizing, and tightening up the site plan, he estimated a $100,000 overall utility cost saving, primarily in sewer and water system installation.

REDUCE SIZE EXPECTATIONS

Size of rooms, number of bedrooms, etc. all impact significantly on cost. Seek to balance your expectations with your financial capacity, as a group and as an individual.

ENLARGE THE COMMON HOUSE

Consider contributing more to the common spaces. Savings can be achieved by choosing a smaller private space and contributing your purchasing power to improving and enlarging the common facilities. Why not share the "spare room" and the "rec room?" You can multiply the benefits by working together as a community.

CONSIDER STACKING UNITS

The greatest cost savings are achieved by reducing the number of foundations and roofs you will need to build, as well as the number of roofs through which you will lose heat. Stacking units will save in capital costs and operating costs.

STANDARDIZATION

A major way to achieve affordability is through standardization. In the same way that standardization reduced the price of manufacturing cars and other goods, standardizing housing reduces the cost of making housing.

The standardized kitchen is the most common and generally accepted way of achieving this economy. A well-designed, modest kitchen that can be modified to suit individual needs after moving in, will go a long way toward reducing project costs. Also consider standardizing hardware and equipment where possible. Common plumbing fixtures, moldings, windows, etc., all add up to cost savings.

CUSTOMIZATION

Do not allow any customization during the initial construction process. This will be a major cost savings to the entire community. For those who insist on individuality and uniqueness, ask them to wait until after moving in.

SWEAT EQUITY

It may seem that there is no reason why you can't do all the work to build your community yourselves. There may be members of your group who would prefer this, but there are some difficulties and disadvantages which limit practicality.

In order to build your project yourselves, you have to have the money. You will have a hard time borrowing money to build it yourselves. Bank financing requires security and predictability, and for the bank this means an experienced and licensed contractor, and a short construction time-frame. Communities that have built for themselves have done so over a very long period, and lived with substantial hardship during the process. It often precludes working elsewhere, meaning there is no source of income for the funds necessary to sustain your family, much less buy the building materials necessary for construction.

If you don't need to borrow money and you have the time, consider building it yourselves. If not, consider paying to have it built and arrange to help where you can, such as with landscaping or site clean-up.

Cost and value

There is a difference between cost and value. Cost is what the group had to pay for the land, and to have the contractor build the buildings. Value is what it is worth after it is completed, on the open market, or to a banker. The banker will ask an independent appraiser to establish a value.

Price is what a member actually pays the community to purchase the completed dwelling unit and/or share of the community facilities. In theory, as a not-for-profit enterprise, your prices should reflect actual cost. Also in theory, your values should be higher than your costs. Have a look at the Cost and Value illustration.

Professional roles in finance and budget

THE DEVELOPER

The developer (and/or your group's development consultant) is responsible for establishing the project budget, reviewing and modifying that budget as your assumptions change. After establishing a budget, you predict the required cash flow and then adjust your assumptions about those predictions so that you have an idea about what cash will be needed and when.

During the construction process you manage the construction draws, evaluating what your contractor has actually done and what is appropriate to pay.

THE ARCHITECT

The Architect is responsible for designing the project to meet the requirements of the established budget. Architects tend to push the budget, asking for more money or saying that what you want can't be done for the amount of money you want to spend, etc. The architect will push and you will push back, so expect some give and take.

During construction, the bank will normally have an architect inspect the project regularly, certifying percentage of completion when the contractor is asking for money.

THE ESTIMATOR

Architects and contractors often use an estimator to predict what the actual costs will be before the plans are complete. During the design process this helps to establish what you can afford, and what is within your budget. After construction plans are complete, the estimator can also assist in evaluating competitive bids from subcontractors.

THE APPRAISER

The appraiser is important. Lenders need to be assured that the collateral they hold (your land and buildings) has value. They will want a professional appraiser to tell them what the collateral is worth, and then they will lend you a percentage of that value. (Unless a mortgage is insured by someone else, a lender will usually only lend you 50% to 80% of what something is worth.)

In addition, the mortgage lenders for the take-out financing will want an appraiser to tell them what your individual units are worth. Before completing construction you will either need a revision to the project appraisal, or private unit appraisals for the take-out financing.

Remember that the appraiser's first responsibility is to the bank, and not to you. Even though you are paying them, directly or indirectly, their reputation with the banks is what keeps them in business.

THE CONSTRUCTION LENDER

The construction lender will be loaning you short-term, relatively high-risk money, secured at first by the land, and later by the completed portions of the project. Before you start construction they will commit to lending the money. During construction they will advance money based on their commitment, as well as the percentage of the construction completed.

THE CONTRACTOR

The contractor is responsible for building the project at the agreed-upon cost. You can bring in a contractor during the design development phase for design evaluation and assistance in estimating the costs. During construction, the contractor is going to be making draw requests, which get approved by the developer and the architect as they look at the progress.

THE TAKE-OUT LENDER

Those members who won't be buying their unit with cash will need to borrow money long term to own their home. They will get this money from the take-out lender, or private mortgage lender. Often, the construction lender will require that the take-out lender issue a "take-out commitment." This is a promise, in writing, to lend each family the money to buy its unit when construction is complete.

The bank with the take-out commitment pays off the construction lender at the close of construction. It will need to know the value of the unit used for collateral on the loan. The construction and the take-out lenders can be the same lender.

Cash calls and member assessments

When you begin, all the money you need will have to come out of your own pockets. Most groups start with a small amount to cover administrative costs, with everybody putting in $100 to $300. This money will serve your needs until it's time to enter the development game.

At the point of looking for land, most groups begin to realize how much cash is going to be required and set up a series of regular "cash calls," allowing members to budget for the coming payment requirements. Those who are serious and have the financial capacity to continue will begin putting in the thousands of dollars required. (See also Eight Major Thresholds, in Chapter 3, The Development Process.)

Rewarding early members for taking a risk

It is often suggested that early members should get some benefit from putting up their money and taking the risk early in the project. In many communities a system is worked out so that later members pay slightly more for the same membership position.

A system created at Winslow increased the equity membership payment requirement by 1% each month, meaning that after a year the value of your membership was something like 12% more than it had been a year before. As fair and equitable as this sounded, it was never implemented for several reasons.

First, the requirements to maintain the tax benefit status on the mortgages was such that they couldn't actually charge late-comers more money without losing the benefit (see your tax accountant). And second, after setting up the system, approving it and deciding to implement it, the mem-

Mortgage Qualification Assistance Sheet

Mortgage lenders will generally look at your gross monthly income and require that the mortgage payment not exceed 28% of income, and that the mortgage payment plus other monthly debt payments not exceed 36% of monthly income.

Please refer to the filled out sample sheet, "Mortgage Financing Qualification Analysis".

Unit Purchase Price: Estimate unit size X $85/square foot for unit cost, added to a prorated portion of the common house (say 200sf. for 20 units) X $60.

sample: 1,000 sf. unit	@ $85/sf.	= $85,000
200 sf. common house		
	@ $60/sf	= <u>12,000</u>
Unit Purchase Price		$97,000

Downpayment: = 20% of Unit Purchase Price

sample: $97,000 X .20   = $19,000

Mortgage Loan: = Unit Purchase Price less Downpayment.

sample: $97,000 - $19,000   = $78,000

Estimated Annual: **Property Tax** = 1.3% of Unit Purchase Price.

sample:	$97,000 X .013	= $1,261
	Insurance	=.25% of Unit Purchase Price
sample:	$97,000 X .0025	= $242.50 rounded to $250.

Mortgage payment: principal and interest =
                mortgage loan X mortgage loan constant
                (assuming 10.5%, 30 year amortization)

sample: $78,000 X .00938   =731.64 rounded to $732.

1/12 annual escrow deposit: = Property tax + Property insurance / 12.

sample: $1, 511/12   =$125.92, rounded to $126.

1/12 annual Homeowners Dues: Estimate $600/year, or $50/mo.

Monthly debt includes: outstanding loans, credit card accounts, store charge accounts, alimony or child support.

Two Ratios: should be 28% and 36%, or less

Mortgage Financing Qualification Analysis

Estimated Annual:

Unit Purchase Price:	$ 97,000	Property tax:	$ 1,261
Less: Downpayment:	(19,000)	Property ins.:	$ 250
Mortgage Loan:	$ 78,000	Escrow deposit:	$ 1,511

Mortgage payment (prin/int.) monthly	$ 732
Plus: 1/12 of annual escrow deposit	$ 126
Plus: 1/12 of annual Homeowners Dues	$ 50
Total:	$ 908
	(A)

Monthly debt payment:

Credit cards	$	
Auto	$	
Loans	$	150
Alimony/Child Support	$	
Other recurring debt	$	50

Total:	$ 200
	(B)

Gross monthly income:
(If self-employed, may be adjusted gross income from Federal Tax Return averaged for last two years divided by 24 months.) $ 3,300
                                                                                                                          (C)

Two ratios are considered:

1. Mortgage payment/gross monthly income =

$ 908 / $ 3,300   28%
(A)   (C)   (should be 28% or less)

2.   Mortgage
Payment + mo. debt/gross monthly income =

$ 1,108 / $ 3,300   34%
(A+B)   (C)   (should be 36% or less)

Name: _____ Date: _____
Name: _____ Date: _____

Mortgage Financing Qualification Analysis

	Estimated Annual:
Unit Purchase Price: $	Property tax: $
Less: Downpayment:	Property ins.: $
Mortgage Loan: $	Escrow deposit: $

Mortgage payment (prin/int.) monthly	$
Plus: 1/12 of annual escrow deposit	$
Plus: 1/12 of annual Homeowners Dues	$
Total:	$
	(A)

Monthly debt payment:

Credit cards	$
Auto	$
Loans	$
Alimony/Child Support	$
Other recurring debt	$

Total:	$
	(B)

Gross monthly income:

(If self-employed, may be adjusted gross income from Federal Tax Return averaged for last two years divided by 24 months.) $

(C)

Two ratios are considered:

1. Mortgage payment/gross monthly income =

   $ / $ %

   (A)   **(C)**   (should be 28% or less)

2.   Mortgage

Payment + mo. debt/gross monthly income =

   $ / $ %

   (A+B)   **(C)**   (should be 36% or less)

Name: _____ Date: _____

Name: _____ Date: _____

bers of Winslow could not bring ourselves to ask new people to pay $110 for the something we had agreed to pay $100 for.

While it seems fair to create a system that takes into account the high value and high risk of early investment, it is very hard to implement such a system.

Unit pricing

Setting the price of the individual units is crucial, because it is essential that prices are both fair and appropriate. Early on, before your design is finished and your plans are complete, you will want to establish rough or estimated pricing for individual units. The price you set for all the units in your project must add up to the total cost of creating your project. This will establish the income necessary to pay off the construction and development costs.

Establishing prices for individual units will help you to determine if your pricing is appropriate for local market conditions, and it will allow members to begin the process of selecting a unit which they can comfortably afford. It would seem logical that the pricing should be done by an outside person, such as an appraiser, but you may find it difficult to hire an appraiser for this task. Unfortunately, appraisers need completed, detailed plans, which won't be available at this time. Consider doing the preliminary pricing yourselves, or have a cohousing development consultant do it for you.

In establishing the value of individual units for the bank, an appraiser will consider a number of site location variables, including;
- views (e.g., of trees, a distant skyline, or mountains)
- proximity to the road or driveways
- proximity to parking (positive or negative, depending on your perspective)
- proximity to the common house (again, could be positive or negative)
- end units vs. middle units with no end wall
- upper vs. lower units when units are stacked
- generous back yard conditions

It is important to note that these location variables are extremely variable. A view can be worth $5,000 or it can be worth $50,000 depending on what a buyer is willing to pay. I suggest that you arrange to visit at least one townhouse project (or a project similar to what you hope to build) so that you can look carefully at their unit pricing structure. Compare units of similar size and floor plan which are located in different places on the site. Ask the marketing agents about pricing and see what they have to say.

Establishing preliminary unit pricing

You will want to establish preliminary unit prices early, long before you actually have plans completed. The following strategy works quite well to set your unit prices fairly, if someone in your group has computer spreadsheet experience. (If not, I recommend that you hire someone to assist you.)

Fairness is what this is really all about. It is not an attempt to determine a market value for the bank. Your intent is to set your preliminary unit prices so that each individual member feels they are fair. You must agree beforehand to live with the results of the following unit pricing process to make this process worthwhile.

You will want to call a special meeting of all those interested in participating in the unit pricing process. The group can be 3 or 4 people, or it could be 20. (The larger the group, the better it needs to be facilitated.)

Put a large site plan up on the wall, with individual unit locations clearly marked and numbered. The unit type (two-bedroom, etc.) should be indicated for each location on the site plan. Also have floor plans of each individual unit type up on the wall. Post a list of the site location variables to aid later discussion. Write the bottom line number for your project budget up on the wall, in large clear print.

Plan to spend several hours going through the following procedure:

1. Imagine that all your units have two bedrooms with exactly the same floor plan.

2. Discuss the common reasons why units in different locations should have different prices. Talk about the various locations on your site and see what people think about views, road noise, end units and back yards.

3. Have everyone price every unit by themselves (as two-bedroom identical units) using a pre-printed listing of unit numbers. Don't require that the prices add up to the total project cost yet. The computer will do that later, adjusting all prices up or down proportionally as necessary to cover actual costs.

4. Turn in the lists to the person on the computer and have him or her enter the data in a spreadsheet while the group discusses what they have just done, and what they are about to do next.

5. The person on the computer should set up a table listing each individual participant down the left side with a blank row between each, and each unit location across the top. Calculate the sum of each participant's unit prices in a PROJECT TOTALS column to the far right. In the blank line below each participant's prices, create a formula that will automatically increase or decrease the price for each unit in proportion to the PROJECT TOTAL's relation to the Actual Project Budget posted on the wall. Set up a UNIT AVERAGES row at the very bottom and calculate an average for the "adjusted" prices for each unit location. Print this out and discuss it.

6. Come to consensus as a group about the pricing of these hypothetical two-bedroom units based on site location. Be sure that each participant is comfortable that the averaged price for each unit location seems fair. Adjust the prices as required to achieve consensus.

7. Beginning with the average two-bedroom unit prices, propose prices for typical studios, one-bedroom, three-bedroom and four-bedroom units. Discuss the merits of the proposed average unit prices for the various unit sizes and types, without regard to the actual unit locations.

8. Come to consensus as a group about relative pricing of the various unit types without regard to location.

9. Adjourn the meeting and let the computer people finish the following calculations.

10. If the averaged two-bedroom unit prices in step 6 above were adjusted to achieve consensus, increase or decrease them all proportionally so that they add up to the project budget.

11. Using the hypothetical, all two-bedroom units spreadsheet, set up a formula to calculate the LOCATION ADJUSTMENT. It will be a percentage (or a ratio) calculated by dividing the agreed two-bedroom unit price for each location, by the average two-bedroom unit price. These will result in both positive and negative numbers, and they should add up to zero. They represent the percentage that each unit location is valued above or below the average unit location.

12. Create a table of unit prices by type and location using the site plan and the decision from step 8 above, as well as the Location Adjustment factor from step 11 above. When you are finished you should have four columns labeled Unit Number, Unit Type, Unadjusted Price, and Location Adjustment Factor. Check your data en-

try very carefully. Ask someone else to check as well. You don't want to have a mistake here.

13. In a fifth column on your spreadsheet, calculate the Preliminary Unit Price for each unit by location. The formula should be: Unadjusted Price multiplied by Location Adjustment Factor. Check the sum of the Preliminary Unit Price column to make sure you are still coming up with the Total Project Cost. Since different-sized units are in different locations there will probably be some adjustment required. As before, increase or decrease all unit prices proportionally to achieve the necessary number.

14. Present the Preliminary Unit Price results to the group.

After your plans are substantially complete, get an official appraisal to include in your loan package. Use an appraiser who will be acceptable to the banks where you plan to submit your package. Ask the banks and they will usually give you a list of the appraisers they use.

It is a good idea to work as closely with your appraiser as possible, providing him or her with your Preliminary Unit Pricing and an understanding of your group's feelings about the fairness of those prices. Also share information about why cohousing is of value to each of you. Consider providing copies of positive appraisals from other cohousing projects. (Cohousing development consultants will usually have copies from other projects.) Since your individual unit financing (your final take-out mortgages) will be based on the appraised value of each unit, you may need to adjust the Final Unit Pricing to be consistent with the appraised values. This doesn't mean they should match the appraised values, but it does mean that your unit prices should be relatively proportional to the appraised values.

Allocation of common costs

The allocation of the common costs, for instance the construction cost of the common house, is generally proportional to unit value. Usually they are included in the purchase price of each unit. The exception to this seems to be when a community chooses to develop a project as individual building lots, and lot purchasers build their own homes whenever they wish. In this situation it makes sense to have the common costs allocated in proportion to the established sale price of each lot.

Some groups attempt to distribute common costs either by unit size (rather than value), or equally by number of units. In my experience neither of these methods actually works when there is a wide range of unit sizes, and when members have to pay for their share of the common costs as part of a mortgage.

Post-occupancy development fees

The Winslow community discovered a fairness issue you might want to consider. Private units were designed to be easily expanded, since the intent was to make it easy for people to enlarge their units themselves after moving in. Based on appraised value, three-bedroom units were priced at about $140,000, about $20,000 more than two-bedroom units. (Typically units are priced and financed based on appraised value.) One family figured out that they could add a third bedroom to a two-bedroom unit for about four thousand dollars in material costs if they did the work themselves, meaning that they could end up in a three-bedroom unit for $124,000 instead of $140,000.

When this became known the demand for two-bedroom units went up. Everyone wanted one, and nobody wanted the three-bedroom or four-bedroom units. One option was to build only two-bedroom units, but that had a surprising effect on costs. If we built only the less expensive two-bedroom units, the costs (and therefore the purchase prices) went up to about $135,000 for each two-bedroom unit.

For those who wanted only two bedrooms in the first place, this was bad news. For those who wanted three bedrooms the apparent savings was gone. The culprit in all this was the cost of land and the soft costs which had to be spread over the smaller, less costly to build units. By keeping the unit mix as originally planned, with ones, twos, threes and fours, the larger and more valuable units absorbed a proportionally larger share of the land and soft costs.

After much calculation, debate, gnashing of teeth and recalculation, we discovered that the $20,000 difference in value between a two-bedroom and a three-bedroom unit was about $4,000 in materials, another $4,000 in labor, and about $12,000 in land and soft costs.

In the end we settled on a development fee for those who wanted to add a third bedroom to their two-bedroom unit, to be paid to the community to cover a proportional share of the land and soft costs. The group decided that this money would then be made available for the community to use for the common house or other community improvements.

Unit size

The size of units is of concern for the appraiser when it comes to determining the unit value. The bankers are concerned about the security of their loan and they depend on the appraiser to give them accurate information about the unit's true value. The challenge will often be to educate

Cardiff Place
Unit Size Table

sf = square feet

Total Area 17 Private Units 15,863 sf
Usable Common Area 2,600 sf

Floor	Special Features	# of Bed	# of Bath	Deck Size sf	Net Size sf	Percent of Total	Share of Common sf	Gross Size sf
Loowill Manor								
Lower	East facing, low ceiling	1	1	0	641	4.04%	105	746
Main	East facing, high ceiling	1	1	0	635	4.00%	104	739
Main	West facing, high ceiling	1	1	0	713	4.49%	117	830
2nd	East facing	2	1	0	785	4.95%	129	914
2nd	West facing	2	1	0	697	4.39%	114	811
Attic	Ocean VIEW!!	3	2	0	1,076	6.78%	176	1252
New Building								
2nd Floor	NE, with laundry	2	1	90	1,157	7.29%	190	1347
2nd Floor	Southeast facing	2	2	65	879	5.54%	144	1023
2nd Floor	NW, Storage++	2	2	130	1,153	7.27%	189	1342
2nd Floor	Southwest facing	2	1.5	65	905	5.71%	148	1053
3rd Floor	NE, with laundry	3	2	90	1,360	8.57%	223	1583
3rd Floor	Southeast facing	2	2	65	874	5.51%	143	1017
3rd Floor	Northwest facing	1	1	130	814	5.13%	133	947
3rd Floor	Southwest facing	2	1.5	65	905	5.71%	148	1053
4th Floor	Northeast facing	2	1.5	95	998	6.29%	164	1162
4th Floor	South Views, Laundry	3	2	70	1,212	7.64%	199	1411
4th Floor	Northwest facing	2	1.5	100	1,059	6.68%	174	1233
Sub-Totals		33	25	965	15,863	100%	2,600	18,463

Sample unit size table

the bankers and the appraisers regarding the value of the common house so that they are not comparing 1,000-square-foot cohousing units with 1,000-square-foot townhouse units. Often they will come to understand that each unit actually owns a real and valuable share of the common facilities. [sample unit size table] I have often provided bankers and appraisers with a table listing units by type and size, indicating exact share of the common facilities in square feet, adding it to the "net square feet" for each unit to come up with a "gross square feet" for each unit. (See Chapter 6, The Design Process and Chapter 7, Design Considerations for additional comments on unit and common house sizing.)

Summary

It takes money to build. But it also takes money to get your group to the point where the buildings can be built. With a clear understanding of pro forma development, budget management and cash flow planning processes, members of your community will feel much more secure about making the financial commitment necessary to bring your project to life.

11

Marketing and Membership

Why marketing and membership? • Who are cohousing people?
• What attracts people to cohousing? • The marketing plan •
Using "The Four Sale Approach" • Implementing the plan — a few
recommendations • New members • Database and waiting list
maintenance • Samples • Summary

Why marketing and membership?

When it's time for your group to grow, it's time to think seriously about marketing and membership. There are two questions to answer. Where will your new members come from and how will they be integrated into the existing group? In this chapter we will consider how to develop a marketing plan and some strategies for implementing that plan. We will also consider the integration of new members into your group. How do you get to know them? How do you "bring them up to speed," or help them understand and appreciate your group's history and process? How do you include them in your process and make them a part of your growing community?

Marketing cohousing is quite different from marketing conventional housing. Cohousing is both a concept and a lifestyle. The housing product, while important, is far less important during the marketing and membership process. You are primarily interested in finding people who want to become members of your community, not just people who are looking for a new home.

Fritz Radandt, a resident at the Cardiff Place community, refers to the "buying cycle" being different for cohousing. He points out that most people require several months, or even years, before they are ready to commit to buying membership in a cohousing community, and their decision is made incrementally. Generally they:

- learn about the cohousing concept
- create a new vision for themselves living in community
- become comfortable with the other members of the group
- like the location of the site
- like the housing forms that have been designed
- determine that they are able to afford a unit

Once convinced about the merits of cohousing, people will go to great lengths to find a way to become a part of your project.

Who are cohousing people?

People who are interested in cohousing come from various social and economic classes, but a survey of residents at completed projects in North America indicates some interesting patterns:

- Most cohousing residents have higher than average levels of education and many are professionals.
- Most selected cohousing to improve their quality of life.
- Many have chosen to work at lower paying, or more fulfilling positions, or are working only part time. (The president of Kitsap Federal Credit Union, who did all the construction and take-out financing, once called the members at Winslow Cohousing "over-educated and under-employed professionals.")
- Many have chosen to work at home.
- Many have a higher than expected level of financial resources, generally from having owned a home before.
- An unusual number of cohousing residents are debt-free.
- They are proactive people, often involved in a number of other organizations and community activities.
- They tend to be of European descent.

- They range in age from early thirties into retirement age.
- They include all family types – singles and couples, with kids and without.

Race and ethnicity in cohousing

It seems that cohousing is attractive mainly to white middle-class folks. But is this perception accurate, and if so, why? Theories abound. It has been suggested that many visible minorities in our society already have a sense of community where they live. It has also been suggested that the white middle class who have moved to suburbia have lost their sense of community. These suburbanites have found themselves increasingly isolated and alone in their single family homes with their extended families often thousands of miles away.

Several groups have tried to set up membership quotas, hoping to create a community that is racially and ethnically diverse. Unfortunately, this doesn't seem to work. It is hard enough to find people who want to participate in your project and turning them away because they do not meet your quota requirements can stall your project completely.

Try attracting people of different ethnic and racial backgrounds without using quotas. Try advertising in specialty newspapers and putting up posters in a wide range of neighborhoods. Attract diversity, don't strangle your community in the making by regulating diversity.

There may be increasing racial diversity in cohousing. According to recent research by Dorit Fromm, approximately 13% of the residents in existing cohousing communities in North America are non-whites, including African-Americans, Hispanics and Asians. And there are cohousing communities in development which are primarily for people of color, such as the Harrambee Homes cohousing group in the Chicago area.

What attracts people to cohousing?

In developing your marketing and membership strategies you should keep in mind those things that attracted you to cohousing. Consider also the following:

- safety and security
- raising children
- an end to alienation
- contribution to a community
- opportunities for social interaction
- flexibility and choice in such things as meals, socializing, etc.
- environment
- lower living costs
- time savings
- control
- spontaneity of social interaction
- intergenerational living

The marketing plan

A marketing plan for your group should be able to answer the questions, "Who will be interested?" and "How do we reach them?" It will be a guide to effectively spending your time, your money and your effort toward achieving a clearly stated set of membership goals.

In the process of formulating your plan you will need to carefully assess the current situation for your group and the local area. You will try to anticipate what will be attractive to whom. You will consider your own strengths and weaknesses as a group, as well as the opportunities and constraints in the local housing market and larger community.

A typical marketing plan for a cohousing group would include the following:

- Overview
  - A one-page summary of the entire plan
  - Situational Analysis
  - Project Overview
  - What is the current project status?
  - When is it likely to be completed?
- Goals and objectives of the existing group
  - What specific goals and objectives have been established by the group?
  - How big will the community be?
  - What are the goals for diversity, family types, etc?

- Site and location
  - What is the neighborhood like and how will cohousing be received?
  - What special attributes of the site and location might affect who will be interested in buying or joining?
  - Local housing market
  - Is the local housing market growing or shrinking?
  - What types of housing are being built?
  - What are people buying?
- Cohousing interest in the area
  - What interest is there in cohousing in the area?
  - Are other groups active in the area?
- Alternatives to cohousing
  - What housing is currently available in the area?
  - Is there anything like cohousing around?
- Identifiable opportunities and constraints
  - Are there identifiable opportunities which should be pursued? Opportunities include an available site, a large group, special skills, etc.?
  - What about constraints, such as local zoning bylaws, or cost, etc.?
- Review marketing and membership alternatives
  - Grassroots
  - Do you want to do all the marketing yourselves?
  - Is word of mouth adequate to get the word out?
- Marketing consultant
  - Who will develop your marketing plan?
  - Who will implement the plan and oversee the marketing effort?
  - Are you willing to hire an experienced marketing consultant?
- Conventional marketing
  - What approach to marketing will you use?
  - Will you use standard "developer" techniques, such as signs, newspaper ads, and a sales center on site?
- Seeking designated markets
  - Are you seeking special groups, such as the retired, families with children, etc.?

- · How will you target those who might be interested and who can afford to buy cohousing?
- · Are there special considerations for marketing to these designated groups?
- Implementation strategies

  Based on your defined goals, the local situation and your budget, what are your strategies for:
  - · An awareness campaign
  - · How are you going to get the word out that you exist?
  - · What are the most probable sources for new members?
  - · What organizations, neighborhoods, and publications are the most promising?
  - · Response management
  - · How are you going to deal with all the calls you will get in response to your advertising, or in response to a recent newspaper article?
  - · Participation
  - · How will potential members be encouraged to participate during their evaluation and education stage?
  - · How will you keep potential new members from feeling like outsiders?
  - · Completion
  - · What will be the process for integrating new members into the existing group?

Budget

Crucial to establishing a marketing and membership plan you must determine your financial capabilities. Ask yourselves, "What is available to spend?" and "How much do we need to spend?" Some early groups, such as Winslow, found that they didn't need to do much marketing. The media took such an interest in cohousing that they had all the free advertising they could want in the form of newspaper articles, TV segments, etc. Today however, cohousing isn't exactly new. You will need to spend some money to make sure those who might be interested know that you exist.

In addition to knowing how much you have to spend, you will need to evaluate the marketing budget carefully, asking yourselves, "How do we want to spend it?" "Do we focus our limited funds on media advertising, or do we spend more on site signage, or special events?"

BY ZEV PAISS, SUPPORT FINANCIAL SERVICES

Using "The Four Sale Approach"

The process of bringing in new committed members to your cohousing group is more complicated than the normal method of marketing housing. As groups move toward or into the construction phase of their community, the ability to satisfy new member needs becomes increasingly more challenging. This is because you are actually required to make four "sales" for every new member. First they need to be sold on the concept of Cohousing. As we have all experienced, the Cohousing idea isn't for everyone. Secondly they need to be sold on the community of existing members. This is especially important when the group is small, and unique personalities are more obvious. First impressions can make the difference at this point. Thirdly the potential members need to be sold on the location of your project. Just like purchasing a home in a conventional neighborhood, location is important. Before land is selected many people will hesitate before knowing where there future home will be located, but once a site is selected it then needs to work for all future members. Finally, potential members need to be sold on the home they will be buying. They need to believe that it is worth the price. If they join the community early enough, they may be able to influence the home styles and available features. Later members need to find an available site or unit which works for their individual situation.

WHO WILL DO IT?

How will you implement your plan? Who will actually take the time to do the work? Who will arrange for advertising, special events or signage? Who will keep track of your database, respond to phone calls, and keep track of who needs to be called back?

Do you have members in your group who have the time to do what's necessary? Are there members who have the skills and the energy? Or do you need to consider hiring someone?

MANAGEMENT

Someone needs to track the budget, and account for the money you have agreed to spend. Someone needs to make sure that those who volunteer to do things actually get them done. Who is going to keep the marketing effort on track and make sure your money is wisely spent?

MONITORING EFFECTIVENESS

Sit down together periodically and ask yourselves, "How well are we doing?" "How many phone calls are we getting?" "Are we spending our money wisely?" "Should we make adjustments to our plan?" This should be an ongoing process.

ACTION PLAN

Awareness Campaign: How will we make people aware of our project?

- paid advertising
- printed materials: brochures, posters, etc.
- site signs
- public information meetings and presentations
- public displays: e.g., at a shopping center
- media news coverage: press releases, etc.
- speaker's bureau: offering to speak to interested community groups
- site tours and open houses
- submission of articles for publication in newspapers and magazines

Response management: How will we manage all the responses we will get from our awareness campaign?

Existing membership: What role will the existing membership play in this process?

Community relations: How will we manage our relationships with the surrounding neighborhood and the larger community?

Implementing the plan – a few recommendations

The media

Dealing with the media can be tricky. You want them to write about you, but you can't control what they write. Be patient with them. Don't expect very much. Provide them with written information when possible. Give them articles that have been written about other cohousing projects, especially articles that present cohousing in a positive light. In the end you may have to accept that there is some truth to what a politician once said, "All publicity is good publicity."

Word of mouth outreach

Your members are the outreach and sales team. One member, or a hired staff person, may be responsible for keeping everything on track, but it is the members of your group who have already made the decision that co-housing is right for them, who are the most effective sales and outreach people. Members should try to invite friends to come out to meetings. They should carry brochures. There is no need for them to adopt a high-pressure sales approach. A little bit of enthusiasm will be more effective.

Attracting new members

Some proven methods of attracting new members include:
- Phasing the membership program
  - Different types of people will be interested in your project at different times in the process. You can tailor membership efforts to reach and attract the early members who will be more pioneering and later members who may be more traditional "buyers."
- Using professionals appropriately
  - Once you have engaged the services of professionals you will appear more credible to many people. Take advantage of this by inviting potential members to join in the consultations with those professionals.
- Consider "levels" of membership
  - Allow your membership program to have more than one level of commitment and participation. This allows people to make small first steps, such as becoming "associate members."
- Focus on "Our Community"
  - Be inclusive. Talk about "our community" to include those who are associates, or who are just considering joining your group.
- Focus on your unique site
  - Once you have a site, focus your membership efforts around site and neighborhood-specific activities. Have a campout on site. Have your meetings nearby.
- Make sure you look competent
  - For many, it will be hard to believe that you are really going to make this dream happen. Look competent, act competent, and be competent.

- Use free public relations in the media
  - There are lots of ways to take advantage of free media. Cable TV stations, newspapers and other media sometimes offer free listings for events which are open to the public. Some newspapers and magazines will be interested in doing a story about your group, your project or cohousing in general.
- Schedule special events
  - Have a big celebration and invite the public to join you. Make it special and invite the media to cover it.
- Have an open house at your site
  - Have an open house on your site. Invite politicians, the media, and prospective new members.
- Target specific publications for advertising
  - After carefully reviewing the audience of your local media, select specific media for advertising. Generally, small long-term ads are more effective than large one-time ads. What kind of people are interested in cohousing and what media do they read or watch or listen to?
- Emphasize the telephone response process
  - Keep in mind that attracting new people is only half the equation. You must also answer the phone, respond to their needs and keep track of who called. Then you must have a good system for following up and staying in touch.
- Members invite guests to function
  - Set up special events for current members and their "prospective member" guests. Your membership will do the best job of sharing the excitement and enthusiasm about your project.
- Develop package of printed materials
  - Develop a complete package of printed materials for mail-out, handing out or posting. This can range from a simple one-page brochure to a detailed package of information about who you are and what you plan to build.
- Emphasize local markets
  - Many, if not all of your new members will be local to your area. All you have to do is get the word out that you exist.
- Encourage neighborhood relations

- Establish contact with your neighbors and continue to stay in touch. They may have friends who are interested, and they may eventually get interested themselves.
- Distribute posters and brochures regularly
  - Develop a regular routine for distributing posters and brochures. Update and replace them as necessary.
- Maintain a database
  - Keep track of who has called and who has come to meetings. Maintain a database of names, addresses and phone numbers, and develop a method for staying in touch.
- Consider direct mailings – invitations, etc.
  - Do a mailing to everyone on your database once in a while, keeping them apprised of your progress.

Spontaneous brainstorming

The tendency at general meetings of a group, especially during the report from the marketing and membership committee, is to begin a process of brainstorming. People start throwing out ideas, often very good ones, about how to bring in new members. Where to put up posters, how to advertise, when to schedule an event, etc.

Don't squash this rich and productive process, but anticipate it, and take advantage of it. Don't let it sidetrack your marketing and membership plan. Keep track of the new ideas and incorporate them into the next revision of your marketing plan, after reviewing and considering them at your next membership committee meeting. Don't let spontaneous brainstorming drive the marketing effort in the meantime, as it will tend to divert you from implementing your well-considered marketing plan.

Training members

Selling cohousing is different from selling a product. Cohousing is a way of life, it is a set of relationships, it is the design of the built environment, and most of all, it is the experience of community. In some ways, cohousing is also a product, and many of the ideas used in selling a product or service have some application that make them useful in presenting cohousing to a person for the first time.

Try what is called "Needs Satisfaction Selling." It is generally accepted that in the sale of a product or service a person buys something to satisfy a need. It may be a basic need, such as shelter. It may also be a psychological need, such as the need to feel good about yourself, or to improve the qualify of your life.

Following this logic, let's assume that people who come to an open house at your site have a need they are trying to satify. Your job is to find out what that need is. They may or may not be able to identify that need when you ask, so you may need to pry a little. Be patient, and most of all, listen.

You might think you can anticipate a person's needs, but it is important that you ask. Make no assumptions. Ask! Ask people about their expectations, ask about their assumptions, ask about their feelings. Ask about their everyday life, and then *listen*!

Some questions you could ask to help identify a person's perceived needs include:
- Why are you interested in cohousing?
- Do you like your current living arrangements?
- Do you feel that privacy is important to you?
- What do you think about sharing child care?
- Have you considered the benefits of sharing meals once in a while?
- Have you thought about the benefits of having a supportive community?

Remember, you want to find out what they think they need, from *their* point of view. Don't put words in their mouth. This means you have to really listen. Show respect, listen actively. Repeat what you have heard and ask for clarification if necessary.

One note: If a person describes a need your project won't satisfy, don't dwell on it, and don't try to fix it for them. For instance, someone may have her heart set on a fireplace in her private unit when your group may have already chosen to have a fireplace only in the common house. Move on with the conversation. Cohousing doesn't satisfy every need, and cohousing isn't for everybody.

The rules for members when reaching out to potential new members:
- *Listen, listen* and *listen* some more!
- *Do not argue.*
- *Do not challenge.*
- And please, *do not lecture.* Some of us tend to just keep talking, going on and on about the history of cohousing, why we think

cohousing is great, and so on. Share your personal stories, but do not lecture.
- Do not put words in their mouth.
- Show respect.

Telephones and follow-up

Follow-up is extremely important, so secure phone numbers and addresses whenever possible. Successful cohousing groups generally have at least one "telephone person" who feels comfortable talking on the phone almost every evening. This is a crucial part of building community, helping people feel that they are important, and that they belong.

If a person comes to one meeting, follow up during the week after the meeting. Assign members as "buddies" to stay in touch with visitors. Call the interested people again, just before the next meeting. Offer to pick them up and bring them to the meeting. Or invite them to dinner in your own home.

The closer – ready to sign them up

Don't neglect the closing function within sales. This is the process of moving from thinking about it to doing something about it. Identifying potential new members is only a part of the process. Someone needs to follow through and be the "closer," helping new members actually sign on the dotted line.

Generally, the closer is the member of your group who is a natural sales person. They seem to know instinctively when a person is ready to make the next step. When it is finally time to close the deal, sign them up and deposit their check.

New members

Acceptance or selection of new members

Many groups talk about establishing a selection process for considering new members. On the face of it, it seems like a good idea to carefully consider who you want your new neighbors to be. You certainly don't want someone who has been convicted of molesting children to join your group. What is the real risk that an unsavory sort will either join your group or want to make a home in your community? What kind of people are interested in cohousing and who is likely to become your new neighbor?

Most groups eventually settle on a self-selection process. The reason, I think, is due primarily to a growing trust in the type of people who are attracted to cohousing. Maybe more importantly, it is based on a realization of what type of person is not interested.

First, those attracted to cohousing are generally proactive, make-it-happen, get-it-done kinds of people. They don't tend to think of the world as happening to them. Instead they think of themselves as making the world happen. Also, they are seeking more community in their lives, finding the level of privacy they now have to be just too much. Generally they are relatively well educated, if not formally then informally, or self-educated. Well-traveled, interesting, and socially concerned people, they are religiously and politically diverse.

Conversely, those not interested in cohousing are generally satisfied with the current level of privacy in their lives. They are not seeking participation in community, at least not any more than they are already experiencing.

Participation in community requires exposing oneself somewhat to others. It requires a level of honesty and participation. It also requires a degree of engagement on a daily basis.

Based on my experience it is unnecessary to set up a selection process because the self-selection process works fine. Those who have joined and find it doesn't work simply leave. The process gives them time to figure out what works, and whether or not their expectations can be met. It also allows existing members to get to know potential new members before they actually commit to joining, eliminating the biggest fear of all: uncertainty.

Education of new members

As potential members consider joining the group they will want to know what to expect. What has been decided? How is it going to work? Who is responsible for what? Presenting this information in a matter-of-fact and nonthreatening way is the key to bringing new members on board. Keeping good records, maintaining a decision log and having them available to refer to are crucial to making a potential member feel comfortable.

After a new member joins the group a major task will be educating them regarding all that has gone before. The more they get involved, the more interested they will become in exactly what is planned, what is expected, and why. Proactive types that they are, they will likely want to have a say themselves. Sometimes they will ask why something which has already been decided can't be changed, without being aware of the long involved process that went into making that particular decision the first time.

New members will need to learn the basics of the development process. They should each read this book, for instance. The topics for review with each new member should include:

- Cohousing overview and group goals and objectives
- Group process: group history, decision-making process, committee structure, issues still to be decided or discussed, expectations about participation
- Finance: group history, current budget, current cash flow plan, individual financial responsibility and expectations
- Legal: organizing agreements, ownership structure, rights and responsibilities
- Development process: group history, decisions which have been made, expectations about development strategy
- Design process: group history, status of design process, etc.
- Marketing and membership process: group history, current status of the marketing plan
- Working with professionals: group history, introduction to individual professionals, expectations about contact and access
- Construction: current status, expectations about the construction process, expectations about sweat equity construction

Bringing new members up to speed is a major part of building community together, helping them understand what has been decided and why. A key seems to be really including them in what is happening as they are considering joining. Ask for help in dealing with the work that still needs to be done.

Unit selection

Unit selection can be a delicate issue. Who gets first choice, and what is fair? Most groups (maybe all groups) decide early on to select units based on the sequence in which a household has joined the group as an equity member. This sounds straightforward and relatively easy, but several issues should be anticipated.

The most obvious is special needs. How do you deal with a member who needs a wheelchair-accessible unit when only a portion of the project has been designed that way? What about a family who needs a three-bedroom, can't afford a four-bedroom, and is worried about the small number of three-bedroom units available? And what about the person who can only afford a very small unit when you are planning to build only one of them?

Well, it all works out. First, don't select specific units until after the project design is complete. Make sure that there are sufficient units of the types and sizes required to meet the needs of all the members you have before the initial unit selection, plus those you anticipate will be joining. For those with really special needs consider planning for more than one unit that will meet their needs.

You have probably agreed to a first-come, first-served selection process. If more than one household joins on the same date simply have those households draw straws. This worked quite well for us at Winslow.

Generally, the original group will be making their unit selections all at the same time. Simply schedule a day to have a unit selection meeting. You might want to do a few practice rounds of choosing a unit. Have each member indicate where they think they might want to be. Allow more than one household to select the same unit and ask each household to specify first and second choices. Final choices may not be strictly in order since some will choose to defer to those with special needs.

After some discussion all groups seem to be able to find a way to make everyone happy. Some people with early choices find that it really doesn't matter where they are going to live. Some are there for the community first and the unit location is of little consequence for them. Those with specific needs can usually have their needs met quite easily.

New members who join after the first unit selection process has been completed will know what is taken. They can select from what is still available. If you have planned your unit mix well they will find a unit that is right for them. With eight units left at WindSong the mix was still quite good, including two one-bedroom + den units, three three-bedroom units, and four four-bedroom units.

The "scale down" phenomenon

People often choose a unit bigger than they really need or can afford. Keep this in mind as you establish your unit mix, and later during the unit selection process. Typically, a few households who fully intended to purchase a three-bedroom unit will scale down to a two-bedroom unit just before the start of construction. A significant shuffling of units can result. I suspect that several factors contribute to this phenomenon, including:

- increasing trust in the use and availability of the common house to meet family needs, such as guest rooms, shared office spaces, and children's play rooms.
- increasing appreciation for and understanding of the life of children in a community or village, resulting in a lower priority on the private bedroom space for each child.
- realizing that as time passes and the group ages, children will leave.
- and last but not least, financial reality strikes.

Database and waiting list maintenance

Early in your process you will want to start keeping track of members and potential members on some type of list. More and more people keep records on a simple computer database.

At first this is useful for contacting members to schedule meetings, etc. Later it will become an important part of the marketing and membership process. You will want to contact people who came to a meeting three months ago, to invite them to the next open house, and keep them informed of your progress, hoping that the time may come when they are ready to make a commitment.

Later still you will want a list of all those who have expressed interest in becoming a part of your community. Send them your internal newsletter. Think of it as a waiting list, or think of it as "friends of the community." This list, if well maintained, will be invaluable to those who eventually have to leave the community. It will also make those who stay more comfortable knowing who might become their new neighbors.

Maintain your database. You will be glad you did.

Samples

I have included sample marketing and membership materials for you to use as a guide to creating your own materials. Feel free to extract liberally from the text of the various posters and brochures. These descriptions of cohousing have been written and rewritten, passed on, revised and rewritten again. What is important to your group may not be expressed in these examples, so customize them to fit your specific needs. Samples include:

Statement of Purpose
Membership Application
Introduction to Cohousing
Benefits of cohousing
"Most Commonly Asked Questions"

Summary

Most groups are comfortable staying small for some time. With three to five households it is easier to find a place to have meetings, decision making is easier, and selecting land is certainly easier. The time comes when you will need to raise the money to buy the land, or existing members may get nervous about making plans to build a community larger than the current membership. That's the time to seriously consider marketing and membership for your group.

Where will new members come from and how will they be integrated into the existing group? A well thought out marketing and membership plan can be a big help in establishing your goals and objectives and clarifying your intended course of action.

Winslow
Cohousing Core Group
of Bainbridge Island

STATEMENT OF PURPOSE

IT IS THE INTENT OF THE WINSLOW COHOUSING CORE GROUP TO DEVELOP A COHOUSING PROJECT IN WINSLOW, WASHINGTON.

THE COHOUSING CONCEPT: The concept of Cohousing presented by Kathryn McCamant and Charles Durrett in their book Cohousing, shall be used as the basis for our mutual understanding of this new term. They have described it as:

> "Cohousing developments consist of individual family dwelling units and a large common house situated in a pedestrian oriented environment. Most community facilities are located at the common house usually include a common dining room and kitchen, children's playrooms, workshops, a living/meeting room, guest rooms, laundry facilities, a cooperative store, a photo darkroom, a music room and perhaps garden areas. Although each individual house has a complete kitchen, common dinners are available for those who wish to participate. Dinner often becomes an important aspect of community life for both social and practical reasons. The common house provides a place for a wide variety of activities which range from organized childcare to spontaneous afternoon teas with the neighbors."

WE FURTHER INTEND THAT OUR COHOUSING SHALL INCLUDE THE FOLLOWING:

PARTICIPATORY PROCESS: The future residents of our Cohousing development shall organize, plan, and participate in the design process of our development. We are responsible as a group for all final decisions.

INTENTIONAL NEIGHBORHOOD DESIGN: It is our intention that the physical design of our Cohousing development will facilitate a sense of community, and that the practical and social activities of our residents shall also further that end. Our community will be a pedestrian environment with overnight parking segregated from the residential area.

EXTENSIVE COMMON FACILITIES: It is our intent to design the common areas of our Cohousing development in order to make them an integral part of the community. We intend to use them on a daily basis, and to have them provide a practical supplement to our private dwellings. Our common facilities shall include but not be limited to; dining area, kitchen and guest rooms.

SELF MANAGEMENT: It is our intent that all decisions of common concern to our group shall be made by members of the group before, during and after development. The group shall use the assistance of skilled professionals where needed.

VARIANCE FROM THE DANISH PROTOTYPE: Since the model for this new housing type is Danish it is reasonable to assume that its specific application here on Bainbridge Island may be somewhat different with regard to physical design, ownership, or management. It is the intention of this group to identify those variations and agree to them specifically.

AGREED THIS 11TH DAY OF MARCH 1989:

name _____   phone _____

address _____

Victoria Cohousing Development Society
Membership Application and Agreement

I _____(name)

of _____ (street)

_____ (city, prov, code)

_____ (phone)

hereby apply for membership in the Victoria Cohousing Development Society.

I understand and support the purposes set down for the Society. I will read and make every effort to support all past decisions of the Society. In order to understand the history of cohousing and to better appreciate the expectations of members of the Society I will read the book *Cohousing, A Contemporary Approach to Housing Ourselves.*

Being accepted for membership in the Society, I shall participate in regular meetings and other affairs of the Society when I can, abiding by the Constitution and Bylaws of the Society. I shall participate in the development of and support the implementation of administrative policies for running meetings and making decisions. I shall notify the Society if I wish to terminate my membership.

I understand that Membership in the Society entitles me/us to be given the first opportunity to purchase a suite at **Cardiff Place**, to invest in a rental suite at **Cardiff Place**, or to rent one of the cohousing suites at **Cardiff Place** owned and/or managed by the Society. If this is my choice, I will meet the requirements to be a purchaser and enter into a Contract of Purchase and Sale with the Society.

My membership fee of $100 are submitted herewith.

Signed this _____day of _____ 1994

_____
(signature of new member)

Accepted for Membership _____ date _____
　　　　　　　　　　　　　Director

2/19/94

Victoria Cohousing Development Society
DRAFT of Proposed Membership Policy

The purposes of the Society are to:
a) provide information to interested members of the public on cohousing models
b) assist members of the Society in the development of cohousing projects
c) develop cohousing projects for the sale to members of the Society and to the public
d) ownership and management of rental units in a cohousing project

The Society has entered into an agreement to purchase all 17 suites at **Cardiff Place** from the builder who owns the land and the Development Permit. The project was designed and approved for development before the Society came into being. Current members of the Society have participated in the adaptation of the building interiors, as well as the creation of a new connection between the two buildings, in order to make the project work for cohousing. Please review the plans and see what you think.

The Society is seeking your support and participation. Please consider joining us.

Membership in the Society
Anyone interested in cohousing can become a member of the Society by simply applying for membership. A one time membership fee of $100 will cover the Society's administrative costs for copies and mailing. We ask that members of the Society read the cohousing book, come to at least one meeting about cohousing to talk with others who are already participating, and sign an agreement about decision making and participation. Copies of the Membership Application and Agreement are available for you to review.

Membership in the Society entitles you to purchase a suite at **Cardiff Place**, to invest in a rental suite at **Cardiff Place**, or to rent one of the cohousing suites at **Cardiff Place** owned and/or managed by the Society, or to make a loan to the Society. The Society has decided to pay 6% on loans from interested members.

Purchasing a Suite at Cardiff Place
Any member who wishes to purchase a suite at **Cardiff Place**, to live in immediately or as an investment, will be required to loan the Society an amount equal to 10% of the purchase price of that suite and enter into a Loan Agreement with the Society at the same time as signing a Contract for Purchase and Sale with the Society for the purchase of the suite. See the Price Sheet for availability and purchase prices.

Purchasers must first attend a total of three meetings of the Society, participate in a clearness committee process, disclose their financial capacity to make the purchase, and then sign a purchaser's agreement. The Society expects ongoing participation from purchasers during the remainder of the development process.

How will things be run?
The actual operation and management of the community has not been worked out, however, most cohousing communities choose to manage their own property. Their will be a Strata Council in the normal way, made up of owners of the suites. The Society will also continue to exist to provide a structure for managing and/or owning rental units. There may also be a resident's association.

2/19/94

COHOUSING

NEIGHBORHOOD

A successful reality in Denmark, Cohousing offers a contemporary model for recreating a secure sense of family and neighborhood. It is a workable alternative to the isolation felt by families and individuals because of today's changed lifestyles. Cohousing provides the privacy of individual homes and the community of common areas, sharing certain resources but maintaining independence. Inter-generational with mixed family types, it's a great place for kids to grow up, and a great place to retire.

**YOU AND YOUR FAMILY ARE INVITED
TO JOIN OUR COHOUSING GROUP**

If you are interested in living in a close-knit and diverse community with modest private homes and generous common facilities, Cohousing may be for you.

Members of our group own a wooded site, an easy walk from schools and stores. The clustered, pedestrian oriented community has a projected occupancy date of mid-1990 and will be home to 20-30 families. We anticipate building units ranging in price from $50,000 to $120,000.

Design is now underway on site, dwellings and common facilities and we're looking forward to the input of our future neighbors.

If you'd like detailed information or would like to attend one of our meetings, and can finance a moderately priced home, please call one of the members listed below.

Introduction to Cohousing

Commonly Asked Questions About Cohousing

Is there a screening process? How do I become a member?

Most cohousing communities do not screen new residents. If potential residents understand the nature of the community and their expectations for their own participation, they will be able to choose whether or not the community meets their needs.

Does everyone have to eat in the common house?

Participation in common meals is voluntary; residents take part as often or as seldom as they want.

How does resale work?

Cohousing has a standard strata title ownership structure like any other condominium or town house development. This means you own your own unit as well as a share of the com-mon facilities. When you sell, your unit is sold like any other condominium. In Europe, homes in existing cohousing communities are highly prized - buyers receive the benefits without all of the development work!

What about pets?

Each community must decide its own pet policy based on the size of the site, etc. Most communities are happy to accomodate pets.

How is a community managed?

Residents manage their communities as they choose. Normally residents form committees to carry out the work of the community.

How much participation is required?

Each community must decide for itself. A minimum level typically includes cooking dinner in the common house once a month and participating on a work committee or two.

What if I don't like someone in the group?

It is not essential for everyone in a cohousing community to like each other. In fact, a variety of personalities adds interest to community life. Cohousing residents need only share a goal of making their lives more efficient and enjoyable through cooperating with their neighbours. Since cohousing offers more opportunities for interaction with neighbours, residents learn to develop their conflict resolution and mediation skills.

How is Cohousing different from a co-op?

In Canada, most housing co-ops are a government sponsored affordable housing program. Residents do not build equity in their units. Many residents join co-ops primarily because they are affordable. In cohousing, all homes are owned by the residents. Residents become a part of cohousing because they want to be part of a vibrant community. Cohousing communities have considerably more common facilities than most co-ops.

What is the ideal size of a cohousing community?

Anywhere from 10 up to 35 or 40 households seems to work best. If a community is any smaller, its smooth operation depends too much on specific individuals; if larger, some of the sense of community becomes lost.

The Benefits of Cohousing

Safe and Supportive Environment

In a world of increasing crime its nice to know there are people around who will look out for each other. Since all residents know each other, strangers are spotted and questioned instantly.

Opportunities for Social Interaction

Many persons are tired of being isolated; cohousing provides the option for regular human interaction without sacrificing privacy.

Contribution

Cohousers appreciate the opportunity to share their skills and talents with other members of the community such as music, fixing bikes, cooking, gardening.

Sharing Resources

By sharing resources, people living in cohousing have access to many more facilities than they would on their own. Gardens, play areas, workshops, darkrooms, crafts rooms, lounges and kitchen and dining areas are often part of cohousing common facilities.

Raising Children

Given the stresses on modern parents, cohousing is an ideal way to raise children with support from others - especially for single parents. Children have safe places and appropriate facilities in which to play outside of their homes. Children have playmates within their community. Parents have others to share child minding duties with.

Environmentally Friendly

Sharing resources with others puts less strain on the environment. Working as a group, there are more opportunities to reduce, reuse and recycle.

Preserve Green Space

By clustering the homes, cohousing communities preserve much of the green space on the site where a traditional neighbourhood would use every last inch for houses, streets and parking.

Lower Living Costs

Shared meals, bulk buying, sharing of resources such, car pooling, sharing baby-sitting, trading goods and less travel due to more on-site activities are some examples of how daily living costs can be reduced.

Time Saving

Cohousers have more free time because of shared meals, shared chores, less travel time due to more on-site activities, and less time minding the kids.

Resident Participation

Consensus decision making empowers all residents. Everyone's point of view must be heard and considered in planning and managing the community.

Diverse Intergenerational Community

Living with people of all ages provides a diversity of experience for both young and old. Most communities separate ages and family status - cohousing brings them together.

12

Scheduling and Planning

Project tasks and milestones • Schedule charts • Sample
schedule charts • Scheduling software • Summary

There are several graphic project management techniques which may be
beneficial for organizing, understanding and sharing information about
when your project is going to happen and when you will need to make decisions. Two common methods are the Gantt chart and the Critical Path
Method (CPM) chart. Some computer programs allow you to enter data
about your project and they will generate either type of chart. (See Scheduling Software, below.)

Project tasks and milestones

Begin by identifying your project tasks. A major part of the scheduling
process is trying to anticipate what must happen for your project to become a reality. A major benefit to listing your project tasks and then developing a schedule is anticipating what decisions will need to be made, and
when. In addition to tasks, identify the milestones along the way, such as
"building permit approved" or "Move In!"

Some experience with the development process or a careful reading of this book will be necessary before you will feel comfortable with your list of project tasks and milestones. Below, broken into several categories, is a list of "typical" project tasks. It is important to note that every project is different, and therefore every project task list will be different, but the sample list will assist you in understanding what types of tasks and milestones need to be identified and anticipated.

Sample list of project tasks (by category)

GROUP PROCESS
- agree on decision-making structure
- develop administrative procedures
- develop marketing and membership plan
- public meeting and open house #1
- group process skills workshop
- plan move-in process

LEGAL
- evaluate possible ownership structures
- choose ownership structure for the development process
- choose ownership structure for living there
- select a lawyer
- review contract with architect
- review contract with builder

LAND
- mapping process
- land search
- make offer
- feasibility analysis
- completion of land purchase

FINANCE
- develop project pro forma
- develop cash flow plan
- cash call #1 (of many?)
- assemble construction financing package
- submit financing packages
- select lender

- appraisal
- construction loan commitment
- arrange individual mortgages
- construction loan funded

DESIGN

- project programming
- site
- survey
- site analysis
- schematic design
- design development
- construction documents
- common house
- schematic design
- design development
- construction documents
- private units
- schematic design
- design development
- construction documents
- schematic design approval
- first cost review
- design development approval
- second cost review
- construction documents approval

GOVERNMENT APPROVALS

- land use (zoning) application
- public hearing
- land use (zoning) approval
- building permit application
- post construction bonds
- building permit issued

CONSTRUCTION

- contractor plan review/cost estimating
- contractor selected

- contract signed
- construction start
- select interior finish options
- construction complete

Schedule charts

Scheduling a project helps you to define it, making it more real. It also helps you anticipate when you will have to do those big things, like selling your house, or making a decision about the color of the common house. There are many ways to plan a project, and many ways to represent that project's schedule. I will focus on two methods which are in common use and which each work quite well for the purposes intended. They each require that you start with a list of project tasks, such as "design common house," and project milestones, such as "start of construction."

The most important reason to create a scheduling chart is to be able to communicate this information to others. It helps when you are trying to explain the project to new members, or when you are trying to arrange for a loan at the bank.

The Gantt chart

The Gantt chart is a horizontal bar graph with a list of project tasks down the left side of the page and time stretching across the page from left to right. It is a simple but effective method of visually understanding what happens when. If the list of tasks is well organized, it can provide insight into what has to be done first. It does not, however, indicate the critical relationships which sometimes exist between tasks, such as which ones are dependent on which other ones, and so on.

The CPM (Critical Path Method) chart

The other commonly used scheduling method is the CPM, or Critical Path Method, chart. As is evident from the name, the strength of this method is the graphic representation of the project's critical path, the series of tasks, sequentially dependent upon one another, which will take the longest to accomplish. If any task on the critical path is delayed, the project is delayed. This can be true of other tasks as well, especially if the delays are lengthy. However, those tasks identified as being on the critical path are the ones which must be accomplished, in order, on time, for the project to be completed as scheduled. This information is not available on the Gantt chart.

COHO Design Schedule

	JANUARY	FEBRUARY	MARCH	APRIL	MAY	JUNE	JULY	AUGUST	SEPTEMB
SHORT LIST INTERVIEWS	▓								
FINAL INTERVIEWS	▓								
CONSULTANT SELECTION		▓							
SITE DOCUMENTS AVAILABLE		▓							
REVIEW SITE DOCUMENTS		▓							
REVIEW PROGRAMMING									
LAND USE									
SITE ANALYSIS		▓							
COHO REVIEW		●							
SITE USE ALTERNATIVES			▓						
COHO REVIEW			● ●						
FINAL LAND USE PLAN				▓					
COHO REVIEW				● ●					
PERMIT DOCUMENTS					▓				
COHO REVIEW					● ●				
PERMIT APPLICATION						▓			
ARCHITECTURAL									
PROGRAMMING			▓						
CONCEPTUAL DESIGN			▓						
COHO REVIEW				● ●					
DESIGN DEVELOPMENT				▓					
COHO REVIEW					● ● ●				
CONTRACT DOCUMENTS						▓			
COHO REVIEW							● ●		
BUILDING PERMIT SUBMIT'L								▓	
BIDDING/NEGOTIATION									

Sample Gantt chart

The timeline game

The CoHousing Timeline Game uses a series of cards defining specific events in the development process. It utilizes the CPM method of illustrating a project schedule and makes it fun to create. It was developed by Bruce Coldham for use by Pine Street CoHousing in Amherst, Massachusetts, where he now lives. It was designed to illustrate the scheduling process in the form of a CPM chart.

An architect, Bruce has led many other start-up groups through the game to assist them with their development process. In October 1994, Bruce presented the Timeline Game in a workshop at the First North American CoHousing Conference at Boulder, Colorado. On a voluntary basis, Bruce Coldham, Mac Thompson and Scott Freudenthal revised the game material so that it can be used by any group without special assistance.

Copies of the CoHousing Timeline Game can be purchased from The CoHousing Network for $25. Proceeds go to the CoHousing Network. The game is available as computer files via Internet, on disk, or you can get it by fax. Their address is P.O. Box 2584, Berkeley, CA 94702.

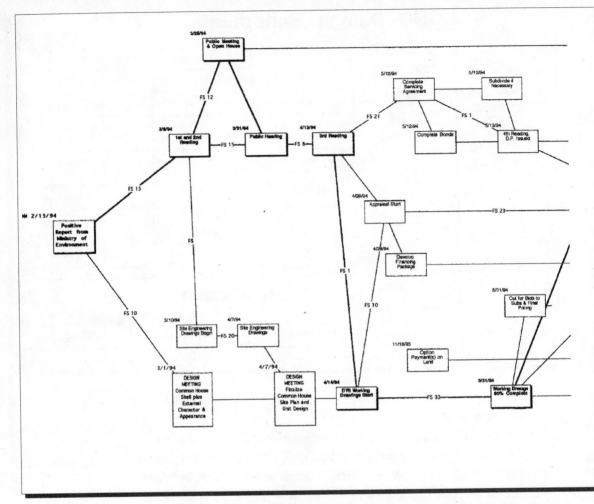

A one-hour audiotape of the Timeline Game as facilitated by Bruce Coldham at the First North American CoHousing Conference is available from the Rocky Mountain CoHousing Association. Contact them at (303) 584-3237.

Sample schedule charts

The samples I have included reflect two real cohousing projects viewed after the fact. Each is simplified to include basic tasks and milestones. It is an interesting process to look at the early predictions and compare them to what really happened.

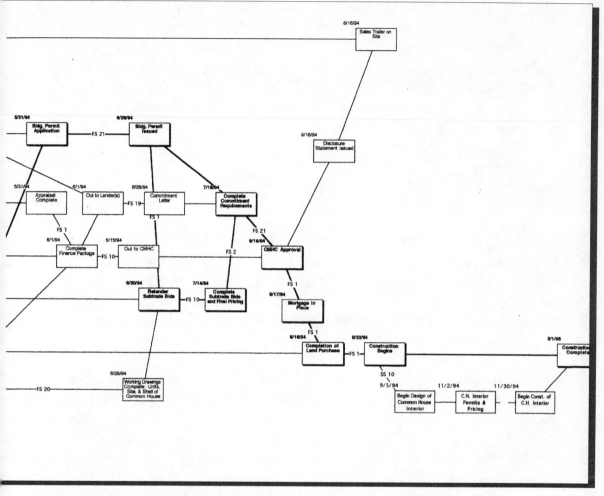

When planning your project and developing a schedule of events and activities it is important to find a balance between the extreme level of detail that is possible and the general overview of key tasks that must be represented. Too much detail is not useful to those who can't or won't take the time to fully understand and appreciate it. Too little may get the big picture across, but it is not useful when you need to schedule group decision making.

Scheduling software

Numerous software programs are available which will assist you in creating a schedule chart. They vary in their complexity, flexibility and ease of use, so if you want to do your scheduling on a computer, choose something that fits your needs. Check out the following:

MacProject (by Claris)
ClarisImpact
Microsoft Project
Project Scheduler
JobTracker
TimeLine
Project Director

Back in the mid 1980s I started using MacProject, a simple CPM chart program. Straightforward, graphic, and easy to use, I learned the benefits of presenting a project schedule in the CPM format. Since then the same program has evolved into a much bigger, more powerful and much more complex program. It is also very expensive now.

Several years ago I took advantage of a special offer from Microsoft and "upgraded" to their product, Microsoft Project. Normally a very expensive program, the special offer made it affordable to try. It was very complex. It has much more power than I could ever use. I'm sure there are professional project managers who use it regularly, but frankly, it put me off project scheduling altogether for awhile. Eventually I sold it and went back to a version of MacProject, now called MacProject Pro. It is still more complex than I need, but at least I know how to use its basic features.

The ads and reviews I read in the computer magazines indicate that many other programs are available. Unfortunately, as such a small segment of the software market, they don't get very much attention.

Summary

Planning your project will help you know what to expect and when. It will help you be realistic about your expectations, and will help you share those expectations with others. For many it is a way of anticipating the necessary decisions, allowing your group to prepare for them with research and discussion.

Many people will complete a project and never use a graphic timeline or schedule, but I find that the personal experience of the cohousing process is eased by graphically representing a proposed schedule. This can really help some people feel better about committing and participating. It helps many people cope with the complexities inherent in a project of this size.

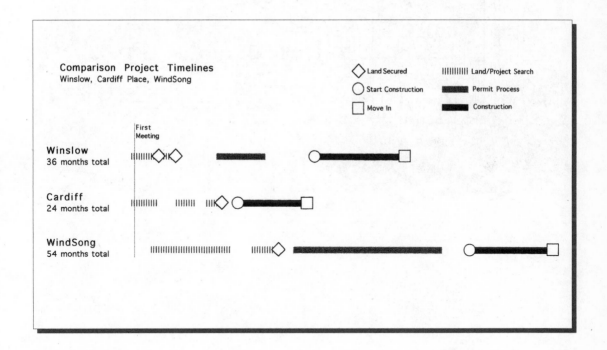

13

Permits and Approvals

Land use approvals • Building permits (fire and life safety
approvals) • The common house kitchen • Appealable
actions • Common types of government approvals • Other
considerations • Three examples of the approval process •
Number of housing units allowed • Speeding up the process

Wherever you want to create your community you will have to obtain permits and approvals from local or regional government, and sometimes from more than one level of government. If you are within a federal jurisdiction, such as on a shoreline or next to a salmon-bearing stream, you will also be subject to federal review and approvals. In most cases you will have to get land use permission to use the land the way you want, and then you will have to get a building permit to ensure that you meet local fire and life safety requirements, such as seismic or ventilation requirements.

The depth and complexity of government involvement in construction and land use is illustrated by the following. Working as a permit specialist for the City of Seattle back in 1979, I itemized all the codes, ordinances, laws and regulations, including those documents adopted by reference within the local ordinances. At that point the Department of Construction and Land Use, with 207 staff members, was responsible for implementing more than 11,000 pages of requirements.

When working with the staff in your building department it is good to keep in mind that most of them have very specialized jobs. Each individual might have read and be responsible for only a small part of the whole picture. Very few if any individuals will have read, much less understood, everything their building department is responsible for implementing.

Land use approvals

As soon as you secure your site you will want to confirm the approved land uses and controls. Your design team will need to know such things as, "How many units can be built?" and "What are the required building setbacks?"

In the broadest sense, the land use approval process is intended to ensure that you use the land in a way that is consistent with zoning and other land use laws, reflecting the social and political expectations of local government and the citizens of your community. This approval process may have a number of different names specific to your community. (See the sidebar: Common Types of Government Approvals.)

Land use approvals are based on the traditions of the established zoning in your area. They will generally reflect the most recent comprehensive or local area planning for your municipality or region. It is important to keep the purpose of zoning in mind when doing your land search, or when proposing any changes to the existing land use system. Set up to protect property rights, zoning was originally intended to prevent inappropriate mixtures of building types, such as loud or noxious factories locating next door to private residences. Over time it has also become a way of protecting property values, and a method of directing growth, or commercial activity.

Zoning and other land use traditions can be very specific to your municipality. It is wise to seek advice from those accustomed to working in your area before making any assumptions about what you may or may not be able to do on the land you might choose for your community.

Building permits (fire and life safety approvals)

The building permit is the primary means for government to provide fire and life safety protection for every citizen. You might think of it as an early form of consumer protection. Unfortunately, as with most consumer protection, there is a cost in the form of bureaucracy, as well as limitations on what you can build where.

Generally, your architect or your contractor will apply for your building permit and associated fire and life safety approvals when your construction documents are substantially complete. In most jurisdictions this means that the land use permits have already been separately approved.

The building permit approval process includes the review of the following types of conditions and situations in your proposed buildings:

- structural safety and adequacy, such as posts, beams and materials
- stairways, such as tread, riser, handrail and shape requirements
- special seismic (earthquake) requirements
- egress requirements (the means of escape in case of fire or other disaster), such as corridors, stairways, doorways, and windows in sleeping rooms
- alarms systems, such as heat or smoke detectors
- fire fighting
- truck and equipment access, turnarounds, etc.
- hose length and hose draw conditions
- fire hydrant locations
- adequate "fire flow," meaning hydrant water pressure and sustained flow rates
- sprinkler requirements
- minimum room sizes and other basic housing standards
- ventilation requirements
- energy usage requirements, such as insulation, limitations on door and window openings, and limitations on heating or cooling systems
- and much, much more

Plumbing, electrical, mechanical and sometimes health permits are also required. In some jurisdictions they are a part of the building permit. Plumbing permits usually include water supply and sewer. Electrical permits usually include power supply and communications, such as telephone. Mechanical permits usually include heating, cooling, ventilation and other special systems. Health approvals generally govern water supply, kitchens which serve the public, and related matters.

The common house kitchen

A tricky, often confusing situation exists when the health officials look at plans for a common house kitchen in a normal cohousing community. Their immediate assumption, based primarily on the size and equipment being specified, is that your kitchen will be used to serve the public.

With a mandate to protect the public health, they will often insist that you provide fire protection, ventilation, plumbing, handwashing and dishwashing in accordance with commercial kitchen standards. This doesn't sound like such a bad idea, except for the cost. The typical commercial kitchen designed to feed 50 people each night for dinner might cost $25,000 to $75,000. The requirements generally include such expensive items as a specially designed stainless-steel range hood with built-in fire suppression system.

Your common house kitchen could be treated quite differently if you carefully present it as being accessory to your private homes, like a party room kitchen in a community clubhouse building. There are several things you can do to facilitate this less expensive interpretation. Consider the following:

- Specify only residential-grade appliances where possible.
- Don't specify stainless-steel counters on your plans.
- Don't specify a large range hood on your plans.
- Don't specify a dish washing-up area on your plans.
- Don't specify a commercial-grade dishwasher. If you want one, install it later, after you move in.
- Generally, make your kitchen look small and modest, like a clubhouse kitchen.
- Consider renovating after you have moved in if necessary.

Architects who have designed cohousing before will be familiar with this challenging and rather expensive dilemma. I especially recommend the services of Charles Durrett at The CoHousing Company. Seek his advice.

Appealable actions

Appealable actions are those proposed land use actions which are outside the administrative authority of the local building official. These might include:

- proposals to change or modify the existing zoning, such as a change from one zone designation to another

- a variance request, for an exception to zoning requirements
- conditional use approvals, where, for example a daycare center for children might be allowable in a certain zone but only through a process of setting conditions, which are then appealable.

Typically, if you want to provide a licensed daycare facility as a part of your community you will trigger the requirements for a conditional use. In your application you will have to meet the guidelines laid out in the your land use code. You will also have to present your proposal at a public hearing. Generally, those people living within 300 to 500 feet will have received written invitations to attend and make comments. In providing the required outdoor playground for the children, your neighbors may complain about potential noise. The municipality may then require that you provide sound control mitigation, such as extra fencing, landscaping or even an earthen berm or barrier. These special requirements are the conditions of approval from which the "conditional use" gets its name.

Common types of government approvals

Here is a list of the types of government approvals your group may need. Contact your local building department for more information about which types of approvals will apply, as well as specific terminology in your area.

Land use approvals
- Use Permit
- Development Permit
- Zoning Approval, or Rezoning Approval
- Local Area Plan Approval, or Revision
- Site Plan Review
- Master Use Permit
- Conditional Use Permit
- Shoreline Permit
- Subdivisions, or Plats
- Short Subdivision or Short Plat
- Planned Unit Development (PUD) Permit
- Planned Residential Development (PRD) Permit
- Water Rights Approval
- Septic System Approval
- Curb Crossing and Road Access Approvals
- Surface Water Management Approval (Storm Water and Drainage)

Fire and life safety approvals
- Building Permit
- Electrical Permit
- Mechanical Permit
- Plumbing Permit
- Health Permit

Other considerations

Environmental protection issues

Most jurisdictions have special environmental protection requirements. These range from completely banning further development to the mapping and control of environmentally sensitive areas within an urban setting. Be aware of the following types of environmental protection requirements which may exist in your area:

- slope protection in hilly areas
- wildlife habitat protection, including set-aside areas and corridors between these areas
- wetland areas protection
- storm and surface water management controls to protect streams and wetlands from the effects of development
- shoreline protection in areas with rivers and coastlines
- and much more

Water and water rights

Your project must have access to water. The need for drinking water is obvious, but in most locations you will also need an adequate supply of water for fire protection.

In cities and towns you can usually connect to an existing water system, unless that system is at or above capacity. It may not, however, have adequate flow rates to meet local requirements for fire protection. You may need to work closely with fire officials to work out an acceptable alternative.

In rural areas access to water becomes much more complicated. If you don't have access to an existing system (public or approved private) you will have to drill wells, and/or create some form of acceptable catchment system. Then you will have to deal with all the costs and complexities of storage and distribution on site.

In some locations and under certain conditions you may be required to apply for water rights. This can be a simple process, but it can also be time-consuming and complex. One rural cohousing group in Washington State was stopped cold by the prospect of waiting five years for their water rights approval, not even being allowed to make their land use permit applications until the water rights were in place.

Sewer and septic systems

In cities and towns there is a good chance you can connect to an existing sewer system, if it still has capacity. In rural areas you will probably have to deal with your sewage on site and meet all the associated health requirements.

Health departments generally accept standard septic tank and filtration bed systems when the soil conditions are acceptable. But soil conditions are not always acceptable, such as the rocky 100-plus-acre site in New England that a cohousing group sought to develop. They discovered after much work that only one unit of housing could be built on the site since the soil didn't percolate adequately for a larger septic system.

Above-ground biofiltration systems are becoming popular with would-be communities everywhere. The Solar Aquatics sewerage system is being used effectively in a number of locations and is being considered by the health departments of other municipalities. Care should be taken, however. Do not assume that your local health officials will embrace something unknown to them.

Roads, driveways and access

Often overlooked, a major issue in getting municipal approvals is the identification of a mutually acceptable driveway access location. Where a street has curbs, it may be called a curb cut, the location where your driveway will cross the curb and allow vehicle access onto your property. Generally curb cuts should not be located close to street intersections. On a busy street you may be limited to a single curb cut, or required to enter your site off a side street, or even an alley. The issue to be aware of is traffic control and safety. Negotiate access with the engineering department early. It will be a necessary part of your site planning process, and as you can imagine, it will have a huge impact on how your site will be developed.

Three examples of the approval process

The experience of getting land use approvals and a building permit can be quite different from a small town to a big city. Rural areas provide a special challenge because they have little engineering infrastructure in place. Attitudes about development differ. Size of the government bureaucracy differs. And neighborhood involvement differs. Consider the following three examples of what it can be like to get your project approved.

Small town approvals (The Winslow example)

As an example of a small town let's consider what happened at Winslow Cohousing on Bainbridge Island in Washington State. A small town of about 2,400 people, the town of Winslow had a comprehensive plan and a zoning ordinance with a map indicating areas where specific uses were allowed. Certain areas were shown as being intended for multi-family housing, while others were for various types or intensities of commercial use. The low intensity commercial use zone designation, intended for offices, clinics, etc., also allowed multi-family housing since it was considered a compatible use.

After we located the land and assured ourselves that it could be used the way we intended, the City of Winslow required that we make an application for a land use permit. During the land use permit review process we were required to make a presentation at a City Council meeting which was open to the public. Members of the public were asked to comment and make presentations for or against our proposed project, or specific aspects of our proposal.

Being a small town, the building department was small and easy to work with. There were about five staff members. They helped us consider all the different aspects of our approval requirements and made suggestions about making a successful presentation at the public hearing with the City Council.

In hindsight, the most important part of process was the meetings with the fire chief. Above all, he had to be satisfied that our pedestrian street plan would not hinder his efforts at fire fighting.

After receiving indications of the satisfactory nature of our proposal, and before receiving the final land use permit, we made our building permit application. A complete set of technical drawings were submitted, including all the specifics of building, mechanical, electrical and plumbing. With the issuance of the building permit we received approval for the plumbing, electrical and mechanical systems which had been designed. In all, the permit process took about eight months from initial contact with the City to final approval.

Big city approvals (The Cardiff Place example)

Development in a big city is a little more complex. As an example, let's review what happened for the 17 unit Cardiff Place cohousing community in Victoria, B.C. While Victoria is not a large city, the permit process there is complex enough to be representative of what it is like to get your permits and approvals in big cities everywhere.

The land use approval process started with a request for proposal from the City who was the owner of the land. A number of builders and developers responded, proposing various methods of developing the property within the guidelines established by the City.

After being selected as the winning proposal, the developer had to make applications for land use approvals, including the rezoning which was required. The review process included submissions and presentations to the Building Department, the Advisory Design Panel, the Planning Commission, as well as the City Council. Materials necessary for presentations at these various reviewing bodies included:

- Schematic design plans for site and buildings, including floor plans and elevations
- Renderings (artist's drawings in color) of what the building would look like from the street
- A complete site model, showing building massing and certain other details
- Narrative description of the project and how it was intended to fit into the neighborhood.

Located on a relatively busy neighborhood street, at the corner with a small side street, the site was originally developed with two single-family houses. One of the houses, called Loowill Mansion, was quite large. It had been legally converted into an apartment building more than 50 years earlier. The developer's proposal was to remove the smaller house but to retain and renovate the mansion, adding a new apartment style building in an "L" shape around the older building.

The permits and approvals required the complete reconstruction of the old building to current building code and seismic standards, while retaining the look and feel of the original mock Tudor style. To accomplish this the developer had to strip the building to its wood frame shell, add a completely new foundation and structural system inside the old shell to meet current seismic and building code requirements, and then rebuild the inside of the building as if it were new construction. The cost was more than what it would have been for new construction.

The project required not only rezoning, but an amendment to the Official Community Plan. Several special studies were also required, including reports from traffic, parking and environmental specialists. During the development permit process there was a special site plan review as well. The developer made several public presentations, and several presentations to the City Council. The neighborhood got involved, making specific suggestions for how to shield the parking so they didn't have to look at it. The City's social planner and the local rental advocacy group got involved, suggesting and eventually requiring several rental units as a part of the project.

From the time of the first response to the City's request for proposals it took more than two years before the project was ready for construction. The cohousing group did not affect this approval process, indeed they did not even know of the project until a few weeks before the start of construction. In a big city it can take several years for an experienced developer to get final building permit approvals.

Rural area approvals (The South Surrey example)

It is extremely difficult to develop a cohousing project in a rural area. Even though there is a great deal of undeveloped land in North America, most areas of Canada and the United States have adopted growth control measures to prevent the continued destruction of the natural environment.

As an example of rural area development, let's look at the process undertaken by the Eco-Village Association of South Surrey, a rural area southeast of Vancouver, and just north of the U.S. border at Blaine, Washington. The group was eager to create an eco-village using the concepts of fourth generation cohousing (see Chapter 7, Design Considerations). They were looking for land which was ten acres or larger, where several cohousing neighborhoods could be clustered together into a larger community.

They were looking in an area where future development was anticipated and being planned for by the Municipality of Surrey. They located a 16 acre site developed as a single-family "hobby farm" within the proposed development area and made what seemed like a reasonable offer on the land.

As we completed a detailed Feasibility Analysis for the project we uncovered several very risky conditions. These included:

• Limited water availability
• Insufficient fire flows (not enough sustainable water volume and/or pressure)
• No sewer, with limited on site sewer capacity and a less than warm reception for the group's proposal to use Solar Aquatics instead of a traditional septic system

• A long range plan to build sewer in the area, with no certainty of the alignment, making site planning extremely difficult.

The site would have required rezoning. Although the area was partially within the new development area there was some disagreement about how much of the site could be included. As a result there was no assurance as to how many housing units might be allowed on the property after rezoning. Estimates ranged from 30 units to over 100 units, with the highest probability at the low end of the range.

Number of housing units allowed

(excerpt from the feasibility report done for the Eco-Village Association of South Surrey)

Current zoning will not allow the development of a cohousing or eco-village community. It is understood by all parties that it will be necessary to obtain appropriate rezoning approval. It is not possible at this time to determine what the final density will be after rezoning is approved, assuming it is approved.

It seems that the maximum density achievable on this site, using the most liberal interpretation of the local area plan, is 78 housing units. Previous estimates ranged widely, from 20 units to nearly 100 units. The Surrey Planner responsible for the area feels that 20 units can be assured but 30 units may be pushing the limit. The architect's research has led him to the conclusion that 30 units can be assured, 60 units are very possible, but 78 units can be rationalized. The owner of the land previously indicated that 96 units would be allowed.

Achieving 78 units is based on converting the minimum amount of land to one acre lots (approximately 3.35 acres when providing roadway) and calculating 6 units per acre density over the entire remainder of the site. The minimal one acre conversion might be seen as tokenism. More significantly, there is real doubt whether the entire property can be used in the 6 unit per acre calculation, or if the "unbuildable area" should be removed before making the calculation.

Both the planner and the architect are quite clear that 96 units is not even possible at this time. The local area plan, adopted less than a year ago, shows that a part of this site should be developed as one acre single-family lots. To request an Comprehensive Plan amendment now, as would be necessary to achieve 96 units. The neighborhood plan that has been in place for less than a year, would be difficult if not impossible to change. The major difficulty of course is that it would be a politically unacceptable change to the Plan.

Eco Village Association
of South Surrey

How many units will be approved?

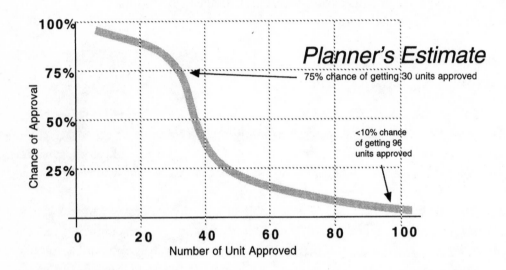

Planner's Estimate

75% chance of getting 30 units approved

<10% chance of getting 96 units approved

Chance of Approval

Number of Unit Approved

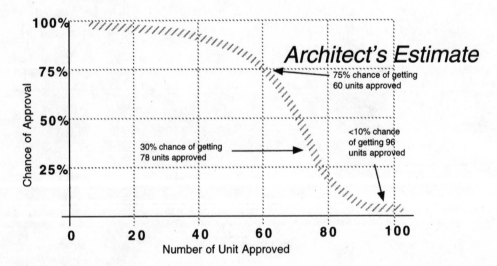

Architect's Estimate

75% chance of getting 60 units approved

30% chance of getting 78 units approved

<10% chance of getting 96 units approved

Chance of Approval

Number of Unit Approved

Feasibility Report
Cohousing Resources

Section 1.3

With all this uncertainty the group made an appropriate decision to pull back and wait, letting go of their option on a very beautiful piece of land. A developer with lots of money and a good hunch may have chosen to hang in there and take the risk. However, for a cohousing group the land cost was high. Much could have been lost if option money was spent, soft costs incurred, or the purchase completed, only to find that the group's intentions were not permitted. Although the group still exists, many of the members of the Eco-Village Association of South Surrey subsequently joined WindSong, which was about to start construction at the same time. Most still hope that someday they can create an eco-village project in South Surrey.

Having found themselves in similar situations, some groups have tried to persevere, and some have lost money. Doing development in rural areas can be very risky, and it is also damaging to the environment.

Speeding up the process

The bureaucracy of a municipal building department is often large and complex. In addition, your project will usually need to be approved by several other municipal departments, and these must be coordinated with the building department.

Bureaucracies have substantial inertia, the tendency to continue moving along at their normal rate, and a resistance to being changed. My suggestion is that you not try to change them, just try to understand them and work with them.

After a few years of working in a building department and then many more years helping clients work effectively with local building departments, I have found a few strategies which help speed up the process. They include:

- Smile. Be a real person and treat building officials like real people.
- Read the law. Ignorance is costly, causing frustration as well as expense.
- Try to make your written or verbal presentations in the language of the building official. Ask to see samples of their previous reports or presentations.
- Do not 'demand' anything.
- Keep in mind that the people across that counter are trying to do their jobs. Even though what they are saying may sound silly, un-

reasonable or expensive, it is their job to implement the laws which were passed by your elected legislators. If you get really frustrated, you may need to look at changing the law.

• And above all, BE PATIENT.

When I worked at the Seattle Building Department (which became the Department of Construction and Land Use) we proudly displayed a sign and pointed to it often. The sign read – "Lack of Prior Planning on Your Part Does Not Constitute an Emergency on Our Part."

14

The Construction Process

Typical construction schedule • Letting go • Design changes • Making sweat equity practical • Managing the contingency fund • Summary

---

A few comments on the construction process are in order since this will be a major effort undertaken by someone else on your behalf, involving a major expenditure of your money. Assuming you hire a contractor to build your project for you (or one part or phase of your project) all sorts of opportunities exist for costs to get out of control. The relationship between the community and the contractor is a complex one.

Typical construction schedule

The new construction of a typical 30-unit cohousing community will generally take from six to ten months to complete, depending on a number of variables. These include:

- type of construction – concrete, wood frame, etc.
- weather – snow and rain can slow down foundations, etc.
- subsurface soil conditions – type, structural capacity, etc.
- site access or other special site conditions
- project phasing – building the project in stages
- skill and experience of the on-site project manager

WindSong actual schedule

If your project is a renovation it could be completed more quickly, especially if the work is limited to indoor activity. Some renovation projects can actually take longer than new construction, however, due to the complexity and the vast number of unknown conditions which have to be dealt with on a daily basis.

Planning a construction project is complex, such as scheduling the work of 50 or more subtrades and arranging for the ordering, delivery and storage of materials and equipment. The sample WindSong Construction Schedule chart illustrates how a project manager plans and tracks what will happen and when during the construction process. Several factors affected how this project was scheduled. Project financing requirements (dependent on membership numbers) delayed the start of this project until November of 1995. A decision was made to bear the extra risk and cost of wintertime construction rather than pay the substantial carrying costs of delaying the start until springtime. (While there isn't much snow in the Vancouver area, the winter rainy season begins in October and runs through March, with up to six inches of rain expected each month.) The project was designed with an underground parking garage plus three large basement slabs, requiring more than 1,300 cubic yards of concrete. Building the parking garage during the winter rains made it difficult to schedule the major concrete pours, especially for the five exposed floor slabs, since they each needed to be poured and finished on a long dry day. In addition, construction was slowed or shut down over the week between Christmas and New Year's.

Once the concrete is in place and the framing can be started the scheduling becomes much more predictable. A contractor who has experience working with the local subtrades knows pretty much what can expected in the way of performance. How long will each trade take to complete its work? How much overlap of the trades will result in efficient construction without having one trade constantly getting in the way of the next? How many people will be on site and much parking is required? Where will all the materials be unloaded and stored?

Study the WindSong Construction Schedule to get an idea of how this works, but remember, your project schedule will likely be very different.

Letting go

Letting go and staying out of the way is the most important thing you can do during the construction process. Meddling, interfering or in any manner getting in the way of the contractor's progress will quite simply cost the community money.

The simplest and most difficult part of letting go is staying off the job site. There are obvious reasons to stay off the job site, including safety. But there will be a temptation to make sure the contractor is doing a good job. There will also be a natural desire to watch the progress, or even to help. Control your urges if you can and stay out of the way. Trust your professionals to monitor quality of construction as well as conformance with the approved plans.

Design changes

The temptation to make changes during the construction process is enormous, but making changes is a *big* risk to the community. Don't change anything at this stage, even if you think the change is really important to make things better long term. Accept what you and your design team have done and let the contractor build it as it was designed and specified. In the end this will reduce the risk that costs will rise or that the schedule will slip, forcing costs to rise even more. Accept the fact that you will have to make any required changes after completing construction and moving in.

The contractor will ask for a few changes, called change orders, mostly based on errors, inconsistencies or inaccuracies in the construction drawings. No architectural drawings are ever perfect or complete, so expect these minor change requests, but don't allow the budget to creep up on you.

In my opinion, the customization of private units should never be allowed. The risk to the community is too great. As costs escalate, financially marginal members will have to leave the community. This is not an appropriate sacrifice for a custom kitchen or an extra closet. All customization should be left until after construction is complete.

Here again, the temptation is enormous. Existing members will think of things they want to change. New members will say to you, "If I could have a bigger deck off my unit I would consider joining the community." You will be tempted to accommodate them in order to get them to join, but don't. If that is what their membership is based on, you probably don't really want them as neighbors. And besides, they can modify their deck later. (See also Chapter 7, Design Considerations: Private Unit Designs.)

Making sweat equity practical

Sweat equity, doing some of the construction yourself to save money, is possible only in a limited way. If you have borrowed money to do the construction the bank will hold the contractor responsible for making sure all the work is completed.

Typically cohousing groups can talk their contractors into letting them assist with the installation of the required landscaping. They can sometimes arrange to come in on weekends and clean up the site, managing the recycling of materials, for instance. This can save the contractor money and they may be willing to give you the credit. But remember, they are responsible to the bank for getting the project done on time and on budget. If you arrange to provide any of the work the contractor will still be responsible for making sure it gets done and doing it if you don't.

Take care to be safe. Establish and maintain your own liability insurance as a group and respect the insurance requirements of your contractor.

Managing the contingency fund

If your group is the developer, or if you have chosen to establish a relationship with a developer that requires you to take some responsibility for the development process, then you will have set aside a contingency fund in your project budget. The more responsibility you have as a group, the higher that amount ought to be. (See Chapter 10, Finance and Budget.)

The contingency fund protects you from unplanned, unforeseen circumstances. These might include:
- soil conditions and subsurface geology affecting the construction of foundations (clay where you hoped there was sand, for instance)
- errors and omissions on the drawings; things the designers forgot
- material and equipment availability problems or delays
- unavoidable delays due to weather
- accidents
- labor disputes
- additional interest charges due to construction delays

Most groups try not to spend their contingency fund until after the risks are reduced. When the foundations are in and the framing is well underway, the risk of subsurface soil problems and weather delays are reduced. But still, it is best to hold onto the money until late in the construction process. Commit to spending parts of it only after you are absolutely sure you will not need it.

Groups tend to use what remains of their contingency fund for completing and furnishing the common house, expanding the landscaping, or building that barn you had to cut from the budget. Some members may suggest that any money left over should be redistributed to the members. It has been my experience, however, that every community can come up with a list of wishes and desires for spending that money which far exceeds the amount that will be available.

Summary

The construction is the fun part: watching it go up, seeing the physical manifestation of all your dreams taking shape. Imagining yourself living there, seeing and feeling the place where you and your community are going to live in the near future. Let it happen. Don't let your controlling nature get in the way of letting your project achieve its completion smoothly and economically.

You might start planning for the move in. Maybe schedule a workshop called "Living There." Consider inviting a few residents from completed cohousing communities to spend the weekend, helping you as a group anticipate what it will be like in a few months when you have moved in.

15

Moving In

Move-in packet • Plan your move – individually, and as a
community • Move-in schedule • Planning for the future •
Burn-out • Summary

This is what you've been waiting for. It's time to actually think about moving in. During the construction process you need something else to think about while you are trying to "let go" and stay out of the way.

Take some time to plan your move in, and think about what it will be like to live there. You might want to talk to members of other communities about what it was like when they first moved in. Consider assembling a package of information for members, including maps, community center schedules, etc.

Move-in packet

At Winslow several members got together and assembled a remarkably comprehensive package they called a move-in packet. It included the following items:
- Cover letter, welcoming people to their new homes and listing the contents of the package
- Congratulation letter from the development consultants, The Northwest Community Housing Foundation
- Welcome letter from the Earth Stewards and The Peace Trees Project on Bainbridge Island

- Transition: A Survival Summary – tricks and tools for making the most of transition, excerpted from a book called *Transitions*, by William Bridges
- Countdown: Planning Your Move – a checklist of what to do and when
- Unit Acceptance Procedures – from the development committee
- A list of 50 proven stress reducers – #17 is "Make friends with non-worriers." #40 is "Laugh."
- Moving Tips and Fun Things to Do (pamphlet)
- Caution! New Home Health Hazards (pamphlet)
- A list of utilities, their addresses and phone numbers
- Parking on Our Site – space assignments and more
- Child Care Plans
- Self Management and the "Sweatola System"
- Memo from the Meals Planning subgroup
- Amended Articles of Incorporation
- Final accounting of change order items and costs
- Punch list of known deficiencies still to be completed by the contractor
- Flyer for an upcoming Community Building Workshop being put on by the Foundation for Community Encouragement (based on the work of M. Scott Peck)
- Status report and review of visioning process for the landscape committee
- 8 1/2 x 11 plans of the unit
- List of all members' new addresses, phone numbers, etc.
- Waiting list information and proposals for review
- Map and welcome brochure from the Chamber of Commerce listing public transportation, parks, boat docks, and statistics about the Island
- Letter from the Chamber of Commerce with piles of additional information about banks, realtors, seniors housing projects, churches, recycling depots, licensing locations, voting, services clubs, etc.
- Letter from the Chamber of Commerce with additional information about schools on the Island
- Brochure from the City of Winslow, with map, list of shops, etc.
- Info brochure from cable TV supplier

- Newsletter from the power company
- An excellent area map from a local realtor
- Local swimming pool schedule

Simplify or expand your move-in packet, but try to include similar materials. It will be a tremendous help during a very stressful period.

Plan your move –individually, and as a community

It may seem obvious, but one key to a trouble-free move is preparation. Think through what it will be like as a community to all move in at the same time, or almost the same time. The motivation to move into cohousing sometimes results in very significant moves for people, across the State or across the country. Many of your members will be perpetual movers, as I seem to be. But some will have lived in the same home for many years and will not have the benefit of a recent move to remind them what this process is all about. Moving is stressful for anybody. As a community you have the opportunity to plan and work together to reduce this stress.

Provide each member with information about your new community

Move-in schedule

The following pre-move-in countdown schedule can help each family plan its move. While this list is not comprehensive, it will get you off to a good start.

EIGHT WEEKS BEFORE
- Collect estimates and select a mover. Consider cooperating with several other members and try to get a bulk discount. Check details on cost, packing, loading, delivery, and claims procedures.
- Arrange to transfer children's school records.
- Notify the incoming school about all the children in the community, providing them with one list of names, addresses, ages, classes, special needs, etc.
- Use the floor plan of your new home to determine what to take, what to get rid of, and where it will all go. This is important in cohousing, since many families are moving from larger houses to smaller private spaces.

FOUR WEEKS BEFORE
- Clean out closets. Get rid of unwanted clothing.
- Hold a garage sale to sell furniture and other items you don't want to move and you know the community won't need in the common house. Donate to charities.
- Obtain boxes, tape, twine, labels, and supplies.
- If your mover is to handle the packing, arrange to have it done one or two days before loading begins. If you'll be packing yourself start by placing items that aren't used often. Try to keep each box under 30 pounds. Pack books and other heavy items in small boxes.
- Send furniture, drapes, and carpets for repair or cleaning as needed.
- Review your homeowner's insurance policy to determine whether your possessions are covered during your move! If in doubt, ask your insurance agent.
- Get change-of-address forms from the post office and send them out. (It often takes a month for magazine publishers and other businesses to adjust their records.)

THREE WEEKS BEFORE
- Make any motel or other reservations.

- Set a date to cancel utilities and to have them switched on at your new home.
- Ready car registration and insurance records for transfer.

TWO WEEKS BEFORE

- Arrange to transfer your bank accounts if necessary. Notify any creditors that you'll be moving.
- Make arrangements to move pets. Check with your mover about moving house plants. (Some won't take them.)
- Cancel newspaper delivery.
- Ask your doctor and dentist for your records if you'll be moving out of the area.

TWO DAYS BEFORE

- Have mover pack your goods (unless you're doing it yourself).
- Defrost and dry refrigerators and freezers to be moved.
- If you're moving a long distance, arrange for cash or traveler's checks for the trip, and for paying the mover.
- Set aside jewelry, vital documents, money, and valuable small items to carry with you.

MOVING DAY

- Be on hand to answer questions and give directions to the movers.
- Save your muscles by letting the moving crew take apart beds, roll up carpets, and put mattresses in bags or boxes.
- Carefully read the bill of lading – the contract between you and the mover – before you sign it. Keep it with you until your things are delivered, the charges are paid and any claims are settled.

DELIVERY DAY

- Be on hand to answer questions and give directions.
- Be prepared to pay the driver before your goods are unloaded. (This is a federal requirement for interstate moves in the U.S.)
- Note on the inventory any damaged boxes or obvious damage to unboxed items before you sign. This is necessary to process any claims.

A number of things can be done as a community to make the move-in transition smoother. You may obtain ownership and occupancy in stages over a period of a few days or weeks. But you may receive ownership and occupancy on the same day, so plan your move-in schedule carefully, as a community. Find out which members want to move on which days. Consider hiring the same mover(s). Consider renting a truck together, sharing boxes, etc.

Many cohousing groups find that members have brought too much furniture with them when they move in. Coming from a larger house, it is sometimes very hard to judge what will fit. Some members of your community will probably feel that everything they don't need should go to furnish the common house. Others aren't sure where to put things, so they stack extras (such as freezers they weren't thinking about) on the front porch, upsetting their new cohousing neighbors for weeks or months to come.

I suggest preparing for these events by establishing a "Common House Furnishings Committee." The committee, consisting of any members who care to be involved, can take responsibility for determining what furniture is needed in the common house and then sorting through the furniture donated by members. As you can imagine, many members will have old furniture they want to donate, not realizing that other members would prefer not to have it in the common house for aesthetic reasons. If a committee takes the responsibility for organizing donations and making the determination, it tends to reduce the bad feelings that might otherwise occur.

Plan for a "Super Big Multi-Family Garage Sale" several weeks after move in. (A church, of course, would call this a rummage sale.) After your common house committee has had a chance to select the best items for use in the common house, have a big sale for everything that's left. Advertise it well, and dedicate the proceeds toward buying china, tools for the workshop, or that hot tub you didn't think you could afford.

Planning for the Future

Anticipate the fact that not everyone will stay after they move in. Some may find that your community, or your location, doesn't work the way they thought it would. Commuting is worse than expected, the kids are noisier, or the dogs are messier. Dealing with turnover is a natural part of the evolution of community, so don't be too surprised.

BY PATSY ALIA CASEY, WINSLOW COHOUSING

Burn-out

In mid-August here in the Pacific Northwest, the days are exquisite, the heavy heat of summer already past. Through the fresh sea air, the sun is a warm carress on the bare skin. The gardens are starting to peak into a glory of colors — purples, pinks, lavenders, blues with orange, yellow and white counterpoints.

It was such a day, a Saturday, and I had just finished giving a tour. I was speaking with someone in the courtyard and glanced away to see my dear Swiss friend, Thérèse, slender, brown-haired, mother of Lucas and Nina, wife of Kim, my confi-dante, my laughingmate, walking toward me, up the village path from the meander-ing Northeast Knoll. Thérèse's gait is distinctive, slightly off, naturally so because, as she explains, "I have weird hips." Born that way, Lucas also has weird hips and to see the two of them walking together always leaves me smiling. They amble in their wandering, awkward way, bumping each other along. Now, as Thérèse gets closer, I can see her mood is not amiable. She strides up to me and reaches out with both hands to grip my shoulders.

The last two weeks had been harried for Thérèse and me. Work, kids, projects . . . juggle, juggle, juggle. Our talks have been brief, quick exchanges snatched on the path-ways. To make matters worse for me, it seemed that all of the cohousing children had suddenly become insatiable data banks. Their sweet observations about life had dis-appeared and been replaced by constant queries about how long, how far, how much, how many? Fun experiences had become nightmares. How long before the cookies are done? How much sugar is in a package? How many nuts are in a cup? How many cookies will we have? How many do we each get? How many do we save for Nathan? How far away is the bakery?

These children were suddenly, definitely not cute. Especially when my answers were usually met with, "Yes, but why? How do you know?" In desperation and for peace of mind I began saying, "Hmm, interesting question. However, I can't answer it because something happened to me this summer. I changed. I don't do numbers anymore." And when the next big-eyed data bank asked me a question, I'd remind him or her, "Remember. I don't do numbers." Then a day or so later, it happened: Aidan admonished Isabel, "Don't ask her that. Patsy doesn't do numbers." I was home-free.

I had shared all this with Thérèse the week before in front of the common house. We laughed and separated with smiles on our faces.

There was no smile on Thérèse's face now as her brown eyes gazed directly into mine while her hands held my shoulders square to hers. I waited for her soft Swiss accent, which so often undermines her firmness, to begin. She took a deep breath and began, pausing for emphasis after each statement. "Patsy, this is very important! I have decided. There is no changing this. I don't do numbers . . . I don't do time . . . I don't do meetings . . . I don't do pets . . . I don't do forms . . . I don't do children . . . I don't do husbands. . . . " Here, she stopped. Letting it all sink in, ignoring the beginnings of my smile. Then her parting shot. "I only do hot tubs!" And she marched off.

It is one of my treasured moments.

Why do people leave? The reasons vary, but generally it's because lives change or expectations aren't being met. Will the pioneers leave? The short answer is yes, many of them will, eventually. Don't worry about it, though. They did their part. It may take pioneers to get it built, but it takes sustainers to keep your community healthy and alive.

A major issue to anticipate is the process of integrating new resident members who replace those who move out. Living there is not the same as the development process. No big meetings about spending lots of money, no design discussions, and very few sessions devoted to creating dreams together. Instead you will be dealing with everyday life. Questions about how to raise children in community, co-parenting, etc. Who is parking where, when and how often? Whose dog is leaving little piles in the garden? Talk to older cohousing communities about their experiences. See how they have done things, and ask what works. (Don't reinvent the wheel.)

When a member does need to move on, the stress will be significantly reduced if you have maintained a data base of interested people. Some of them might be ready to buy a home in your community if one becomes available. The seller benefits by having a ready buyer. The community benefits since those who want to move in are already known to those who live there.

Summary

The transition from the creative process to "living the goal" is a change from "doing" to "being." The community will change dramatically, from being focused on getting a project built to figuring out how to live this new and different lifestyle. Planning and anticipation are the key, I think, to reducing the stress and making life in your community the pleasurable experience you were looking for.

One of the first things you will notice after moving in is the apparent exhaustion and even depression in a few members. Those who managed to keep things going during the development process may no longer have to do so.

This is normal. It is a part of the process of change. To some extent you can anticipate these changes and facilitate the process by assembling a package of information to help with the transition.

16

Resources

A number of resources are available to assist you in creating your cohousing community. You will find below a list of books, organizations, professionals, journals, videos, related resources and sample materials I have found to be helpful.

   If you are a cohousing professional and you are not listed below, or if you know of other resources, please let me know so that I can update this list for the next edition of this book. Contact Chris Hanson at CHanson17@aol.com.

Selected Books:

After the Crash: The Emergence of the Rainbow Economy. By Guy Dauncey, Third Ed. 1996 Greenprint, London

Boundaries of Home: Mapping for Local Empowerment. Edited by Doug Aberley, 1994 New Society Publishers

Cohousing: A Contemporary Approach to Housing Ourselves. Second Edition. By McCamant & Durrett with Hertzman, 1994, Ten Speed Press Communities Directory by Fellowship for Intentional Community, Rt. 4, Box 169, Louisa, VA 23093 (540) 894-5126

Creating Community Anywhere: Finding Support & Connection in a Fragmented World. By Carolyn Shaffer and Kristin Amundsen, 1993 G.P. Putnum's Sons, New York, NY.

Ecocity Berkeley: Building Cities for a Healthy Future. By Richard Register, 1987 North Atlantic Books, Berkeley, CA

Egograms, by John M. Dusay, M.D.

Futures by Design: The Practice of Ecological Planning. Edited by Doug Aberley, 1994 New Society Publishers

Gifts Differing, 1980 Consulting Psychologists Press

Games People Play by Eric Berne, 1985 Ballantine

Housing as if People Mattered by Clare Cooper Marcus and Wendy Sarkissian, 1986 University of California Press, Berkeley

How Buildings Learn: What Happens After They're Built. By Stewart Brand, 1995 Penguin

Living Longer, Living Better: Adventures in Community Housing for Those in the Second Half of Life. By Jane Porcino, 1991 Crossroad, NY

No Contest: The Case Against Competition. By Alfie Kohn, 1992 Houghton Mifflin Company, New York, NY

A Primer on Sustainable Building, by Barnett and Browning, 1995 Rocky Mountain Institute

Rebuilding Community in America: Housing for Ecological Living, Personal Empowerment, and the New Extended Family. By Ken Norwood and Kathleen Smith, 1995 Shared Living Resource Center, Berkeley, CA

Redesigning the American Dream. By Dolores Hayden, 1984 W.W. Norton & Co., NY

Voluntary Simplicity: Towards a Way of Life That is Outwardly Simple, Inwardly Rich. By Duane Elgin, 1981 William Morrow and Co. New York, NY

Who Am I? Personality Types for Self Discovery. By Robert Frager, 1994 Putnam

Organizations & Professionals:

American Institute of Architects, Local Chapters. Source for standard contracts, etc.

Boston CoHousing Network, Stella Tarnay, 45 Rice Street, Cambridge, MA 02140 (617)491-4392

The Cohousing Center, Marc Daigle, 103 Morse Street, Watertown, MA 02172 (617) 923-1300

Patsy Casey, Story Teller and Hypnotherapist, Winslow Cohousing, 353 Wallace Way NE, #30, Bainbridge Island, WA 98110

The CoHousing Company, Katie McCamant & Chuck Durrett, 1250 Addison St. #113, Berkeley, CA 94702 (510)549-9980, Email: CoHousngCo@aol.com

The Cohousing Network, Don Lindemann, PO Box 2584, Berkeley, CA 94702 (510) 526-6124

The Cohousing Network, BC Chapter, Alan Carpenter, #27 - 20543 96th Avenue, Langley, BC V1M 3W3

Bruce Coldham, Architect, Pine Street Cohousing, 155 Pine Street, Amherst, MA 01002 (413)549-3616

Community Bookshelf, East Wind Community, Box CM5, Tecumseh, MO 65760 (417)679-4682

Guy Dauncey, Sustainable Communities Consultancy, (604) 592-4473, Email: gdauncey@islandnet.com

Caroline Estes, Alpha Institue, Deadwood, OR 97430 (503) 964-5102

Fellowship for Intentional Community, Rt. 1, Box 155, Rutledge, MO 63563

Growing Community Associates, PO Box 5415-C, Berkeley CA 94705 (510) 869-4878

Chris Hanson, Cohousing Resources, CHanson17@aol.com

Stanley King, CoDesign Architect, 738 Millyard St., Vancouver, BC V5Z 4A1 (604) 873-3547

Mary Kraus, Architect, Pioneer Valley Cohousing, 67 N. Pleasant Street, Amherst, MA 01002 (413) 253-4090

Jim Leach, Wonderland Hill Development Co. Email: Madhat500@aol.com

Living Village Design, PO Box 1734, Boulder, CO 80306 (303) 449-4264

Tom Moench, Organizational Consultant, Winslow Cohousing, 353 Wallace Way NE, #18, Bainbridge Island, WA 98110

Puget Sound Cohousing Network, Rob Sandelin, (206) 936-7157

Fritz Radandt, Cardiff Place Cohousing, Marketing and Computers, 403- 1246 Fairfield Ave., Victoria, BC V8V 3B5 (604) 920-9984

Richard Register, Ecocity Builders, 5427 Telegraph Ave, W2, Oakland, CA 94609 (510) 649-1817

Rock Mountain CoHousing Association, 1705 14th Street #160, Boulder, CO 80302 (303) 584-3237

Shared Living Resource Center, Ken Norwood, 2375 Shattuck Ave, Berkeley, CA 94704 (510) 548-6608

David Simpson, Architect, Davidson Yuen Simpson Architects, 2nd Floor, 321 Water Street, Vancouver, BC V6B 1B8 (604) 669-7710

Dan Suchman, Attorney, Winslow Cohousing, 353 Wallace Way NE, #26, Bainbridge Island, WA 98110 (206) 842-9700

Support Financial Services, Inc., Zev Paiss, 3577 Nyland Way North, Lafayette, CO 80026 (303) 499-8189

Village Habitat, Greg Ramsey, 2001 Westminster Way, Atlanta, GA 30307 (404) 325-9033

David Wright, Landscape Architect, WindSong Cohousing, #31 - 20543 96th Avenue, Langley, BC V1M 3W3 (604) 882-3627

Journals, Videos and Other Resources:

CoHousing: Contemporary Approaches to Housing Ourselves. Quarterly Journal of the CoHousing Network, PO Box 2584, Berkeley, CA 94702 (510)526-6124 Email: cohomag@aol.com

cohousing-L on the INTERNET, send Email message to: subscribe cohousing-L <your name> to listproc@cohousing.org

CoHousing: Neighborhoods for People, Video by Paiss Productions 1995, RMCA, 1705 14th Street, #160, Boulder, CO 80302

Communities, Journal of Cooperative Living. Rt. 1, Box 155, Rutledge, MO 63563 (540)894-5126

Ecocity Builder Bulletin, 5427 Telegraph Ave, W2, Oakland, CA 94609 (510)649-1817

EcoDesign Resource Society, Journal and Web Site, PO Box 3981-MPO, Vancouver, BC, V6B3Z4 (604)689-7622 Email: ecodesign@freenet.vancouver.bc.ca

Home Power Magazine, PO Box 520, Ashland, OR 97520 (916)475-3179

The Timeline Game, 862 County Road 503, Bayfield, CO 81122 (970)884-2196

Sample Documents:

Bylaws of a cohousing group (prototypical)

I.   MEMBERSHIP

1.   The Public Relations Committee shall be responsible for recruiting prospective members. The People Committee shall receive all applications for membership and shall be responsible for educating prospective members and orienting and integrating new members. The Finance Committee shall help persons interested in becoming members to review their financial situation and ability to qualify for necessary financing.

2.   After an orientation meeting with the People Committee and a review of their financial situation with the Finance Committee, anyone who wishes to become a member of the association must:

 a) attend three regular meetings (a requirement which may only be waived under exceptional circumstances),

 b) sign the Articles of Association and the Bylaws, and

 c) pay a nonrefundable initiation fee of $100 per member.

3.   To promote the long-term health and viability of our community, we desire members representing a mix of ages, races, gender and sexual orientation, with sufficient children for them to feel community with one another.

4.   Any member who wishes to withdraw from membership must do so in writing to the Secretary, effective when received. Any member who fails to withdraw in writing will continue to be liable for commitments made by the association on their behalf.

II.   DUES AND FEES

1.   Monthly dues of $5.00/household shall be contributed by the first of each month to cover general operating and office expenses of the association.

2.   Members of the association shall be responsible for pre-development soft costs. Members who join after June 1 shall pay their share of the pre-development costs from June 1 in a lump sum, or otherwise as agreed by the association.

3.   Members joining after the down payment has been made for the purchase of land shall contribute an amount to be set by the association which shall reflect any increased value resulting from the time and effort already invested by the association.

4.   Members who withdraw from the association shall receive a refund of any contributions as agreed by the association on a case-by-case basis

depending on the phase of development at the time, but the down payment portion of the purchase price of land shall not be returned until all units are pre-sold.

III. BUSINESS MEETINGS

1. The secretary shall see that all members receive notice by phone, by first-class mail or in person of the time and place of meetings at least five days before regularly scheduled meetings.

2. No meeting may be convened without 2/3's of the member households represented in person but the meeting may continue despite the withdrawal of enough members to leave less than a quorum. At the start of the meeting, a dated 5" x 8" index card shall be signed by all the members present and used to divide the card file into a section for each meeting.

3. All members may participate in decision-making and voting on proposals.

4. Only one person has the right to speak at any one time during a meeting. Anyone else wishing to speak shall so indicate nonverbally and the recorder shall list them in the order they will be called.

5. Only one proposal may be discussed at any one time, and no other business shall be conducted until that proposal is either decided upon or postponed until a later meeting.

6. A facilitator and recorder shall be chosen for each meeting. The facilitator shall enforce these rules, arrange the agenda, and arbitrate disputes between members. The facilitator shall help members to come to a decision and shall not participate in discussions. If need be, the facilitator may appoint someone as temporary facilitator for a given issue. The recorder shall recognize members to speak and make sure that all who wish to speak are heard in order. The recorder shall also ensure that comments, objections and a summary are

posted as made. The facilitator and recorder shall see that tabled decisions and ongoing business are set for the next agenda. The secretary shall be responsible for ensuring that decisions are recorded.

7. The order of business at meetings shall be:
    a) Call to order by facilitator and quiet time;
    b) Brief report of the last meeting by reviewing the agenda cards, short committee reports, announcements/comments and report of actions taken by the Management Board since the last meeting;
    c) Agenda items with tabled decisions first, followed by ongoing business, and last, new business;
    d) Announcement of next meeting time and place;
    e) Closure.

8. Only business on the agenda shall be considered during a meeting. For an item to be placed on the agenda it must be written on one side of a 5" x 8" index card and given to the facilitator at least one week before the scheduled meeting. For good reason, the facilitator may fill out an agenda card and place an item on the agenda if requested by a member no later than 24 hours before the meeting.

9. After an item has been disposed of, the recorder shall note the disposition and date on the back of the agenda card. Agenda cards shall constitute the record of business and shall be kept by the secretary for reference by all members accompanied by the list of members present at the meeting.

10. Any item left pending or tabled shall be placed on the agenda of the next meeting.

IV. COOPERATIVE DECISION-MAKING

1. A decision on each issue presented to the meeting in the form of a written proposal shall be determined by first seeking consensus.

2. Consensus shall be understood to mean general agreement or concord. Everyone's opinion shall be sought and the proposal modified until concerns are met and a solution found that everyone can live with.

3. After an agreed-upon length of time (determined by the members in light of the importance of the issue under discussion) and in order to see how much agreement exists, a poll shall be called by the facilitator by asking for objections or by asking if everyone can live with the proposed solution. The facilitator or any member may also ask how the group feels at any appropriate time during the discussion.

4. Pools shall be taken by the following method:

  a) Each member shall have five cards to represent five classes of opinions in regard to their feelings about the proposal.

  b) The appropriate class shall be written on each card:

    1) Green = Approve

    2) Blue or White = Acceptable/ neutral

    3) Yellow = Unsure/unclear

    4) Orange = Not preferred

    5) Red = Definitely opposed

5. Yellows may explain what is unsure or unclear. The facilitator decides if clarification or discussion is needed on the points raised.

6. Orange and red must speak, even if only to say, "My objection has been spoken to."

7. After steps 5 and 6 are completed, a second poll shall be taken. If objections still remain as shown by orange or red cards, the proposal shall be tabled until the next meeting and an ad hoc team appointed to see if a creative solution can be found to address the concerns raised.

8. The last form of the proposal and any new solutions shall be presented at the next meeting. If after discussion consensus cannot be reached because of definite opposition and a decision must be made quickly, a "yes" or "no" vote shall be asked for.

9. No proposal shall pass if fewer than 3/4's of the members present are in favor or if in the seven days following the meeting, 3/4's of the members entitled to vote do not agree in writing.

V. MANAGEMENT

1. This association shall be represented by a management board of no fewer than five members.

2. Each of the five standing committees of the association shall appoint one representative to the Management Board for staggered terms of three, six, nine and twelve months.

3. The five standing committees shall be: Finance, Architectural Review, Legal, People and Public Relations.

4. The Board shall have the power to make all day-to-day decisions in the ordinary course of association business but shall not enter into a contract with a third person, sell property of the association or incur expenditures of more than $_____ without the express written consent of the association members.

5. The members of the association may by written consent expressly authorize any member of the Management Board to enter into any contract and deliver any instrument in the name of and on behalf of the association.

6. The Management Board shall hold regularly scheduled meetings and notice of the time and place of meetings shall be given to each board member by phone, by first-class mail or in person at least forty-eight hours before a meeting. All meetings of the Board shall be open to all association members, but members other than Board members may not participate in any discussion or deliberation unless expressly authorized to do so by the Board.

7.   The Board shall set its own procedure for decision-making based on the consensus model.

8.   Every act performed and decision made by the Board at a duly held meeting at which four of the five members are present shall be regarded as the act of the Board.

9.   Any action required or permitted to be taken by the Board may be taken without a meeting, if all the members of the Board consent in writing to the action. Such action by written consent shall have the same force and effect as a unanimous vote of the board.

10.   The Board shall keep a complete record of all its acts, and the transactions of any meeting of the Board or action taken without a meeting shall be explained to the association members at the next scheduled meeting of the association.

11.   The members of the Board shall not be personally liable to the association or its members for monetary damages for acts or omissions as a Board member that did not involve intentional misconduct or a knowing violation of law, or a transaction from which the Board member personally received a benefit in money, property or services to which they were not legally entitled.

VI.   SECRETARY AND TREASURER

1.   The members of the association shall select a treasurer who shall maintain a bank account, be responsible for all funds of the association, disburse funds for business of the association taking vouchers for such disbursements, and keep adequate and correct financial records and books of account. When and if it becomes necessary for the association to hire a bookkeeper or accountant, the treasurer shall make recommendations to the members about, and shall be responsible for overseeing the work of, the bookkeeper or accountant.

2.   The members of the association shall select a secretary to keep minutes and records of all meetings and maintain the agenda card index and membership list current.

VII.   ADOPTION, AMENDMENT, REPEAL

1.   These bylaws shall be adopted by the agreement and written consent of all the members.

2.   They may be amended or repealed, in whole or in part, by the agreement and the written consent of all the members. If all the members cannot agree, then these bylaws shall be amended or repealed by the vote or written consent of 3/4's of the members.

We, the undersigned, are all of the members of this association, and hereby consent to and adopt the above bylaws as the bylaws of the association.

Operating Guidelines
Victoria Cohousing Development Society Cardiff Place Development Committee Draft 2.0 April. 9, 94

PURPOSE
On February 15th, 1994, the Victoria Cohousing Development Society struck the Cardiff Place Development Committee to "manage all affairs of the Society related to the development of Cardiff Place." This committee was also instructed to report to the Society on a regular basis in writing with a record of minutes and decisions. This document outlines the operation of the Cardiff Place Development Committee.

MEMBERSHIP
Membership in the Cardiff Place Development Committee consists of members of the Victoria Cohousing Development Society who are fully subscribed purchasers of suites Cardiff Place. Each suite shall count as one member, irregardless of

the number of adults represented. All adults purchasing a suite are welcome to participate in the meetings but ultimately the suite only has one say in the decision making process.

MEETINGS

The Committee will meet regularly, currently every Saturday at 12:30 PM, to conduct its affairs. This meeting may be canceled if at least 48 hours notice is given to all Committee members. In addition, extraordinary meetings may be called if at least 48 hours notice is given to all Committee Members. Notice shall be in person, by written notice delivered to their residence, or by telephone. Leaving a message on a message machine shall constitute notification. Regularly scheduled meetings do not require additional notice.

ATTENDANCE

Committee members are encouraged to attend every possible meeting to ensure their input is heard, to facilitate communication, and to ensure quorum is reached.

Society members are welcomed and encouraged to attend Committee meetings, as are guests. They can participate in discussions but cannot participate in establishing consensus or voting. Guests are encouraged to contribute to discussions as their knowledge allows but should ask information gathering questions outside of the formal meeting. In this way, valuable meeting time will not be consumed going over old ground.

QUORUM

A meeting shall convene only if a quorum of Committee members are present.

Quorum shall consist of two thirds (2/3) of the members of the Committee. The calculated 2/3 count shall be rounded up to the next whole number.

A member not in attendance can give their proxy to any other Committee member. The proxy must be declared at the start of the meeting and be recorded in the minutes. The proxy has the authority to make judgments on behalf of the absent party, but limited only by the conditions that the absent part has indicated.

MINUTES

Minutes must be taken of every Cardiff Place Development Committee meeting.

A minute taker will be determined at the start of each meeting.

The minutes of the previous meeting will be read at the start of every meeting.

A copy of the minutes must be forwarded to the secretary of the Victoria Cohousing Development Society.

FACILITATION

Every regular Committee meeting will have two facilitators: a *meeting facilitator* and a *process facilitator*.

The meeting facilitator focuses on the agenda items, calls on speaker, facilitates discussions, and keeps the discussion on the current agenda item.

The process facilitator focuses on keeping the meeting on time, ensuring the decision making process is adhered to, and points out any other meeting irregularities such as someone not getting a chance to be heard.

The facilitators are chosen at the start of each meeting. It is hoped that all members will take a turn at the facilitator roles.

DECISION MAKING

The Committee shall make decisions by consensus. Consensus is reached when all members agree the proposal is acceptable to them. Consensus is blocked when even one member cannot agree with the proposal.

PROPOSALS

All significant decisions should be made by a written proposal submitted to the group at least one week prior to the decision. A decision is considered significant if even one members believes it is.

EMERGENCY AND REQUIRED DECISIONS

There will be occasions when consensus is not possible. For example, some decisions must be made very quickly (emergency) or some decisions must be made if the Committee is to move forward (required decisions). To avoid gridlock, the Committee may have to resort to voting.

An emergency decision is any decision the Committee agrees by consensus is an emergency. A required decision is any decision the Committee agrees by consensus is required or is so identified by a Committee consultant. With emergency decisions, the Committee can vote on the proposal immediately. With required decisions, the Committee can vote on the proposal after two meetings of unsuccessful attempts at consensus.

Decisions which are put to a vote must be approved by three quarters (3/4) of Committee members.

REVISITING PREVIOUS DECISIONS

To avoid the continual revisiting of decisions, all decisions are considered final unless two thirds (2/3) of Committee members sign a petition to put the item on a later agenda. All members must be notified the decision is being revisited.

CARD SYSTEM

The Cardiff Place Development Committee will use a colored card system to facilitate the decision making process. *explanation to follow*

TASK GROUPS

The Cardiff Place Development Committee will form task groups as needed to relieve the work-load and the time constraints of the regular Committee meetings.

The task groups will be made of members from the Committee as well as any other volunteers or consultants.

Each task group must have its mandate approved by the Committee. Any activities the task group under takes should be approved by the committee in advance.

Each task group must have its budget approved by the Committee. The task group can then has spending authority as long as it is within the budget.

Task groups will have the opportunity to update the Committee at every general meeting. Task groups should not rehash their discussions at the general meetings. Task groups should use the general meetings to provide concise summaries of their activities, to get feedback about specific issues, or to get approval for a clearly present proposal.

COMMUNICATION

Each Committee member is allocated an envelope with their name on it. These envelopes are kept at the site of the committees' regular meetings. Members and task groups can communicate with other members placing a copy of a document in every member's envelope. In this fashion, every member is assured of receiving all correspondence, even if absent from a meeting.

AGENDAS

A standard agenda format, as set out below, will be used by the Committee for all regular meetings.

The agenda will be compiled by the Administration/Steering task group.

Every task group is allocated a maximum of 5 minutes for each meeting. If a task group requires more time than this, it must contact the focalizer of the Administration/Steering task group no later than 2 days prior to the meeting.

Victoria Cohousing Development Society
Cardiff Place Development Committee
Sample Agenda
Date (eg. Saturday, March 5th, 1994)
Time (eg. 12:30 to 4:00)
Location

#	Topic	Purpose	Who	Time
0.	Envelope stuffing - proposals and other printed materials are put in all members' envelopes	Communication	All	prior to meeting
1.	Checkin - each person has the option of a brief sharing, no questions are allowed	Come-together	All	15 min.
2.	Designation of meeting facilitators, note taker	Organization	All	1 min.
3.	Secretary's Report including last meeting and proxies	Information	Sec.	3 min.
4.	Approve Agenda - add or delete items - prioritize items - set or change time allocated for items - determine length of the meeting	Organization	Fac	10 min.
5.	Task Group Reports & Issues - updates from task group or consultants - discussion and decisions on items relating to the task groups - each task group is automatically granted 5 mins - items requiring more time must be submitted to the admin task group 2 days prior to meeting	Info, discuss, decis.	Various	
6.	Coffee Break about 2 hours into the agenda	Relax	All	10 min.
7.	Other Business - items not yet covered			
8.	Future agenda items	Organization	Fac	5 min.
9.	Next Meeting - decide on date and location	Organization	Fac	1 min.
10.	Announcements - meetings - personal	Information	All	5 min.
11.	Review of Meeting	Growth	Proc. Fac	3 min.

WINSLOW COHOUSING GROUP
PO Box 10661
Winslow, WA 98110
842-0253

Cost of Participation, as of 23 June 1989

The bylaws of our Association require a one time membership fee for voting members. In addition, members of the Winslow Cohousing Group have recently purchased land together with each household contributing an equal share toward those costs.

In order to become a member of the Association it would be necessary for a new household to pay the membership fee and to contribute equally their share of the land cost accumulated to date. It will also be necessary to commit to further land purchase payments and development soft costs, such as permit and professional fees, by signing the subscription agreement being used by the group.

At this point we are planning to close a construction loan sometime early in 1990, hopefully in January. In order to have a construction loan approved we will need to have cash invested in the project at that date. We expect that each family purchasing an average unit of 850 square feet will have made investments totalling $10,000 in cash at the point of the construction loan. Households will be required to contribute a little more or a little less depending on the size of the unit being purchased. The rate and method of that investment has begun as follows:

Membership and land costs for those joining before June 30, 1989.

Membership, per voting adult	$100.00
Ericksen Purchase	900.00
Wallace Purchase	3750.00
TOTAL (one adult)	$4750.00
TOTAL (two adults)	$4850.00

Membership and land costs for those joining 1 July through 15 September 1989.

Membership, per voting adult	$100.00
Land Purchase Contribution	4950.00
TOTAL (one adult)	$5050.00
TOTAL (two adults)	$5150.00

The next definite land investment payments per household are:
$1000.00 on 30 September 1989
$1000.00 on 31 December 1989

The above figures give a total somewhat less than the $10,000 which will be necessary. Our developer is currently evaluating cost requirements for the preconstruction period and the group will make a decision within the next couple of months on what to assess itself in fees to cover those costs. As you can imagine, part of the formula is estimating the number of new members and when they will join. By the end of September we hope to have all households committed to units of specific size which will allow us to begin differentiating costs proportionately.

*Participation
cost analysis*

WCGOPCST.XLS

Winslow Estimated Operating Expenses, 30 Units (8/17/90- KCM & TCG)

Item	Per Unit Monthly	Total Monthly	Total Annual	Per Unit Annual	Assumptions
FIXED COSTS					
Blanket Mortgage	$536.97	$16,109.12	$193,309.44	$6,443.65	Based upon $1.6 million blanket loan
Property Taxes	$121.77	$3,653.17	$43,838.00	$1,461.27	$13 per $1000 valued on cost of construction
Corporate Taxes			$5.00	$0.17	Annual filing fee
Insurance	$22.61	$678.33	$8,140.00	$271.33	Based upon $2.20 per $1000 at $3.7 million value
License/Inspection	$0.69	$20.83	$250.00	$8.33	Assumes hot tub or boiler
L.I.D. Assessment	$12.04	$361.08	$4,333.00	$144.43	
TOTAL FIXED COSTS	$682.05	$20,461.45	$245,542.44	$8,184.75	
OPERATING COST					
Utilities:					
Electricity (common building)	$16.67	$500.00	$6,000.00	$200.00	Electricity for units not included
Water	$30.00	$900.00	$10,800.00	$360.00	Utilities are extrapolations of billing rates for 30 units
Sewer	$30.00	$900.00	$10,800.00	$360.00	
Cable TV	$0.67	$20.00	$240.00	$8.00	One cable line for common house
Garbage	$15.00	$450.00	$5,400.00	$180.00	2 dumpsters picked up once weekly
Intercoms/Telephone	$0.97	$29.17	$350.00	$11.67	One phone line for common house (min. long distance)
Continuing Coop Education	$1.67	$50.00	$600.00	$20.00	Required by Nat. Coop Bank
Pest Control	$1.94	$58.33	$700.00	$23.33	Based upon 4 treatments (tree spraying)
Landscape	$4.17	$125.00	$1,500.00	$50.00	Community work parties and responsibilities assumed
Maintenance	$15.00	$450.00	$5,400.00	$180.00	
Sub total	$101.08	$3,032.50	$36,390.00	$1,213.00	
REPLACEMENT RESERVES:	$23.49	$704.83	$8,457.97	$281.93	Based upon 3% of operating costs
OPERATING RESERVE:	$15.66	$469.89	$5,638.65	$55.36	Based upon 2% of operating budget
ADMINISTRATION:					
Management:	$16.00	$480.00	$5,760.00	$192.00	Assumes self management & a consulting
Legal Services	$0.69	$20.83	$250.00	$8.33	contract @ $480 per mo.
Accounting (Bookkeeping)	$11.81	$354.17	$4,250.00	$141.67	
Office expense	$0.69	$20.83	$250.00	$8.33	
Advertising	$1.67	$50.00	$600.00	$20.00	
Sub total:	$29.19	$875.83	$10,510.00	$350.33	
TOTAL OPERATING COSTS	$153.77	$4,613.16	$55,357.97	$1,845.27	
TOTAL EXPENSES	$835.82	$25,544.51	$306,539.06	$10,030.01	

BLANKET MORT. & SHARE LOAN INTEREST AS WELL AS PROPERTY TAXES ARE TAX DEDUCTIBLE HOME OWNERSHIP EXPENSES

NORTHMARK PROJECTS INC.

SUMMARY OF TOTAL PROJECT COSTS

34 COHOUSES

PROJECT: 205TH ST. & 76 AVE. LANGLEY
BORROWER:
FINANCER:
PROG. CLAIM #

JOB NO: 9301
DATE: July 20, 1994
SHEET NO: 1 OF 1

COST CODE (1)	DESCRIPTION OF WORK	ORIGINAL BUDGET (2)	CHANGE ORDERS (3)	REVISED BUDGET (4)(2+3)	TOTAL WORK IN PLACE PREV. APPLICATION (5)	WORK IN PLACE THIS APPLICATION (6)	TOTAL WORK IN PLACE (7)(5+6)	COST TO COMPLETE (8)(4-7)	LIEN 10% HOLDBACK (9)	TOTAL PAYMENT (10)(7-9)	COST PER UNIT	COST PER SQ.FT
01.000	GENERAL REQUIREMENTS	461,850.00	0.00	461,850.00	0.00	0.00	0.00	461,850.00	0.00	0.00	13,583.82	13.37
02.000	SITE WORK	350,500.00	0.00	350,500.00	0.00	0.00	0.00	350,500.00	0.00	0.00	10,308.82	10.15
03.000	CONCRETE	310,300.00	0.00	310,300.00	0.00	0.00	0.00	310,300.00	0.00	0.00	9,126.47	8.99
04.000	MASONRY	5,000.00	0.00	5,000.00	0.00	0.00	0.00	5,000.00	0.00	0.00	147.06	0.14
05.000	METALS	21,299.44	0.00	21,299.44	0.00	0.00	0.00	21,299.44	0.00	0.00	626.45	0.62
06.000	WOOD & PLASTIC	574,458.92	0.00	574,458.92	0.00	0.00	0.00	574,458.92	0.00	0.00	16,895.85	16.64
07.000	THERMAL & MOIST. PROTEC.	529,482.73	0.00	529,482.73	0.00	0.00	0.00	529,482.73	0.00	0.00	15,573.02	15.33
08.000	DOORS & WINDOWS	124,713.80	0.00	124,713.80	0.00	0.00	0.00	124,713.80	0.00	0.00	3,668.05	3.61
09.000	FINISHES	273,155.92	0.00	273,155.92	0.00	0.00	0.00	273,155.92	0.00	0.00	8,034.00	7.91
10.000	SPECIALTIES	10,462.88	0.00	10,462.88	0.00	0.00	0.00	10,462.88	0.00	0.00	307.73	0.30
11.000	EQUIPMENT	38,301.82	0.00	38,301.82	0.00	0.00	0.00	38,301.82	0.00	0.00	1,126.52	1.11
12.000	FURNISHINGS	12,000.00	0.00	12,000.00	0.00	0.00	0.00	12,000.00	0.00	0.00	352.94	0.35
13.000	SPECIAL CONSTRUCTION	0.00	0.00	0.00	0.00	0.00	0.00	0.00	0.00	0.00	0.00	0.00
14.000	CONVEYING SYSTEMS	0.00	0.00	0.00	0.00	0.00	0.00	0.00	0.00	0.00	0.00	0.00
15.000	MECHANICAL	402,500.00	0.00	402,500.00	0.00	0.00	0.00	402,500.00	0.00	0.00	11,838.24	11.64
16.000	ELECTRICAL	142,500.00	0.00	142,500.00	0.00	0.00	0.00	142,500.00	0.00	0.00	4,191.18	4.13
	SUB TOTAL CONST.	3,256,525.30	0.00	3,256,525.30	0.00	0.00	0.00	3,256,525.30	0.00	0.00	95,780.16	94.30
17.000	CONSULTANTS	638,396.50	0.00	638,396.50	203,918.54	122,308.30	324,086.84	314,309.66	0.00	0.00	18,776.37	18.49
18.000	LAND	1,063,600.00	0.00	1,063,600.00	9,703.65	210,000.00	219,903.65	843,676.35	0.00	0.00	31,282.35	30.80
19.000	MUNICIPAL LEVIES	485,452.00	0.00	485,452.00		2,280.00	2,280.00	483,172.00	0.00	0.00	14,278.00	14.28
20.000	FINANCING	414,624.00	0.00	414,624.00	0.00	0.00	0.00	414,624.00	0.00	0.00	12,194.82	12.01
21.000	SALES	120,000.00	0.00	120,000.00		16,508.48	16,508.48	103,491.52	0.00	0.00	3,529.41	3.48
22.000	CONTINGENCIES	127,000.00	0.00	127,000.00	0.00	0.00	0.00	127,000.00	0.00	0.00	3,791.12	3.74
	SUB TOTAL DEVELOPMENT	2,851,072.50	0.00	2,851,072.50	213,822.19	351,096.78	562,778.97	2,288,293.53	0.00	0.00	83,855.07	82.56
	GRAND TOTAL	6,107,597.80	0.00	6,107,597.80		0.00		5,544,818.83		0.00	179,635.23	176.87

MARGIN TOTAL (less Administration & CoHousing Resources) 5,562,597.80 6,107,597.80 179,635.23 149.21 157.53
which equals— MARGIN (10%) 556,259.78 16,360.58 13.59 14.55
GST (4.48%) 298,540.82 8,780.61 7.29 7.70
PTT (1%) 0.00 0.00 0.00 0.00

Assume no PPT: 1st Time buyers under $200,000

TOTAL 6,962,398.40 204,776.42 170.09

Per Unit	204,776.42	Per Gross	170.09	Per Net SqFt	201.62	+Common House	179.58
						+Common House & Atrium	142.76

34 UNITS @ 40,733 sqft Gross, 34532 sqft Net.
COMMON BUILDING @ 4248 sqft Net costs $350,500.00
Atrium @ 10,000 sqft Covered costs $300,000.00

APPLICATION AND CERTIFICATE FOR PAYMENT   AIA DOCUMENT G702   (Instructions on reverse side)

VENDOR #01580

TO (OWNER): Northwest Co-Housing Foundation
Attn: Tom Gomez
811 1st Ave., Suite #409
Seattle, WA 98104

FROM (CONTRACTOR): J. M. Rafn Company
P.O. Box 4229
Bellevue, WA 98009

PROJECT: Winslow Co-Housing
Job #6008 – Winslow

VIA (ARCHITECT):
INVOICE #12-26-6008GM
DUE & PAYABLE IN FULL BY: 1/10/92

APPLICATION NO: Eight
PERIOD TO: 12/31/91
ARCHITECT'S PROJECT NO:
CONTRACT DATE: May 1, 1991

Distribution to:
☐ OWNER
☐ ARCHITECT
☐ CONTRACTOR
☐
☐

PAGE ONE OF   PAGES

CONTRACT FOR:

Application is made for Payment, as shown below, in connection with the Contract.
Continuation Sheet, AIA Document G703, is attached.

CONTRACTOR'S APPLICATION FOR PAYMENT

CHANGE ORDER SUMMARY

	ADDITIONS	DEDUCTIONS
Change Orders approved in previous months by Owner		28,359.00
Chg. Order No.1 – 3 TOTAL	41,266.47	

Approved this Month

Number	Date Approved		
Chg. Order No. 4		25,815.31	
Chg. Order No. 5		47,381.10	
TOTALS		114,462.88	28,359.00
Net change by Change Orders		86,103.88	

1. ORIGINAL CONTRACT SUM .... $ 2,228,447.00
2. Net change by Change Orders .... $ 86,103.88
3. CONTRACT SUM TO DATE (Line 1 ± 2) .... $ 2,314,550.88
4. TOTAL COMPLETED & STORED TO DATE .... 83% $ 1,913,664.00
   (Column G on G703)
5. RETAINAGE:
   a. _____ % of Completed Work $ 126,486.80   *SEE CONTRACT
      (Column D + E on G703)
   b. _____ % of Stored Material $
      (Column F on G703)
   Total Retainage (Line 5a + 5b or
   Total in Column 1 of G703) .... $ 126,486.80
6. TOTAL EARNED LESS RETAINAGE .... $ 1,787,177.20
   (Line 4 less Line 5 Total)   Plus WSST @7.8   139,399.82
7. LESS PREVIOUS CERTIFICATES FOR   Plus WSST @7.8   1,926,577.02
   PAYMENT (Line 6 from prior Certificate) .... $ 1,813,863.19
8. CURRENT PAYMENT DUE .... $ 112,713.83
9. BALANCE TO FINISH, PLUS RETAINAGE .... $ 527,373.68 *
   (Line 3 less Line 6)   * EXCLUDES W.S.S.

The undersigned Contractor certifies that to the best of the Contractor's knowledge, information and belief the Work covered by this Application for Payment has been completed in accordance with the Contract Documents, that all amounts have been paid by the Contractor for Work for which previous Certificates for Payment were issued and payments received from the Owner, and that current payment shown herein is now due.

CONTRACTOR:

By: _____ Date: 12/26/91

State of: Washington   County of: King
Subscribed and sworn to before me this 26 day of Dec 1991
Notary Public: _____
My Commission expires: 10/25/94

MARY E. LEISSHOW
NOTARY PUBLIC
OCT 25 1994
STATE OF WASHINGTON

ARCHITECT'S CERTIFICATE FOR PAYMENT

In accordance with the Contract Documents, based on on-site observations and the data comprising the above application, the Architect certifies to the Owner that to the best of the Architect's knowledge, information and belief the Work has progressed as indicated, the quality of the Work is in accordance with the Contract Documents, and the Contractor is entitled to payment of the AMOUNT CERTIFIED.

AMOUNT CERTIFIED .... $
(Attach explanation if amount certified differs from the amount applied for.)
ARCHITECT:

By: _____ Date:

This Certificate is not negotiable. The AMOUNT CERTIFIED is payable only to the Contractor named herein. Issuance, payment and acceptance of payment are without prejudice to any rights of the Owner or Contractor under this Contract.

AIA DOCUMENT G702 • APPLICATION AND CERTIFICATE FOR PAYMENT • MAY 1983 EDITION • AIA • © 1983
THE AMERICAN INSTITUTE OF ARCHITECTS, 1735 NEW YORK AVENUE, N.W., WASHINGTON, D.C. 20006

G702-1983

Sample application for payment

WINSLOW CO-HOUSING
PAY REQUEST
JOB #6008

PAGE 2 OF 2
APPLICATION NUMBER: EIGHT
APPLICATION DATE: 12/20/91
PERIOD FROM: 12/1/91
PERIOD TO: 12/31/91

DESCRIPTION	BUDGET	PREVIOUS APPLICATION	THIS APPLICATION WORK IN PLACE	STORED MATERIALS	TOTAL COMPLETED/STORED TO DATE	% COMPLETE	BALANCE TO FINISH
COILING DOOR	3,290	0	0		0		3,290
ALUM/RESIDENT WINDOWS	45,092	45,092	0		45,092	100%	0
FINISH HARDWARE	8,200	1,640	1,640		3,280	40%	4,920
GYPSUM DRYWALL	113,200	67,920	13,584		81,504	72%	31,696
CERAMIC TILE	1,138	0	0		0		1,138
RESILIANT FLOORING	19,347	7,739	2,902	0	10,641	55%	8,706
CARPETING	33,098	22,176	0	0	22,176	67%	10,922
PAINTING	59,456	13,080	13,675		26,755	45%	32,701
SIGNS	1,068	0	0		0		1,068
FIRE EXT. CABINETS	264	0	0		0		264
MAIL BOXES	858	0	0		0		858
TOILET ACCESSORIES	4,847	0	0		0		4,847
WARDROBE SPECIALTIES	2,400	0	0		0		2,400
APPLIANCES	16,338	0	12,254		12,254	75%	4,085
PLUMBING	119,630	89,723	0		89,723	75%	29,908
HEAT SYSTEM	101,086	90,977	0		90,977	90%	10,109
VENTING	29,150	24,486	1,749		26,235	90%	2,915
ENERGY UPGRADE PKG	32,000	10,560	3,840		14,400	45%	17,600
ELECTRICAL	99,745	84,783	0		84,783	85%	14,962
LIGHT FIXTURE	15,100	0	6,040		6,040	40%	9,060
FIRE ALARM	8,000	7,040	0		7,040	88%	960
FIRE PROTECTION	18,605	16,745	0		16,745	90%	1,861
T.V. PREWIRE	1,000	0	0		0		1,000
CHANGE ORDER NO. 1	10,600	10,600	0		10,600	100%	0
CHANGE ORDER NO. 2	30,666	30,666	0		30,666	100%	0
CHANGE ORDER NO. 3	(28,359)	(28,359)	0		(28,359)	100%	0
CHANGE ORDER NO. 4	25,815	25,815	0		25,815	100%	0
CHANGE ORDER NO. 5	47,381	23,691	0		23,691	50%	23,691
		0	0		0		0
LABOR TAXES	42,446	33,211	1,883		35,094	83%	7,352
TAXES AND INSURANCE	28,515	22,311	1,265		23,576	83%	4,939
OVERHEAD AND PROFIT	126,137	98,693	5,597		104,290	83%	21,847
		0	0		0		0
		0	0		0		0
		0	0		0		0
		0	0		0		0
		0	0		0		0
		0	0		0		0
		0	0		0		0
TOTALS	2,314,550	1,809,105	104,558	0	1,913,664	83%	400,886

Contractor's request for payment

About the Author

BACKGROUND

Born in St. Louis, Missouri in 1949, I grew up in Terre Haute, Indiana. I attended the University of Michigan and the University of Maryland's Overseas Division, finally completing my undergraduate degree in architecture at the University of Washington in 1978. After working for 2 years in the Department of Construction and Land Use at the City of Seattle, in 1981 I spent several months working at Arcosanti, Paolo Soleri's experimental archaeology 70 miles north of Phoenix, Arizona.

As a full time development consultant I worked for more than 900 clients in the Seattle area between 1981 and 1987, including home owners, developers, contractors, and land use attorneys. Since 1989 I have focused exclusively on cohousing, recently expanding my interests into the development of eco-villages and sustainable communities. I have provided professional development consulting services to more than 20 cohousing groups, assisting them with all aspects of the cohousing development process, from getting started and land acquisition to project management during construction. The process is fun and the people are great, but the real reward is in getting projects built.

In addition to founding the Winslow Cohousing project near Seattle in 1989, and moving in in 1991, I was a consultant to and later project manager for the Cardiff Place Cohousing group in Victoria, BC during 1992 and 1993. I acted as development consultant and later as project manager for the WindSong Cohousing project completed in July 1996 near Vancouver, BC.

WORKSHOPS AND PRESENTATIONS

I enjoy working interactively with cohousing groups as much as possible, often arranging special workshops on such topics such as:
- Getting Unstuck
- Project Feasibility
- Finances & Commitment
- Understanding the Development Process
- Creating a Proforma and Budget

- Working With Design Professionals
- Making your project Affordable

Special events can be arranged to promote an individual group, or cohousing in general. With a large selection of slides and a growing video collection of cohousing across North America, I provide public presentations, slide shows, and orientations tailored to meet the needs of the specific groups I work with.

HOW TO REACH ME...

If you have questions or suggestions, please don't hesitate to contact me at CHanson17@aol.com. If you don't use electronic mail, pick up a copy of the latest CoHousing journal and you should be able to find my current address and phone under "Products and Services".

Index